THE SANFORD J. GROSSMAN LECTURES IN ECONOMICS SERIES

Every five years, the Department of Economics at the University of Chicago selects a distinguished senior faculty member to serve as the Grossman Prize Lecturer. This scholar develops a new set of lectures that exposes University of Chicago undergraduates to modern developments in economics.

Any opinions expressed herein are those of the author and do not necessarily represent the opinion of Sanford J. Grossman

Information,
Incentives,
AND
Education Policy

DEREK A. NEAL

Harvard University Press

Cambridge, Massachusetts

London, England

2018

Library of Congress Cataloging-in-Publication Data

Names: Neal, Derek A., author.
Title: Information, incentives, and education policy / Derek A. Neal.
Description: Cambridge, Massachusetts : Harvard University Press, 2018. |
Series: Sanford J. Grossman lectures in economics series | Includes
bibliographical references and index.
Identifiers: LCCN 2017049345 | ISBN 9780674050907 (alk. paper)
Subjects: LCSH: Education and state. | Education–Economic aspects. |
Educational planning. | Educational indicators. | Education–Aims and
objectives.
Classification: LCC LC71 .N43 2018 | DDC 379—dc23
LC record available at https://lccn.loc.gov/2017049345

In memory of
Roy Allen Neal, Jr.
who taught by example

Contents

Preface

In 2004, Sanford J. Grossman endowed the Grossman Prize Lecture Series in economics at the University of Chicago. Senior faculty who receive the prize develop courses that expose undergraduates to modern developments in economic research. In the fall of 2010, I proposed a new course on the Economics of Education, and the department bestowed upon me the honor of serving as the Grossman Prize Lecturer from the spring of 2011 through the spring of 2015.

This monograph contains the lectures that now serve as the core material for the class. The lectures explain key economic insights concerning the role of education in modern societies and analyze many important public policy questions that surround the funding and regulation of schools. The lectures necessarily contain some math, but students who understand basic economics and statistics should be able to follow the arguments in the main text. Most chapters also contain appendices that explore technical details that are beyond the grasp of some undergraduates. Students who have a solid command of microeconomics, calculus, and statistics should be able to follow the arguments in these appendices.

I assign these lectures and a collection of supplementary materials as required reading for my class, and during each class meeting, I lead students through discussions of these readings. Given this format, I wrote the lectures as conversations with my students. Thus, "we" refers to my students and me, while "you" refers to the students who are reading these lectures in preparation for my class. My hope is that, over time, "you" will encompass students taking classes in undergraduate programs, professional schools, and PhD programs around the world.

Over the past fifty years, social scientists from the University of Chicago have produced an impressive collection of path-breaking research on education. Sociologist James Coleman produced several large-scale studies that shaped empirical research on schools for decades. In economics, T. W. Schultz conducted pioneering work on the relationship between education and economic development, and over more than the past half century, Gary Becker and James Heckman have developed the analytical frameworks that numerous scholars use to study how preschools, schools, and families invest in the human capacities of children and young adults.

When I began my career at Chicago in 1991, I attended a workshop organized by Coleman and Heckman that sparked my interest in education research. I am grateful that, in the years that followed, both men taught me a great deal about how researchers should think about education and other investments in human capacities.

I owe special thanks to my dear friend Sherwin Rosen. Sherwin wrote few papers on education per se, but through years of coffee breaks, lunches, and tutoring sessions at his chalkboard, Sherwin impressed upon me many of the important ideas that I seek to convey in these lectures. Sherwin taught me most of what I know about life-cycle models of human capital investment, and his work with Edward Lazear forms the foundation for much of my work on incentives in education. I deeply regret that Sherwin did not live to see this return on his many investments in my education.

I thank my colleagues from the Committee on Education, especially Steve Raudenbush, who has been a great source of stimulation and encouragement for me over the past decade. I thank Charles Payne for useful conversations about urban education. I also thank Steve Levitt and John List, whom I value as colleagues both in economics and on the Committee.

I thank Gadi Barlevy and Diane Schanzenbach for working with me on projects that shaped my thinking about this field. I learned much of what I understand about this area by struggling together with them to produce research.

I thank Canice Prendergast and Robert Gibbons for many conversations about information, incentive schemes, and organizations. They helped me understand how the literatures on personnel policies and organizational practices should inform policies that govern the operation on schools and school systems.

I thank Douglas Staiger for many conversations about value-added models and empirical-Bayes methods. One of the appendices could have been titled, "What Doug Taught Me about Measuring Teacher Quality."

I thank Parag Pathak for fruitful exchanges concerning the literature on school assignment mechanisms. These exchanges shaped my thinking about the material in Chapter 3. I thank Chris Walters for useful conversations about the literature on charter schools and various drafts of Appendix 4.5, and for useful conversations about several other chapters. I thank Dennis Epple for reviewing an earlier draft and proposing important revisions.

I thank Sanford J. Grossman for making this exciting experience possible, and I also thank Lindy and Michael Keiser for research support through the University of Chicago's Committee on Education. These lectures contain numerous summaries of my own research as well as original research conducted specifically for this project. The Keisers' gift to the Committee supported the research assistants who worked on these projects.

I thank all of the graduate students who served so well as research or teaching assistants during the past six years: Ian Fillmore, Sarah Gordon Komisarow, Jorge Patricio Rodriguez Osorio, Russell Bittmann, Ezra Karger, Mythili Vinnakota, Andrew Jordan, Jorge L. Garcia G.-Menedez, Grant Gannaway, Charles Yuan, Max Samels, and Neil Cholli.

Finally, I thank the students who took Economics of Education over the past seven years. I learned a great deal from your questions and challenges, and I remain proud that, in 2016, the University of Chicago honored our work together when it bestowed upon me the Llewellyn John and Harriet Manchester Quantrell Award for Excellence in Undergraduate Teaching.

Information,
Incentives,
AND
Education Policy

Introduction

The typical course offerings in most economics departments contain no courses on the economics of machine tools, the market for software, or the economics of furniture. Economists rarely develop courses that explore the market for a single factor of production or a single consumer good. When students study public finance, industrial organization, international trade, or regulation, they are not studying any particular market but rather specific types of market interactions that are features of many markets.

Nonetheless, there are exceptions to this rule. Most universities do offer a class in labor economics, even though labor economics is the detailed analysis of the market for a single factor of production. This exception is easy to understand. The productive capacities of human beings account for most of aggregate wealth in modern societies. Roughly 65 percent of national income in the US goes to labor,[1] and Gollin (2002) argues that national income accounts often understate labor's share in total income because payments for the labor services of owner-managers in small firms are often counted as capital income. Gollin estimates that between .65 and .75 of national income goes to labor in most developed economies.

During the last half of the twentieth century, Gary Becker, Jacob Mincer, T. W. Schultz, and others popularized the concept of "human capital."[2] Human capital theory asserts that individual productive capacities are determined by individual stocks of productive attributes, such as health, skills, knowledge, etc., and that investment decisions determine the evolutions of these stocks. In this framework, job training, formal education, health care, and many other activities are investments in human capital. Modern societies differ significantly in terms of how much of their incomes they devote

1

to health care, but almost all developed countries spend between 5% and 8% of national output on education.[3]

Today, most wealth is held in the form of human capital, and modern societies make large investments in human capital through expenditures on education. Thus, how societies provide education to their citizens may matter greatly for the creation and distribution of wealth in modern economies.

1.1 Humans as Machines

The term human capital suggests a comparison between investments in humans and machines. If a factory owner upgrades the quality of his capital stock by investing in more sophisticated machinery, he expects the new machinery to increase his factory's output enough to justify the cost of improving his machinery. Likewise, many young adults invest in education hoping that the skills they acquire will increase their capacity to produce and therefore earn. They also hope that this increase in future earnings will be great enough to justify the cost of their education.

This line of reasoning first appears in chapter 10 of *The Wealth of Nations*. Adam Smith wrote during a time when most people had little formal schooling, but his observations about the relationship between adult earnings in a given skilled trade and the nature of the apprenticeships in that trade inspired much modern research on education and human capital. Smith wrote:

> Secondly, the wages of labour vary with the easiness and cheapness, or the difficulty and expense of learning the business. When any expensive machine is erected, the extraordinary work to be performed by it before it is worn out, it must be expected, will replace the capital laid out upon it, with at least the ordinary profits. A man educated at the expense of much labour and time to any of those employments which require extraordinary dexterity and skill, may be compared to one of those expensive machines. The work which he learns to perform, it must be expected, over and above the usual wages of common labour, will replace to him the whole expense of his education, with at least the ordinary profits of an equally valuable capital. (Smith 1827)

Modern research on how investments in post-secondary education influence adult labor market outcomes builds on Smith's insights. Associate degrees, bachelors degrees, and professional degrees are analogous to apprenticeships that require different amounts of training, and the earnings differences observed among adults who have completed different levels of schooling provide information about the returns that individuals earn when they invest in education.

Yet, for our purposes, Smith's focus on "learning to perform work" is the equivalent of starting in the middle of a story. He is discussing decisions that confront young adults, such as to work as a laborer or go through an apprenticeship, or, in our day, to go straight to work or go to college. However, young adults make these decisions in the shadow of experiences at home, elementary school, and secondary school, and a key factor that influences how much a young adult decides to invest in learning to perform work is how well she learned how to learn during childhood.

1.2 Learning and Producing

Many economic models describe decisions to invest in human capital. Some characterize how parents allocate time and money to build the capacities of their children. Others describe how young persons allocate time between formal schooling, learning on the job, and productive work as well as how these allocations change as persons age. The most sophisticated versions of these models involve mathematical tools that are well beyond the prerequisites for this book. Our goal for this chapter is to understand the most important insights from these models within the simplest possible framework.

Human capital models typically describe investments in one type of skill.[4] In such models, potential earnings are proportional to stocks of general skill, and individuals allocate time between either earning income or engaging in schooling or training activities that increase stocks of general skill.

However, a recent economics literature, pioneered by James Heckman, devotes considerable attention to the fact that, when parents and schools invest in the human capital of young persons, these investments create many different types of skills or capacities. Further, these capacities build upon each other over time in complex ways. This framework stresses the idea that investments in certain capacities today may shape human capital investment decisions many years from now.[5]

Here, we explore a simple model with two individual capacities: productive skill and learning efficiency. Productive skill allows individuals to produce goods or services and also facilitates the acquisition of additional productive skills. For example, consider a young accountant who is highly proficient with the spreadsheet tools that businesses use to analyze financial statements. This skill makes the young accountant productive at work, but this skill also makes it easier for her to master the statistical models that firms use to create profit forecasts.

In contrast, learning efficiency has no direct value in production, but more efficient learners pay lower costs to acquire new skills. Consider a college student who has strong math skills. Her command of calculus and statistics does not make her more productive in her part-time job at a local fast food place. However, these skills make it easier for her to acquire productive skills that employers value in many business, science, and engineering fields.

It is difficult to identify skills that only affect learning efficiency and have no value in production. The capacity to read quickly and well enhances output directly in some jobs, and mastery of algebra certainly makes algebra teachers more productive. Nonetheless, there are skills that serve primarily as learning skills. Persons who read well, comprehend mathematical arguments, understand the scientific method, and organize new information quickly are more efficient learners in the sense that they are able to acquire new skills in less time and with less instruction from others.

I.2.1 Thought Experiment

Here, we describe a simple model of life-cycle investments in learning efficiency and productive skill. We purposefully avoid mathematical details for now. Our goal is to understand the logic behind several claims that will motivate our study of the economics of education.

Appendix I.5 at the end of this chapter presents the model formally and derives the results described here. Consider a person who lives for three periods. To make our model more concrete, we can think of period one as childhood. By childhood, we mean the period from age 5 to the age at which children are no longer required to attend school, which in the developed world is typically 16 or 17. The second period is young adulthood. We assume that this period covers the late teen years through roughly age 40. Almost all nonmandatory schooling takes place in period two. Even those who pursue the most advanced degrees have usually finished formal schooling by age 40. The third period covers the interval from age 40 until retirement.

We do not model the retirement period explicitly because we do not consider leisure in our model. All time is devoted to learning or working, and our goal is to describe the optimal allocations of time to different types of learning and production over the life cycle of an individual.

In periods two and three, individuals may allocate time to one of three activities. They can work. They can spend time acquiring productive skill, and they can spend time enhancing their learning efficiency. In period one, child labor laws prevent work, but children, or their parents, must still decide how much time they will spend acquiring productive skill and how much time they will spend building their learning efficiency.

Time is not the only input into skill creation. Books, teachers, tutors, and other inputs determine how much skill a given person acquires for each unit of time the individual trains or studies. Thus, individuals face a life-cycle investment problem. In each period, individuals must decide how much to invest in skills that make them more productive and how much to invest in skills that make them more efficient learners.[6]

All types of learning are forms of investment. Learning requires investments of time and resources, and those who pay learning costs today expect to be more productive and thus to earn more in the future. Given this observation, several results about the timing of different types of investments are immediate.

To begin, individuals will not learn anything during the third period of their lives. They know that, after their third period, they will be retired, and their earnings will be zero whether they are highly productive or not. It makes no sense to take time away from work in period three to acquire new skills that will never be used.

Likewise, individuals never invest in learning efficiency during period two. Since they know that they are not going to learn in period three, they will not devote time or money to improving their learning skills in period two. This implies that all investments in learning efficiency must take place during childhood, that is, in period one.

The logic of our three-period model suggests a life-cycle sequence of events. Children devote time to learning how to learn, and possibly to acquiring some productive skills as well. Young adults use their learning skills to build more productive skills that raise their potential earnings. Older adults devote all of their time to work.

Since period one is age 5 to roughly age 16 or 17, we assume that all children begin period one with the same productive capacity. It seems reasonable to assert that differences among 5-year-olds in their capacities to engage in market work and produce output are second-order concerns since the productive capacities of all children are quite limited. However, we assume that initial learning capacities differ among young children in important ways. A large literature in economics and human development contains results that support this approach. Young children differ in many dimensions of school readiness that are likely proxies for their learning capacities.[7]

For a given child, health endowments and family investments determine initial learning skills and school readiness. During childhood, educational investments determine both the learning capacity and productive capacity that an individual brings to adult life. As Appendix I.5 explains, given rather trivial restrictions on the production function for learning efficiency, our model implies that it is always optimal to invest in learning efficiency during childhood (i.e., period one). Further, numerical solutions to versions of the model that I have considered imply that children should focus most of their educational investments on activities that build learning skills.

We have already noted that during young adulthood, period two, individuals no longer invest in learning efficiency. They only invest in productive skills that help them earn income during their working years. Yet individuals differ greatly in terms of how much time and money they invest in skills that improve their labor market prospects. Some young adults leave school as soon as they are legally allowed to do so. Others finish high school but never complete any post-secondary schooling. Some complete certification programs or associate degree programs that require only a year or two of classes. Some complete four-year college degrees, and a more select group goes on to acquire professional degrees, master's degrees, or doctoral degrees.

What determines how much schooling a given young adult will complete? In our model, it is the learning efficiency that the individual acquires in elementary school, middle school, and the early years of high school. Learning skills increase the expected return from investments in additional education and training, but they do not directly affect the opportunity cost of time spent learning. Thus, an individual who enters young adulthood knowing how to learn finds it optimal to invest greatly in learning how to earn. As a result, experiences in childhood that shape individual learning capacities have a profound effect on the earnings that individuals enjoy in their prime working years.

In our model, initial period-two differences in stocks of productive skills do not affect rates of productive skill growth. Holding constant learning efficiency, higher productive capacity at the beginning of the second period has two offsetting effects on skill investments. Those who are already more productive find it easier to acquire new productive skills, but individuals who are already more productive also face a higher opportunity cost for the time they spend learning rather than producing. In Appendix I.5, we choose functional forms such that these offsetting forces cancel each other out. As a result, the growth of productive skills in period two does not depend on the initial level of productive skills.

I.3 Earnings Inequality

Figures I.1 and I.2 present earnings information for persons born between 1957 and 1964 who participated in the National Longitudinal Survey of Youth 1979 (NLSY79). The participants in this survey have been inter-viewed either annually or bi-annually since 1979 when they were in their late teens and early twenties. The 2014 survey provides the most recent available data.

The figures report earnings in 2013 dollars because the survey asks about earnings in the previous calendar year. Each dot gives an average earnings value for a sample of respondents who share the same gender, age, and final education level. The final education level is education at age 40 (i.e., the end of period two in our model).

To make sure you understand the figure, let us consider one specific dot. In Figure I.1, the second-highest dot above age 30 tells us that, among women who earn college degrees but no graduate degrees by age 40, those who are employed at age 30 earn about $50,000 per year.

Several patterns stand out in these figures.

- Earnings growth increases with final education level.
- The present value of lifetime earnings minus average expenditures on post-secondary education increases with education.
- The first two patterns are much more pronounced among men than women.

The first result is quite obvious. However, the second requires some cal-culations. To begin, we need to extrapolate these curves to age 65 or some other suitable retirement age, which we could allow to differ by education

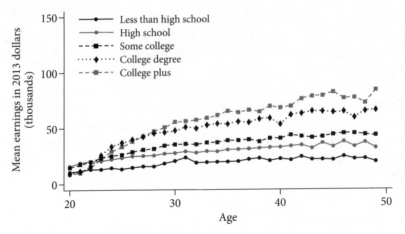

Figure I.1 Age-earnings profile by education level at age 40 (women).

This figure shows the mean of total earnings for women across age and education categories. I use data from the National Longitudinal Survey of Youth 1979 (NLSY79)—specifically, the surveys from 1979 to 1995 (annual basis) and 1996 to 2014 (biennial basis). I express earnings in thousands of 2013 dollars using a wage inflation index based on hourly wages of private nonagricultural industries (source: Obama (2015)). Annual samples exclude the self-employed, those working without pay, and those employed in the military full-time.

group. Next, we need to use a particular discount rate to turn these life-cycle earnings profiles into present value measures of lifetime earnings, that is, to express the value of these profiles in terms of one-time cash transfers at age 20.[8] Finally, we need to estimate the present value of tuition and other expenditures required to complete each level of post-secondary schooling.

One could adopt many different procedures for calculating these net present values for different education groups. Nonetheless, as you will see in the exercises at the end of the chapter, any reasonable procedure produces the same basic result. The present value of lifetime earnings minus post-secondary education expenses increases with education, and the lifetime net income gaps between those who finished college and those who did not are large.

Our third result is expected given the striking differences between Figures I.1 and I.2. Among prime-age workers, earnings grow with education among both men and women, but men earn more than women at every education level. Further, these gender gaps in earnings are greater at higher

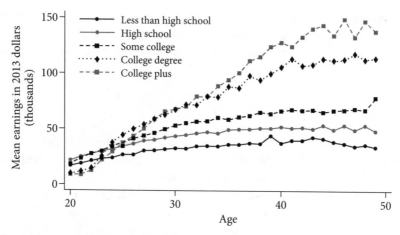

Figure I.2 Age-earnings profile by education level at age 40 (men).
This figure shows the mean of total earnings for men across age and education categories. I use data from the National Longitudinal Survey of Youth 1979 (NLSY79)—specifically, the surveys from 1979 to 1995 (annual basis) and 1996 to 2014 (biennial basis). I express earnings in thousands of 2013 dollars using a wage inflation index based on hourly wages of private nonagricultural industries (source: Obama (2015)). Annual samples exclude the self-employed, those working without pay, and those employed in the military full-time.

education levels. Among those who earn a college or post-graduate degree, men earn almost twice as much as their female peers.

These differences may, in part, reflect labor market discrimination against women, but two other factors are also worth mentioning. First, men are more likely to choose majors in college and graduate school that are associated with high earnings levels for both genders. Second, well educated men work longer hours over their careers and take fewer breaks from full-time employment.[9]

The earnings outcomes in these graphs suggest that, at least in the US, the most well-educated professionals in business, engineering, medicine, and other high-paying fields now earn salaries in their late 40s that are far more than double the salaries of their peers who did not complete any post-secondary schooling. Our model suggests that we observe these patterns because those who become well educated begin their adult lives with much greater capacities to learn than those who do not continue their education. Persons who begin adult life as efficient learners make significant

investments in productive skill, and these educational investments require
them to work less and earn less at the beginning of their adult lives. However, these investments realize large returns over subsequent decades of
employment.

I.3.1 Life-Cycle Behavior

Our simple three-period model invites us to consider the following sequence of events in an individual's life. For a given individual, health endowments and family investments determine school readiness. Next, investments during childhood determine the learning capacity and productive capacity that an individual brings to adult life. Finally, investments in
productive skills determine adult earnings growth and the level of earnings
during prime working years.

Figures I.1 and I.2 strongly suggest that differences in earnings growth
rates are the key drivers of differences in lifetime inequality among various
education groups. In our model, young adult learning efficiency is the key
driver of the adult skill investments that create earnings growth. In Smith's
language, the learning efficiency that an individual acquires at home and in
school during childhood determines whether or not the individual enters
her prime working years as a productive machine that performs substantial
work and receives substantial earnings.

Individuals must learn how to learn before they can learn how to produce. Therefore, in modern societies, the quality of primary and secondary
education directly impacts economic productivity.

I.3.2 Skills or Signals

We have discussed the patterns in Figures I.1 and I.2 under the maintained
assumption that the relationship between education and earnings arises
because education creates skills that make individuals more productive.
However, Spence (1973) argues that educated persons may earn more simply because more productive people find it easier to complete additional
schooling. According to Spence, education and earnings are correlated because education signals something about the productive capacities of individuals to employers and not because schooling enhances the productive
capacities of individuals.

We shall proceed in this book under the assumption that education and other forms of training do enhance productive capacities. Becker (1993) and Mincer (1958) are the seminal modern works on human capital. These works and a large subsequent literature have documented many patterns in life-cycle data on earnings and time allocation that are consistent with the predictions of various human capital models.[10]

In addition, Clark and Martorell (2014) provide evidence that the increase in labor market earnings associated with completing high school cannot be explained as a signaling outcome. They find that, in two states where students must pass an exit exam to receive a diploma, students who completed twelve years of schooling and just passed the diploma exam enjoy future labor market outcomes that are quite similar to those who completed twelve years of schooling and scored just below the passing threshold. This result holds even though there exist strong positive correlations between test scores and earnings and between educational attainment and earnings in their data. In these data, test scores and credits earned do predict labor market outcomes, but holding these factors constant, individuals do not earn an additional benefit from receiving a diploma.

It is difficult to test models that characterize education as a signal. So we cannot rule out the possibility that some part of the empirical relationship between earnings and education is driven by the value of education as a signal of unobserved individual characteristics. Nonetheless, given the relative success of the human capital models over the last half century, we proceed with human capital theory as our default analytical framework.

We do not, however, assume that the empirical relationships in Figures I.1 and I.2 provide all the information we need to calculate the expected returns that individuals face when they make different investments in their education. We do not know what earnings the NLSY college graduates would have enjoyed if they had chosen to finish high school and go straight to work. They may have done better or worse than those who did choose to begin working right after high school. Thus we cannot easily determine what their expected or realized returns to completing college were.

Although we will not explore the large literature that attempts to estimate the gains in expected lifetime earnings that individuals enjoy when they move from one education level to the next,[11] we note that the vast majority of this literature concludes that, on average, the investments that individuals make in post-secondary education raise their future earnings by more than enough to cover the time and money costs associated with their additional schooling. As we proceed, remember that we operate under the maintained assumption that these gains arise primarily because individuals acquire valuable skills through schooling.

1.4 A Role for Government

In developed countries, governments fund the elementary and secondary education that most children receive. Our model describes optimal investments in children, but nothing in our model suggests that these investments should take place in schools or that governments should fund these schools.

So far, we have assumed that individuals or families are able to borrow and lend freely at the market rate of interest. Thus, individuals make all investments that have a positive lifetime return. This assumption is standard in models that characterize investments in post-secondary schooling among adults. However, this assumption is problematic in models that describe investments in elementary schooling for children (i.e., period-one investments).

If a family takes out a loan to build a house, they offer the house as collateral. However, the family cannot take out a loan to build the capacities of their child and then offer the child as collateral. Parents cannot borrow on the child's behalf and legally commit the child to work and repay the loan as an adult. Further, if parents borrow to invest in their child's education and then fail to pay the loan back, the lender has little recourse. Even if the lender gains the legal right to garnish the parents' earnings, the parents have the option to retire early.

Given these credit market frictions, most parents are not able to borrow money to fund educational investments in their young children. So, many parents cannot invest in their children's education without lowering their own consumption, and given this cost, some parents are either not willing or not able to invest efficiently in their children.[12]

If the parents of a child plan to leave a significant bequest to the child, then their inability to borrow on the child's behalf is inconsequential. We expect wealthy parents who are altruistic to simply invest in their child's education using their own resources and deduct these investments (plus the returns that these investments would have earned) from the child's bequest or from other gifts they planned to give the child.[13] Nonetheless, data on bequests and financial transfers between parents and children suggest that most parents are either not wealthy enough or not altruistic enough to make significant transfers to their children.[14]

If significant numbers of parents are not both willing and able to invest efficiently in their children, society may end up in what we might call a "low-skill" trap. If many in the current generation of parents do not commit efficient resources to the education of their children, the adult earnings of these children will turn out to be less than the earnings they would have enjoyed given efficient investment. Because the earnings of this second generation will be inefficiently low, they will likely invest inefficiently in their own children, and subsequent generations may well continue this pattern of underinvestment.

From this starting point, it is easy to imagine that governments can improve welfare by funding education. Assume that Joe is the young child of a single parent who has little education. Joe's mother cannot educate Joe at home because she must work long hours to provide food, clothing, and shelter for Joe, and Joe's mother does not earn enough to both provide for their basic needs and pay for Joe's education.

Now, suppose that the government borrows money to pay for Joe's schooling. Because Joe enters adulthood with more skills, he will expect to earn more during his adult life than he would have with no education, and this increase in the expected present discounted value of Joe's lifetime earnings is a return on the government's investment in his education.

Since we are assuming that it is efficient for children in developed countries to be educated, we expect the rate of return on this investment in Joe's schooling to be greater than the rate of interest. This implies that, in expectation, the government can tax Joe as an adult to pay off the bonds that paid for his schooling, and even in the presence of these additional taxes, the present value of Joe's expected after-tax income minus any expenditures on post-secondary schooling is greater than what he would have enjoyed if the government had never borrowed money to fund his K–12 schooling.[15] If we assume that the government has an infinite time horizon, the government can repeat the same process for Joe's children, Joe's grandchildren, and all subsequent generations.

Children cannot borrow to finance their own education, and some parents are either unable or unwilling to invest efficiently in their children's education. Governments address this market imperfection by taxing one generation to fund the education of the next. As long as the distortions created by higher taxes are small relative to the gains associated with more efficient human capital investment, governments can improve welfare by funding education.[16]

A large literature addresses the possibility that formal education may also help people make better decisions about their health, function more effectively as parents, and generally make better life decisions.[17] We will not explore this literature. Whether or not these additional benefits exist, our observations about the importance of credit market imperfections remain.

Further, while we have focused so far on the ways that formal schooling benefits the individuals who receive it, many social scientists have offered rationales for public funding of education that hinge on social benefits that individuals enjoy when those around them are well educated.[18] Our time together is limited. So we will not explore these literatures, either. It is quite intuitive that I may benefit in several ways from those around me being better educated, and that these educated neighbors and friends may not be able to require me to pay them for these benefits. However, it is difficult to test this idea empirically, and we do not have time to explore the thorny empirical literature that seeks to quantify the social benefits of education.[19]

Our three-period model highlights a sufficient and powerful rationale for the ubiquity of publicly funded schooling. The learning skills that children bring to young adulthood are key determinants of their lifetime incomes. These skills reflect the cumulative effects of investments made throughout childhood, and there are good reasons to believe that, absent any government intervention, many parents would not make these investments efficiently. Governments can mitigate this market imperfection by funding educational investments in children and paying for the investments by taxing the incomes of adults.

I.4.1 Why Is Schooling Mandatory?

These observations help us understand why most developed countries provide free primary and secondary education for children while taxing the income of adults. However, throughout the developed world, primary and secondary schooling is not only free, it is also mandatory. So we must ask why governments not only address the credit market frictions that hamper efficient investment in education but also mandate that children attend school.

If governments simply sent per-child grants to parents that were sufficient to cover the costs of education, some parents would choose to spend some or all of these grants on their own consumption instead of their children's education. If governments sent parents nontransferable vouchers for schooling but did not make schooling mandatory, some parents would still require their children to work at home instead of going to school.

Parents differ not only with respect to their wealth and incomes. Parents also differ in the degree of altruism and care they demonstrate for their children. Schooling is both free and mandatory in developed countries so that children receive an education in instances where their parents lack wealth, altruism, or both.

I.4.2 Policy

For the remainder of this book, we take as given that governments can improve welfare by funding mandatory schooling for children.[20] Yet nothing we have discussed so far provides any guidance concerning how governments should procure education services for children. Should governments operate schools or should governments purchase education services from private providers? Should governments assign students to schools or allow parents to exercise some control over which school educates their child? How should governments determine which schools are eligible to receive government funding? Should governments assess performance bonuses or fines to existing schools based on their performance?

As we approach these questions, we treat government as an agent operating on behalf of children. For our purposes, optimal education policies are optimal procurement policies. Thus, given a particular level of education spending, optimal education policies maximize the social value of the skills that children acquire in school.

In Chapter 1, we review evidence that suggests that traditional public schools do not employ public resources efficiently. Then, in subsequent chapters, we consider different reform agendas. In each of these chapters, we seek to understand the results that competing reforms have produced. Our goal is to employ basic tools from information economics to understand the successes and failures of competing policies and also to propose new mechanisms that may improve the efficiency of publicly funded schools.

I.5 Appendix: Learn to Learn. Learn to Earn. Then Earn.

Here, we describe optimal life-cycle investment in skills. Our goal is to characterize the investments that agents would make in a world with complete information and access to perfect credit markets. To simplify the analysis, we consider the life-cycle investment problem facing one individual.

We assume that the individual is able to borrow freely at a market rate of interest, and we describe the life-cycle investment decisions that maximize the difference between the present value of her lifetime earnings and the present value of her lifetime expenditures on investments in skill. The solution to the problem we describe is a necessary component of a larger utility maximization problem. In order to maximize lifetime utility from consumption, the individual must choose skill investments and time allocations that maximize the present value of her net lifetime resources.[21]

The notation for our model is as follows:

- $t \in \{1, 2, 3\}$ indexes time periods
- k_t productive skill in period t
- h_t learning efficiency in period t
- s_t^k fraction of period t spent acquiring k
- s_t^h fraction of period t spent acquiring h
- x_t^k inputs that facilitate the acquisition of k during period t
- x_t^h inputs that facilitate the acquisition of h during period t
- R rental rate on k
- P common price of x_t^h and x_t^k
- $\beta = \frac{1}{1+r}$ individual discount rate
- r interest rate

The laws of motion that describe how skills evolve are

$$k_{t+1} = k_t + h_t \left(s_t^k k_t x_t^k\right)^{\gamma} \quad \gamma < \frac{1}{2}$$

$$h_{t+1} = h_t + g(h_t, s_t^h, x_t^h)$$

Here, we make an explicit parametric assumption about the law of motion for k_t, but we do not impose a parametric assumption for $g[\cdot, \cdot, \cdot]$. Our law of motion for k is a well-known benchmark in the existing literature on adult investments in human capital,[22] and the key points that motivate future class discussions hold, given several different functional form choices for $g(\cdot, \cdot, \cdot)$. We assume that investments of time and resources are complements, but both investments are subject to diminishing returns, that is, $g_2 > 0$, $g_3 > 0$ and $g_{22} < 0$, $g_{33} < 0$, $g_{23} > 0$.[23]

The initial conditions are $k_1 = 1$ and $h_1 \in (0, 1)$. We return to these assumptions below when we discuss optimal investments during period one.

In our model, an individual chooses investments of money and time that determine the evolution of her skills. The individual makes twelve investment decisions. She lives three periods, and in each period, must decide on both time and money investments that create two types of skill. The twelve investment variables are

$$\{x_1^k, x_2^k, x_3^k, x_1^h, x_2^h, x_3^h, s_1^k, s_2^k, s_3^k, s_1^h, s_2^h, s_3^h\}$$

By assumption, we do not allow the individual to work in period one (i.e., childhood). However, in periods two and three, investment choices also imply work choices since we assume that an adult devotes all of her time to either learning or working.

The objective for the individual is to maximize the present value of lifetime resources available to fund her consumption. She seeks to maximize the difference between the present value of her lifetime earnings,

$$\beta R k_2 (1 - s_2^k - s_2^h) + \beta^2 R k_3 (1 - s_3^k - s_3^h)$$

and the present value of her lifetime expenditures on skill investments,

$$P(x_1^k + x_1^h) + \beta P(x_2^k + x_2^h) + \beta^2 P(x_3^k + x_3^h)$$

I.5.1 Optimal Investments

This is a finite-horizon, dynamic programming problem, and we will adopt the standard solution technique for these problems. We will begin with the last period and work backward.

Consider an individual who begins the third period with production skill k_3 and learning efficiency h_3. We noted earlier that she will make no skill investments in period three. Investments cost money and time today but only earn a return in the future. Since there is no future beyond period three, investments made in period three require costs but generate no returns. Thus, each agent works throughout period three, earns $R k_3$, and spends nothing on investments in skill.

Given this result, we have:

$$V_3(k_3, h_3) = R k_3$$

$V_3(\cdot, \cdot)$ is the period-three value function. It characterizes the maximum value, in terms of the present value of current and future net earnings, that the individual can achieve if she enters period three with stocks (k_3, h_3) and behaves optimally going forward.

We define the period-two value function analogously:

$$V_2(k_2, h_2) = \max_{x_2, s_2} Rk_2(1 - s_2^k - s_2^h) - P(x_2^k + x_2^h) + \beta V_3(k_3, h_3)$$

$$\text{s.t.} \quad k_3 = k_2 + h_2 \left(s_2^k k_2 x_2^k\right)^{\gamma}$$

$$h_3 = h_2 + g(h_2, s_2^h, x_2^h)$$

$$s_2^k + s_2^h \leq 1$$

$V_2(k_2, h_2)$ is the maximum value, in terms of the present value of net earnings, that the individual can achieve if she enters period two given skill stocks (k_2, h_2). This maximization problem involves four choices variables, $\mathbf{x}_2 = \{x_2^k, x_2^h\}$ and $\mathbf{s}_2 = \{s_2^k, s_2^h\}$.

Here, the trade-off between earnings this period and earnings next period is clear. The first term in the maximand is period-two earnings. Potential earnings for period two are Rk_2, but time spent studying is time not spent working, so actual earnings are $Rk_2(1 - s_2^k - s_2^h)$. The next term, $P(x_2^k + x_2^h)$, is the total monetary cost of skill investments. The final term is the discounted value of earnings realized in period three. The laws of motion for k_t and h_t describe how investments in period two determine skill levels in period three. The final constraint requires that total study time be less than or equal to the total time endowment for the period.

Note that by substituting in our solution for $V_3(k_3, h_3)$ and the law of motion for k_t, we can rewrite the period-two value function as

$$V_2(k_2, h_2) = \max_{x_2, s_2} Rk_2(1 - s_2^k - s_2^h) - P(x_2^k + x_2^h) + \beta Rk_2$$

$$+ \beta Rh_2 \left(s_2^k k_2 x_2^k\right)^{\gamma}$$

$$\text{s.t.} \quad s_2^k + s_2^h \leq 1$$

Regardless of your math background, you should be able to see that $x_2^h = s_2^h = 0$ are optimal choices. Since no learning takes place in period three, there is no reason to invest in learning efficiency during period two. On the other hand, the individual does work in period three, so period-two investments $(s_2^k k_2, x_2^k)$ in productive skill earn a return.

Much of modern labor economics explores why different individuals make different skill investments during young adulthood and how these investments shape their earnings during their prime working years. The optimal investment policies for period two are

$$x_2^k = (\beta h_2)^{\frac{1}{1-2\gamma}} * c(\gamma, R, P)$$

$$s_2^k k_2 = x_2^k * \left(\frac{P}{R}\right) \tag{I.1}$$

where $c(\gamma, R, P)$ is a constant determined by prices and the curvature of the production function. Note that, holding the technology of skill production and prices constant, two things determine optimal investments for young adulthood: learning efficiency, h_2, and the interest rate, r, since $\beta = \frac{1}{1+r}$. In this exercise, we are assuming perfect credit markets. So all individuals face the same interest rate. However, individuals do enter young adulthood with different learning skills, and those with weak learning skills are not well positioned to learn how to earn. Experiences in childhood that shape learning capacities determine what career paths are both feasible and optimal for young adults.

I.5.2 Earnings Inequality

We can characterize earnings growth between the two periods of adult life as follows:

$$E_3 - E_2 = R(k_3 - k_2) + Rs_2^k k_2$$

The first term represents the growth in potential earnings between periods two and three. The last term is the earnings growth that occurs because individuals devote all their time to earning and no time to training during period three. Thus, two things determine the growth in earnings between period two and period three: (i) the value of the productive skill the individual acquires during period two, $R(k_3 - k_2)$, and (ii) how much skill investment depresses period-two earnings by reducing time allocated to work, $Rs_2^k k_2$.

Further, equation (I.1) shows that optimal period-two investments in educational resources, x_2^k, are proportional to $s_2^k k_2$. So we know that individuals who forgo the most in terms of period-two earnings, $s_2^k k_2$, also spend the most on education resource investments, x_2^k, and thus experience the largest increases in productive skill, $(k_3 - k_2)$.

Why do some young adults invest more in post-secondary education and training than others? In this model, variation in individual productive capacities, k_2, does not account for individual differences in skill investments among young adults. Here, a higher value of k_2 has two offsetting effects on skill investments. The first is that a higher productive skill level, k_2, facilitates the acquisition of productive skills since skill growth is influenced by effective training time, $(s_2^k k_2)$. However, a higher level of k_2 also increases the opportunity cost, Rk_2, of time spent learning, s_2^k, and this force discourages investments in education and training.

Given our functional form assumptions, these forces cancel each other out and, holding h_2 constant, earnings growth between periods two and three is not a function of k_2. Thus, if young adults differ only in their productive skills, k_2, those who earn more in period two will also earn more in period three, and the earnings gap between any two workers will be the same in both periods.

However, earnings trajectories for individuals who have similar productive skills as young adults, k_2, but different learning efficiencies, h_2, diverge over their careers. Learning efficiency h_2 raises the returns to education and training without affecting the opportunity cost of time spent learning. Thus, high h_2 individuals invest more in education and training and enjoy greater earnings growth between periods two and three.

In sum, productive skills, k_2, affect initial adult earnings capacities but have no clear effect on adult earnings dynamics. Learning efficiency, h_2, does not directly impact earnings capacity in period two but does determine earnings growth during adulthood.

I.5.3 Learning to Learn

If those who enter adulthood as efficient learners are the winners in modern economies, we must step back one more period and ask how adult learning skill, h_2, is determined.

The period-one value function, $V_1(k_1, h_1)$, defines the maximum lifetime present value of net earnings that an individual can obtain if she begins period one with stocks of productive skill and learning skill given by (k_1, h_1) respectively. Period one is age 5 to roughly age 16 or 17, and we normalize initial productive capacity to one, that is, $k_1 = 1$. The specific value used in this normalization is not important. However, it is significant that we are assuming that all individuals begin period one with the same k_1. We are assuming that the differences in the capacities of children to engage in market work and produce output are not important. This is a reasonable assumption because the productive capacities of all children are quite limited.

In contrast, we expect h_1 to vary among children because differences in birth endowments and early childhood experiences create important variation in measures of school readiness. In this book, we devote little attention to the determinants of h_1, but we do not adopt this approach because variation in h_1 is inconsequential. Rather, we take h_1 as given because our focus is the economics of education. It will take a full term to examine K–12 schooling. A more general course on all aspects of human development would require an entire year and a much larger book.

The first-period maximization problem involves three choice variables: x_1^k, x_1^h, and s_1^h. Since children are not allowed to engage in market work, all time not spent building productive skills must be allocated to building learning skills. Given the optimal allocation of time between these types of learning, there exist optimal levels of resource investments (x_1^k, x_1^h) that enhance time spent acquiring productive skill and learning skill, respectively.

The policy functions for (x_1^k, x_1^h, s_1^h) obviously depend on the functional form of $g(h_1, s_1^h, x_1^h)$. I have analyzed several different versions of this model, each using different functional forms and parameterizations for $g(h_1, s_1^h, x_1^h)$.[24] As a rule, it is difficult to derive analytical solutions for the policy functions, (x_1^k, x_1^h, s_1^h). However, two results are clear in all the versions of the model that I have solved analytically or numerically:

- It is always optimal to make investments in the learning efficiency that individuals bring to young adulthood, h_2.
- h_2 is an increasing function of h_1. Young persons who transition to adult life with the greatest stocks of learning skill, h_2, are those who enjoyed the largest stocks of h_1 as preschoolers.

The first result holds given any $g(h_1, s_1^h, x_1^h)$ that satisfies standard Inada conditions. The second result also appears to be quite robust. It is easy to show that $V_2(k_2, h_2)$ is linear in k_2 but convex in h_2. Thus, the second result holds even though the costs of creating additional learning skills, h, are increasing in the current stock of learning skills for most of the $g(h_1, s_1^h, x_1^h)$ specifications I have considered.

I have also numerically solved a version of this model where each year of life is a distinct period. In this model, an optimal life-cycle sequence of activities emerges. During childhood, young children invest almost exclusively in learning how to learn. At some point, youth and young adults begin investing more in productive skills while reducing their investments in learning skills; that is, they transition from learning how to learn to learning how to earn. Finally, as individuals enter their prime-adult working years, they reduce their investments and devote almost all of their time to work.

Our model suggests that the following life-cycle sequence is optimal: learn how to learn, learn how to earn, and then earn. This sequence captures an important progression that we observe among individuals in developed economies. The curriculum for most fifth graders involves only learning skills and no vocational training, but students in medical school are engaged in much vocational training. Finally, while the phrase "life-long learning" is a nice catchphrase, the truth is that most 50-year-olds are not engaged in demanding degree programs or serious training programs at work.

EXERCISES

Our goal is to measure the lifetime earnings associated with different educational choices and to get a feel for what these results may imply about the returns to post-secondary investments in education. We will employ data from the American Community Survey (ACS). The ACS contains a representative sample of the US population along with several demographic and economic variables. Follow these steps to download the data:

- Visit https://usa.ipums.org/usa-action/variables/group and click on "Select Samples."
- Select only the 2012 ACS sample. (An easy way to deselect all samples is to uncheck the "Default sample from each year" button.)
- Click "Submit sample selections."
- Select the following variables (using the "A–Z" drop down menu): "INCWAGE" (wage and salary income), "EMPSTAT" (employment status), "CLASSWKR" (class of worker), "WKSWORK2" (weeks worked last year, intervaled), "UHRSWORK" (usual hours worked per week), "SEX," "EDUC" (educational attainment), and "AGE."
- Click on "View cart" and then on "Create data extract."

- IPUMS will add some default variables to your selection. This is fine. If you would like the data to be in a specific format (e.g., Stata format), select that option at this step.
- Click "Submit Extract."
  - You need to request a free account from IPUMS by entering your email address.
- Now you need to wait for the extract to be created. In the meantime, if you did not ask to download a ".dta" Stata version of the data file, download the Stata command file by clicking on the "Stata" button. This takes you to a page displaying a Stata do-file that you will need to run so you can properly label all the variables you downloaded.
  - Copy and paste the do-file text into your Stata do-file editor.
  - Either change the directory at the top of the do-file (`cd location/folder/`) *or* change the line that says `using filename.dat` to `using location/folder/filename.dat`.
- When your extract is ready, click on the "Data" link.
- Save the data file. (Pay attention to where you save it so you can change the directory in the do-file.)
- Run the labeling do-file that you copied from IPUMS, and save the resulting data set as a new data set named something more intuitive (i.e., econ-of-ed-pset-1.dta).
- Now you have a properly labeled .dta file with the variables you need to complete the exercises below.

▶ First, write 2–3 paragraphs about the ACS sampling strategy and coverage rate. Who is surveyed, how are they surveyed, and how representative is the ACS of the US population as a whole? Does the ACS provide a good snapshot of the US workforce at a given point in time (like on June 1, 2015)?

▶ What is hotdecking? What is topcoding? How do these affect measures of lifetime earnings using the ACS?

▶ Before actually computing the earnings stream, you need to set up your sample. Specifically:

(a) Restrict the sample to employed individuals, working more than 50 weeks in a year and more than 30 hours per week.

(b) Drop from the data self-employed workers.

(c) Consider only individuals between 18 and 65 years old.

(d) Create the following educational categorical variable:

- Less than High School: [8, 11] years of schooling.
- High School: 12 years of schooling.
- Some College: [13, 15] years of schooling.
- College: 16 years of schooling.
- College+: 17 years of schooling.

▶ For each education category and each gender, compute the average earnings at each age level. Prepare a figure showing your results.

▶ Assume that young people have no idea whether they will be average, above average, or below average in any particular career (requiring a certain education level) that they may choose. Also, assume that the economy is in steady state; that is, the wage structure today is going to be the wage structure in the future. Under the steady-state assumption, compute the present value of the earnings stream for each education category for men and women. Perform these calculations for several plausible discount rates, while making explicit assumptions about the ages at which persons who achieve different final education levels begin their full-time careers.

▶ Consider the decision to attend and finish college as opposed to going to work right after high school graduation. Based on the information in the exercises above as well as other information you can find on the internet about the costs of attending college, evaluate whether or not investing in college is a profitable investment in expected value, given several different assumptions about the interest rate that you would have to pay to finance educational expenditures. Do the calculations separately for men and women. Describe and discuss the results and their implications.

ONE

Resources and Outcomes

Table 1.1 presents basic statistics about spending levels in publicly funded schools for a number of developed countries. These data come from 2012. All monetary figures are in 2016 US dollars. These data show that, as a rule, public education authorities in many developed countries spent 10,000 US dollars or more per student. To place this number in context, note that, in 2016 in the US, the median weekly salary among full-time workers implied an annual income of just over 40,000 US dollars.[1]

Table 1.1 Education Spending and Pupil-Teacher Ratio in Developed Countries

Country	Initial Government Funding per Student[a]		Initial Government Funding per Student as % of GDP per capita		Average Pupil-Teacher Ratio	
	Primary	Secondary	Primary	Secondary	Primary	Secondary
Australia	12,898	11,673	18.2	16.5	—	—
France	7,889	11,479	18.5	26.9	17.8	12.8
Germany	7,972	10,669	17.3	23.2	11.7	12.7
Ireland	9,656	13,295	18.8	25.8	16.1	—
Israel	7,848	5,488	23.1	16.1	—	—
Japan	11,492	12,439	22.8	24.7	17.1	11.7
Netherlands	8,817	12,380	17.0	23.9	11.5	13.9
New Zealand	9,439	9,786	23.5	24.4	14.6	14.4
United States	10,702	11,872	20.6	22.8	14.4	14.7

a. 2016 US Dollars

This table contains 2012 data on education funding and pupil-teacher ratios for primary and secondary education. All data is drawn from the United Nations Educational, Scientific, and Cultural Organization (UNESCO) Institute for Statistics.

Many families with two or more school-age children would find it almost impossible to pay for their child's public education out of their own resources. Consider a single parent with two school-age children who earns roughly the median income for a full-time worker. To fully fund her own children's education, she would need to set aside about half of her pretax income. Further, for some families with more children, less income, or both, the comparable fraction would be close to 100% and possibly more.

Private schools often spend less per student than neighboring public schools, but even at these lower spending levels, many disadvantaged families do not have the resources they would need to feed, clothe, and properly educate their own children. Since private lenders are not willing to finance the education of the children in these families, we have argued that governments can improve welfare by funding education directly.

Yet knowing that we can justify government funding for education is not the same as knowing how government should purchase education services. In the balance of this book, we consider different mechanisms that governments could use to purchase education services for children. We begin by discussing the approach that governments employ most often. In the US and many other developed countries, the vast majority of public funds devoted to elementary and secondary schooling are spent in public school systems. We call these systems "public" because educators in these systems work as public employees under administrators who are also public employees, and these administrators report to elected officials.

In Chapters 2 and 3, we consider policies that seek to make traditional public schools more efficient. In Chapters 4 and 5, we consider systems that allow private organizations to operate publicly funded schools. Both charter and voucher systems seek to improve efficiency by requiring all schools that receive public funds to compete for students. In the final chapter, we discuss the components that we expect to find in an optimal education system and note that an optimal system would likely combine elements of all the reform agendas that we study in Chapters 2 through 5. Policy proposals that most legislators and many researchers treat as alternative approaches to education reform may, in reality, be complementary.

1.1 Waste and Calls for Reform

In recent decades, numerous calls for education reform in the United States and elsewhere cite evidence that public school systems, particularly large urban school systems, are often inefficient. Before exploring alternatives to traditional public school systems, we examine this evidence.

We begin by stating exactly what we mean when we say that a school system is inefficient.

A school system is inefficient if it is possible to create a different system that receives less funding but produces the same learning output.

Our definition asserts that efficient school systems minimize the cost of producing the skills children acquire. Given the assumptions we usually make in microeconomics classes, we could have given an equivalent definition that identified inefficient school systems as those that could be replaced by alternatives that produced more learning given the same funding. Either way, efficient school systems do not allow rent-seeking, corruption, or incompetence to divert resources away from their educational mission.

To make our definition useful, we must define the learning output of a school system. For our purposes, the learning output of a school is the value of the skills that students acquire as a result of the services it provides. This definition embodies an important separability assumption. We are assuming that, at least conceptually, we can separate the skill gains that result from the efforts of parents, community groups, private tutors, and students themselves from the skill gains that result directly from the education services provided by schools.

This is a strong assumption, but in practice, we can gather useful evidence about the efficiency of particular types of schools even if we are not able to precisely measure the value of the output created by schools. Whenever schools purchase inputs that do not generate any learning gains for students, there is a prima facie case that schools are operating inefficiently, since these schools could forgo these purchases and produce the same gains for students at lower cost. In short, we can often identify wasteful expenditures even in settings where we are not able to precisely measure all dimensions of school output, and the presence of these wasteful expenditures constitutes direct evidence of inefficiency.

1.1.1 Corruption

On numerous occasions in recent decades, school reform efforts in many large US cities gained public support following investigations by criminal justice officials or local newspapers that revealed significant waste and fraud. Table 1.2 contains summaries of some relatively recent scandals in large public school systems in the US. Table 1.3 (at the end of this chapter) provides a more detailed account of similar scandals during the past twenty-five years.

In large public school systems, scandals that involve the misappropriation or theft of hundreds of thousands, if not millions, of dollars are quite common. Yet the existence of these scandals does not prove that urban public school systems are inefficient relative to other types of organizations. Mismanagement and corruption are also problems in private businesses, private charities, and other government agencies. The Chicago Public Schools spend more than 6 billion dollars annually. In any organization that spends this much, it may be impossible to prevent employees from stealing or wasting millions of dollars.

Nonetheless, some urban school systems have performance records that fall short of any reasonable standard. Here, we discuss one example.

1.1.2 Kansas City

In the 1970s and early 1980s, the Kansas City, MO, public school system was poorly funded, and the vast majority of the students were black. At the same time, surrounding suburban districts with large populations of white students enjoyed better funding. The combination of racial segregation and significant funding disparities invited lawsuits, and in 1985, federal judge Russell Clark ordered the Missouri state government and the local government in Kansas City to raise revenues to fund improvements in the Kansas City schools.

Clark took partial control of the schools and told local officials to tell him what they needed to bring achievement in Kansas City schools up to state norms. In response, officials submitted their wish lists. Funding in the Kansas City system increased dramatically, and school facilities and programs improved in tangible ways. Class sizes shrank, teacher salaries rose, facilities and technology improved, and students gained access to special magnet programs.[2]

Measured in current dollars, Judge Clark oversaw the infusion of more than two billion additional dollars of spending in the Kansas City schools during the period from 1985 to 1995.[3] According to Ciotti (1998), the district's enrollment never exceeded 37,000 students. Thus, in current dollars,

Table 1.2 Recent Corruption Scandals in US Urban School Districts

Chicago

2015	Chicago Public Schools CEO Barbara Byrd-Bennett took kickbacks from vendors in exchange for fraudulently granting them $23 million in no-bid teacher training contracts. (Peters 2015)
2014	Five men stole more than $870,000 from Chicago Public Schools through fraudulent purchasing and reimbursement requests. (Perez and Gormer 2015)

Dallas

2008	The Chief Technology Officer of the Dallas Independent School District took over $1 million in kickbacks from a Houston businessman in exchange for two technology services contracts worth $120 million. (United States Attorney's Office 2008)

Detroit

2013	A former Detroit Public Schools accountant defrauded the 2013 school district of $530,000 via fictitious payments to a shell corporation. (Dixon 2013)
2009	Barbara Byrd-Bennett, who was later prosecuted for corruption as CEO of Chicago Public Schools, directed a $40 million contract to her former and future employer while working for Detroit Public Schools. (Siedel et al. 2015)

Los Angeles

2015	Eight people in Los Angeles and surrounding communities stole $50 million through false invoices from a program designed to offer substance abuse treatment to students. (United States Attorney's Office 2015)
2014	Two men and an L.A. Unified School District employee fraudulently charged the Los Angeles school district $5.4 million by submitting fake invoices for irrigation clocks. (County of Los Angeles District Attorney 2014)

San Francisco

2013	Six employees embezzled more than $15 million from the San Francisco Unified School District by moving money into nonprofits under their personal control. (Winegarner 2013)

Washington, D.C.

2014	A compliance officer in the District of Columbia public schools directed more than $460,000 in fraudulent payments to a transportation company which he owned and operated. (United States Attorney's Office 2014)

Judge Clark oversaw spending increases of more than 5,000 dollars per student per year.

However, test scores for students in grades five and above did not improve, and in many cases, subject-specific scores for students in specific grades fell relative to national norms and relative to the scores reported by other districts in the state.[4] Further, few suburban students chose to enter the Kansas City schools. Families did not relocate to the city, and few students chose to commute from outside the district even though the court mandate created funds to subsidize their commuting costs.[5]

All accounts of Judge Clark's intervention in Kansas City and the results that followed point to the same conclusion. The Kansas City public schools were grossly inefficient in the 1980s and 1990s. Two billion dollars in additional funding produced almost no measurable gains in student achievement.

Still, there are thousands of public school systems in the US. The details of the Kansas City spending experiment are stunning, but these results tells us little about the efficiency of the average public school system.[6]

1.2 Time Series Evidence

In a series of papers, Eric Hanushek points out that spending and achievement data for the nation as a whole exhibit patterns similar to those we see during the 1980s and 1990s in Kansas City.[7] He notes that average per-pupil spending in US schools roughly doubled between 1970 and 2000, but available measures of student achievement provide little evidence of achievement growth over the same time period.

It is difficult to know what to make of these observations because we have no way of knowing what achievement trends would have looked like in a world where governments held spending constant at 1970 levels. Those who studied the Kansas City experiment were able to compare achievement trends in Kansas City over the 1980s and 1990s to trends nationally or in nearby districts that did not receive large increases in funding, but we have no data that would allow us to credibly estimate how achievement would have evolved in a parallel universe where US public schools kept real per-pupil spending constant after 1970.

Further, as Hanushek and Rivkin (2006) acknowledge, there are several reasons to believe that student achievement would have fallen given this scenario. To begin, since 1970 changes in federal law have required public schools to provide additional and often expensive services for students with special needs. Further, single-parent families are much more common now than in 1970, and the trend away from two-parent families may be correlated with declines in the amount of time parents spend helping their children with school work. Finally, compared to many other types of organizations, schools have not benefited from recent changes in technology. Many economists contend that skill-biased technical change has caused the relative cost of educated workers to rise dramatically in recent decades. Yet changes in technology have not greatly impacted the efficiency of classroom instruction. Taken together, these observations suggest that the quality-constant cost of staffing schools may have risen substantially.

While Hanushek and Rivkin argue that these factors cannot account for secular trends in spending in US schools, data do not exist that allow us to definitively evaluate this claim. No reliable time-series data exist concerning the value of parental inputs into their children's schooling. Further, while it is clear that schools have responded to the rising cost of hiring the most skilled college graduates by hiring teachers who have weaker cognitive skills than teachers from previous generations, it is not clear how much it would have cost schools to maintain teacher quality on this dimension.[8]

1.3 More Court Orders

One can imagine an ideal setting where researchers randomly assign changes in funding levels to a large number of public schools or school systems and then measure the accompanying changes in achievement among their student populations. Given the results of such an experiment, researchers could trace out the average relationship between changes in funding and changes in student achievement among public schools.[9] In cases where the affected students come from disadvantaged families that do not tutor their own children or acquire private tutors for them, the changes in student achievement induced by these experiments tell us something about the link between total educational resources and outcomes in public schools.

Any given team of researchers would likely find it impossible to run experiments that randomly change funding levels for large numbers of schools in a given state or the country as a whole. However, in recent decades, courts have issued many orders that forced states and local districts to change their spending levels. The Kansas City intervention grew out of a racial desegregation case, but many courts have ordered changes in education funding in response to plaintiffs who claimed that existing systems of school finance within a state created unconstitutional spending disparities between economically advantaged and disadvantaged districts. Over the past three decades, many researchers have tried to learn something about the relationship between per-pupil spending and student outcomes by treating these court-ordered spending changes as natural experiments.[10]

Researchers who work in this area face several challenges. First, these court decisions often create new, quite complex constraints on how much or how little various school systems may spend. So it can be difficult to pin down how these decisions impact each district or school.[11] Second, because school systems respond to these decisions, the changes in spending that follow them reflect not only the constraints imposed by the new rules but also the efforts of school systems to choose their best response to these new rules. Finally, it is difficult to identify clean control groups, that is, groups of schools that allow researchers to estimate how achievement in the schools affected by court-mandated spending reforms would have evolved if the courts had not mandated the reforms. Court-ordered changes in school finance decisions often affect all districts in a given state at once, and in states where courts deny petitions to change school financing rules, elected officials often change spending rules in response to political pressure created by these efforts.[12]

Given these challenges, it is not surprising that studies in this literature offer a diverse set of findings. Several have found mixed evidence, at best, that court-mandated increases in spending raise achievement.[13] Others conclude that court-ordered changes in spending do improve educational outcomes, future labor market outcomes, or both.[14]

This diversity of findings likely reflects many factors. Here, we note three. First, all researchers in this literature must implicitly or explicitly create estimates of the outcomes that would have occurred in the absence of court-ordered spending changes, but different researchers approach this estimation problem in varied ways. Second, measurement error plagues these studies. In most cases, it is not possible to match individual student data with spending levels in the exact schools each student attended in each grade. Third, not all court-ordered changes in school spending generate the same changes in how schools operate. There is likely much ex ante heterogeneity in the efficiency of schools that experience court-ordered changes in spending. Further, in some cases, court-ordered spending reforms are accompanied by reforms to curricula or accountability systems that directly impact how schools operate.

1.4 Cost-Benefit Analyses Are Not Our Focus

Some of the papers in this literature and other literatures that examine links between school resources and student outcomes contain attempts to calculate whether or not the learning gains induced by new spending are worth more in present value than the costs. However, we will not explore these issues.

Our focus is the extent to which various education policies promote efficient use of public funds allocated to education. Accurate cost-benefit calculations may tell us something about whether or not a policy change, within a given system, produced benefits greater than or equal to required costs. However, these calculations would often tell us nothing about the productive efficiency of the schools operating within the system in question.

Assume that the marginal value of additional spending per student is a decreasing function of the current spending level. Further, assume that the baseline level of spending in a given system is far below the socially optimal level. In this case, the benefits of new spending may exceed costs, even if schools waste a significant portion of the new resources they receive. On the other hand, if the baseline level is far above the optimal level, the benefits of new spending may fall short of the costs, even if all schools are operating efficiently.

We seek to understand how different systems and policies do or do not promote efficient resource use in publicly funded schools. Cost-benefit calculations do not speak directly to this topic unless one is willing to assume that existing institutions represent the only feasible mechanisms for delivering publicly funded education services to children. However, a key aim of this book is to consider alternatives to the traditional public schooling model. We hope to understand whether or not it is possible to serve students better by employing mechanisms that reform, augment, or even replace traditional public schools. Whether or not particular interventions, within the traditional public school model, pass cost-benefit tests is of little interest to us.

1.5 The Education Production Function

To learn more about the efficiency of public schools, we can try to determine whether or not traditional public schools commonly adopt costly policies that generate no benefits for students. Yet, before we can conclude that a given policy produces no gains for students, we must understand the mapping between educational inputs and learning outputs. We need to understand how educators, families, and students jointly produce different types of achievement before we can isolate particular inputs that, at the margin, contribute nothing to student achievement.

Economists refer to this mapping as the education production function. The modern empirical literature on education production begins with the *Equality of Education Opportunity* (1966), also known as the Coleman Report. Over the past fifty years, scholars from many disciplines have developed many empirical models of education production. Almost all of these models are variations on an equation like the following:

$$h_{ijt} = f(h_{ijt-1}, z_{ijt}, x_{it}, e_{ijt}, \varepsilon_{ijt}) \qquad (1.1)$$

Here, h_{ijt} is the human capital of student i in school j at the end of period t. The convention in this literature is to ignore the distinction between learning skills and productive skills that we discussed in our introduction. Instead, this literature classifies skills according to academic fields of study. It is common for researchers to implicitly assume that h_{ijt} can be expressed as a weighted sum of the skills that i possesses in different subject areas, such as math, reading, science, etc. This assumption allows researchers to develop separate models for the production of math, reading, science, and other skill types.

The literature we discuss in this chapter deals primarily with the production of basic reading and math skills in elementary and secondary schools. Thus, our primary concern here is the creation of skills that contribute to the concept of learning efficiency that we discussed in the Introduction.

According to equation (1.1), several factors determine h_{ijt}. As in our three-period model from the Introduction, skill acquired before period t begins, h_{ijt-1}, influences the rate of learning. z_{ijt} denotes the instructional resources provided to student i in school j, and x_{it} captures the instructional resources provided to student i outside school. These resources include supplemental tutoring, help from family members, educational software used at home, etc.

Next, e_{ijt} denotes the study effort of student i enrolled in school j during period t. This effort may be applied during school, at home, and during supplemental programs outside school.

Finally, ε_{ijt} is a shock that captures how life circumstances affect learning. In some years, a given student will suffer health problems or family crises, while in other years, the same student may be fortunate enough to enjoy perfect health and a new set of classmates that she really enjoys. Here, we assume that these factors and others like them are random shocks to the learning process that are beyond the control of individual students, families, or educators.[15]

Our education production function is one simple equation, but it implies a rich and dynamic process for human capital development. Note that, as in the three-period model we explored in the Introduction, a student's own time and skills are inputs in the production of human capital. This means that the production of human capital in period t depends indirectly on the set of human capital investments made in all previous periods.

In addition, although researchers often use the education production framework to organize empirical research on schools, the model highlights the fact that schools do not provide many of the inputs that affect h_{ijt}. The whole history of family investments before and during period t influences skill creation, as does the history of student effort levels.

In empirical work, social scientists often assume that education production functions are linear. Most employ empirical models of education production that are variants of one of these two models:

$$a_{ijt} = \tilde{z}_{jt}\gamma + \tilde{x}_{it}\beta + \eta_{ijt} \qquad (1.2)$$

or

$$a_{ijt} = a_{ijt-1}\alpha + \tilde{z}_{jt}\gamma + \tilde{x}_{it}\beta + v_{ijt} \qquad (1.3)$$

where

- a_{ijt} a measure of achievement for student i at time t in education unit j. This achievement measure is usually a test score, and j can be used to index classrooms, schools, or school districts.
- $\tilde{z}_{jt}$ a vector of characteristics that describe education unit j at time t. These may include per-pupil spending, pupil-teacher ratios, the presence of computers or other instructional equipment, etc.

- $\tilde{x}_{it}$ a vector of demographic characteristics that describe student i or his family at time t. These may include race, gender, parental education, family income, etc.
- η_{ijt} unmeasured determinants of learning that influence achievement for student i in unit j at time t.
- ν_{ijt} unmeasured factors that influence the growth of measured achievement for student i in unit j during time t.

Equation (1.3) is commonly known as a "value-added" model (VAM) because it uses measures of prior achievement as proxies for the skill that students bring to a given school term. Given this conditioning, the coefficients on $\tilde{z}_{jt}$ provide information about the relationship between particular school inputs and the additional learning that takes place during a given school term.

Given modern computers and statistical software, it takes a few seconds to use regression methods to estimate linear models. However, researchers can argue for years about whether or not these regression results provide consistent estimators of the causal parameters in education production functions.

We do not have time to review all that you may or may not have learned about regression models in econometrics. However, let us take time to review some of the most important ideas.[16] In recent years, many researchers have gained access to administrative data that allow them to track student achievement over many years. Thus, VAM specifications similar to equation (1.3) have become standard tools in the education production function literature, and we shall focus our attention on this model.[17]

Let us begin by reviewing some basic principles about Ordinary Least Squares (OLS) regression. OLS always solves a specific prediction problem. If we regress a_{ijt} on a_{ijt-1}, $\tilde{x}_{it}$, and $\tilde{z}_{jt}$, we can form predicted test scores in period t for each student i in each unit j using

$$\hat{a}_{ijt} = a_{ijt-1}\hat{\alpha} + \tilde{z}_{jt}\hat{\gamma} + \tilde{x}_{it}\hat{\beta}$$

where $(\hat{\alpha}, \hat{\gamma}, \hat{\beta})$ are the OLS estimators of (α, γ, β). The vector of $\hat{a}_{ijt}$ values represents the best predictions of a_{ijt} that one can form using linear combinations of $(a_{ijt-1}, \tilde{z}_{jt}, \tilde{x}_{it})$.[18] However, in most cases, education researchers do not run OLS because they want to predict student test scores among existing students. Researchers want to answer specific counterfactual questions.

Here, we consider two types of questions that motivate empirical studies of education production functions. The first is:

Question 1. Holding all other education inputs constant, how would student achievement, a_{ijt}, change if schools were to increase a given school input?

Note that Question 1 is not a direct inquiry about the education production function presented in equation (1.1). We are not asking how the values of student skill stocks change when schools employ more of a given input. To address such a question, we would have to discover much about the mapping between a_{ijt} and h_{ijt}.

The literature on anchoring (e.g., Cunha et al. (2010)) explores the challenges that face researchers who seek to translate test score units, a_{ijt}, into the monetary values of individual skills, h_{ijt}, but most of the existing literature ignores these issues and proceeds under the assumption that measured achievement can be described by the following equation:

$$a_{ijt} = g(h_{ijt}) + \xi_{ijt}$$

where $g(\cdot)$ is a strictly increasing function, and ξ_{ijt} reflects measurement error inherent in achievement testing. If we assume that ξ_{ijt} is mean zero and i.i.d. for all combinations of i, j, and t, this formulation implies that changes in the quality of schooling that raise true skill also raise expected achievement. Thus, if a given change in school investments or school programs produces no gains in expected achievement, researchers assume that this change produced no gains in human capital.

To keep our equations simple, consider the special case, $g(h_{ijt}) = h_{ijt}$, and substitute our equation for a_{ijt} into equation (1.1). We get the following:

$$a_{ijt} = f(a_{ijt-1} - \xi_{ijt-1}, z_{ijt}, x_{it}, e_{ijt}, \varepsilon_{ijt}) + \xi_{ijt}$$

Now it is easy to see that the VAM regression in equation (1.3) is just a linear version of this human capital production function. Further, we see that the error term, v_{ijt}, in equation (1.3) is likely influenced by the following factors:

- unobserved student effort, e_{ijt} ;
- unobserved shocks from life circumstances that affect learning, ε_{ijt};
- measurement errors in achievement tests, ξ_{ijt-1}, and ξ_{ijt};

- differences between $(\tilde{z}_{jt}, \tilde{x}_{it})$ and the complete portfolio of investments in student learning made by schools and families, (z_{jt}, x_{it}).

Consider a researcher who gathers data on a large sample of students from a collection of schools that employ different school resources, $\tilde{z}_{jt}$, and runs an OLS regression of a_{ijt} on $(a_{ijt-1}, \tilde{z}_{jt}, \tilde{x}_{it})$. Given our maintained assumption that the education production function is linear, what do we need to assume about our data collection process in order to claim that the resulting vector, $\hat{\gamma}_{OLS}$, provides unbiased estimates of the causal effects of changes in measured school inputs, $\tilde{z}_{jt}$, on changes in expected achievement, a_{ijt}?

You may remember from econometrics that, if we assume that $E(v_{ijt}|a_{ijt-1}, \tilde{z}_{jt}, \tilde{x}_{it}) = 0$, we can interpret our regression results as estimates of causal parameters, but what does this condition mean? It is just a formal way of asserting that, in expectation, the unmeasured determinants of achievement do not depend on the measured determinants, $(a_{ijt-1}, \tilde{z}_{jt}, \tilde{x}_{it})$, that serve as regressors. However, given our list of factors that influence v_{ijt}, there are good reasons to worry that $E(v_{ijt}|a_{ijt-1}, \tilde{z}_{jt}, \tilde{x}_{it}) \neq 0$.

1.5.1 A Cautionary Tale about VAM Regressions

Assume that a researcher takes the following steps: The researcher creates a sample of fifth-grade math students by randomly selecting one student from each fifth-grade math class in a given state. The researcher then collects fifth-grade math scores for this sample of students as well as fourth-grade math scores from the previous year. Finally, the researcher collects the number of students in each student's math class. With these data, the researcher runs a regression of fifth-grade math scores on fourth-grade math scores and fifth-grade class size.

In this context, would the regression results tell us how expected fifth-grade math achievement for a randomly selected student would change if we were to change the size of her fifth-grade math class while holding other inputs into her education constant? The answer is no if either of the following conjectures are true:

- When school administrators are forced to create larger-than-average classes due to temporary, grade-specific jumps in enrollment, they encourage teachers in the affected grades to take additional personal leave days and thus use substitute teachers more often in these classes.

- Fourth-grade achievement test scores are noisy measures of the true math skill that students bring to fifth grade, and fifth-grade students in districts that have lower-than-average class sizes possess higher-than-average levels of true math skill at the end of fourth grade.

Please note that there is nothing special about the above list of conjectures. You should be able to come up with equally plausible ones that also imply that the regression results in our hypothetical scenario would not yield an unbiased estimate of the relationship between class size and fifth-grade math achievement.

Yet it is important to note that these conjectures have something in common. They both suggest that, conditional on measured fourth-grade achievement, some unmeasured determinant of fifth-grade achievement may be correlated with class size in our cross-section sample of students. In the first, unmeasured differences in the time that students spend on math are correlated with class size, if one assumes that substitute teachers do not keep students on task as well as regular teachers. In the second, students in schools with small classes begin fifth grade, on average, with better math skills than other students, and the measurement error in fourth-grade test scores implies that, even among students who have the same fourth-grade test scores, part of this true skill difference remains.[19]

Since families and schools choose both measured and unmeasured educational inputs simultaneously, it is easy to imagine ways that these measured and unmeasured inputs are linked. If class sizes vary among schools for specific reasons, then unmeasured educational inputs or specific forms of measurement error may vary among schools for the same reasons.

There is nothing about these observations that is specific to inquiries about the effects of class size on achievement. It would be easy to construct similar scenarios that involve researchers using VAM regressions to assess the causal links between student achievement and many different measures of education inputs, such as total spending per student, teacher salaries, or per-student spending on computers.

Given these observations, education research in recent decades has given more attention to results from regression models that employ data from experiments. These researchers hope that, by collecting data from experiments in schools, they can avoid many of the issues that make the interpretation of VAM results problematic given data from observational studies.

1.5.2 Experimental Data

Let us assume that an education authority decides to run an experiment to determine the causal relationship between class size and student achievement. If the education authority randomly assigns class sizes to classrooms and then randomly assigns students to classrooms, it can create random variation in class size that is unrelated to the characteristics of students, their families, or the other characteristics of their classrooms. Given data from such an experiment, the following VAM regression model becomes quite appealing:

$$a_{ijt} = a_{ijt-1}\alpha + \text{size}_{jt}\,\gamma + v_{ijt} \qquad (1.4)$$

where size_{jt} is the randomly assigned size for classroom j at time t.

If the assignment of students to classrooms and the assignment of class sizes to classrooms is truly random in our experiment, then by design, all time-invariant components of v_{ijt} must be statistically independent of both prior achievement, a_{ijt-1}, and class size.

You may be guessing that this independence property implies that $E(v_{ijt}|a_{ijt-1}, \text{size}_{jt}) = 0$ and that $\hat{\gamma}_{ols}$ is an unbiased estimator of the expected change in measured achievement associated with a one-pupil increase in class size. However, we must again proceed with caution. Recall that both parents and schools have the opportunity to take actions, in response to the treatment their students receive in the experiment, that may influence outcomes.

Consider the following possibilities:

- Some parents in the study may be particularly focused on fostering their child's achievement growth. If these parents learn that their child has been randomly assigned to a large class, they may spend extra time helping their child with school work or hire private tutors.
- School administrators may allocate more in-school tutoring or computer resources to students who are randomly assigned to large classes.

In both of these scenarios, behavioral responses to our hypothetical class size experiment could create a correlation between unmeasured determinants of student achievement and class size within the experimental sample. Thus, even when data are gathered through experiments that involve random assignment to treatment and control groups, we cannot be confident that the results from VAM regressions are going to provide unbiased estimates of the true causal impacts of particular education inputs on expected achievement. In sum, Question 1 above is hard to answer because it begins with the phrase "*holding all other education inputs constant.*"

Recall that we began our book by pointing out that, in a world with no public funding for education, some families would not be both willing and able to invest efficiently in their children's education. However, Becker and Tomes (1986) point out that parents who are both wealthy and altruistic would invest efficiently in their children even if governments allocated no funds for education. Thus, we expect that these same parents would increase (decrease) their own educational investments in ways that would fully offset any publicly observed decrease (increase) in the quality of their children's public schools.

Imagine that a community of wealthy families experiences a well-publicized reduction in state funding for local schools. Further, assume that, after this reduction, researchers document little change in student learning outcomes. Would such findings necessarily imply that these schools had been wasting resources before the spending cuts took place? No. In such a community, many parents would be able and willing to, at least partially, offset such spending reductions by making more private investments in their children.

This observation leads us to consider a different question.

Question 2. How would expected student achievement, a_{ijt}, change if education policy makers were to mandate that schools increase a particular measured school input, *given that both parents and schools may adjust their behavior in response to this mandate?*

It should be clear that VAM regressions on experimental data can be used to answer inquiries that take the form of Question 2 as long as the behavioral responses that are permitted within the experiment are the same as those that are allowed under the new mandate.

For example, consider an experiment in which education officials select a random sample of schools for treatment, and these officials give each principal an additional 500 dollars per student but place no restrictions on how these principals may spend the additional resources. Ex post, researchers can use a regression to estimate the expected change in student achievement that would result from implementing a similar increase in funding for all schools, and some would argue that this expected change is a parameter of interest for policy makers.

On the other hand, consider an experiment in which education officials in a given school district randomly select one classroom per school to participate in an experimental program that promotes math achievement using new materials and new teaching methods. Further, assume that education officials do not randomly select the teachers who will teach these new methods but allow principals to make these assignment decisions. If principals in treatment schools systematically select their best teachers to teach the new material in the treatment classes, the results of the experiment cannot be used to infer the changes in achievement that policy makers should expect from introducing the new material and methods in all classrooms. In any universal implementation of the new program, principals would no longer be able to assign only their best teachers to the program. Thus, the treatment that many students would receive in a universal implementation would differ systematically from the treatment that students received, on average, in the experiment.

1.6 Salary Schedules

Now that you have been properly warned about the challenges of interpreting results from the empirical literature on the educational production function, let us ask what the results from this literature teach us about the efficiency of traditional public schools. Does this literature provide evidence that public schools, at least in the US, routinely fund policies or programs that are expensive but produce no learning gains for students? Does this literature demonstrate that public schools refuse to adopt new policies that would both save money and raise student achievement?

Over the past fifty years, social scientists have produced thousands of education production function studies, and debates concerning what this literature teaches us about the efficiency of public schools continue. Yet, as a rule, the studies that raise the most compelling concerns about how public schools allocate resources focus on policies that determine teacher pay and retention.

1.6.1 Master of Education Degrees

Teachers' unions and other political organizations representing public school teachers have lobbied over the past half century or more for salary schedules that link teacher pay to credentials and seniority.[20] As a result, the vast majority of public school districts in the United States now have salary schedules for teachers that mandate automatic raises for all teachers who obtain master's degrees, and according to Chingos and Peterson (2011), seventeen states require that all school districts adopt salary schedules with this feature.

Teachers have responded to these policies. Hanushek and Rivkin (2006) note that the fraction of public school teachers with a master's degree more than doubled between 1970 and 2000. Among the more than 56 percent of US public school teachers in 2000 who had master's degrees, the vast majority held master's degrees in education. In most districts, teachers receive raises for acquiring master's degrees in education. Relatively few teachers receive raises for obtaining master's degrees in particular subjects such as mathematics or biology.

Although the practice of linking teacher pay and master's degrees in education is widespread, the empirical literature on education production provides little or no evidence that the training offered in these programs improves the performance of teachers in the classroom. Chingos and Peterson (2011) cite a number of studies that find no effect of master's degree training on teacher performance. They then examine longitudinal data from Florida that allows them to measure the performance of a given teacher's students before and after the teacher in question completes a master's degree. They too find no evidence that teachers who complete their master's degrees improve their teaching. Holding constant the previous academic records of her students, the expected performance of a given teacher's students on end-of-year exams does not change when she acquires a master's degree.

We stated above that an education system is inefficient if it is possible to design a different system that produces the same social output at lower cost, and it is easy to see how officials could produce the same learning outcomes at lower cost by abandoning existing salary rules related to master's degrees.[21] Education officials could instruct teachers not to pursue traditional master's degrees in education schools but instead promise to grant raises and a master's certification to teachers who spend a fixed period teaching extra classes.[22]

For the purposes of this illustration, we assume that the costs and benefits of this alternative scheme are the same as those associated with existing master's certification programs. As a worst-case scenario, we assume that, similar to the training offered by traditional master's programs, the experience gained from teaching extra classes in the alternative program would not improve teacher performance in the classroom. Further, we can always pick a required amount of extra teaching such that teachers would be indifferent between going through this alternative certification plan or incurring the costs associated with a traditional master's degree program.[23]

Given these assumptions, it is immediate that our alternative master's certification program would dominate the status quo. Under both policies, the requirements for master's certification do not involve activities that improve teaching. However, given the alternative certification program, school systems would need fewer teachers because all teachers seeking their master's certification would be teaching more classes. Thus, under our alternative approach, student learning would not be harmed and schools would save money.[24]

Salary schedules that reward public school teachers for obtaining master's degrees in education are wasteful. In the US, they are also ubiquitous.

1.6.2 Pay by Field

While public school districts do base pay on seniority and credentials, most public school districts do not pay teachers differently according to the subjects or grades they teach. Some may pay secondary school teachers differently than primary school teachers, but often district salary schedules draw no distinctions between teachers who teach different subjects or grades.[25]

This practice is likely wasteful. If any organization pays more for a factor of production than its market price, the organization is wasting resources, and it seems fanciful to imagine that the outside earning opportunities of teachers do not vary with their specialties.

Consider a district that pays all teachers according to a common salary schedule. In this district, a high school teacher who teaches computer programming and AP statistics almost certainly has better earning prospects outside teaching than the typical art teacher who works with students in grades K–3. Thus, two things are possible. The school district is paying both teachers more than their outside options, or the district is paying the art teacher more than her outside option.

In either case, the district is paying more than it needs to pay to deliver the quality of instruction it currently provides. This inefficient practice is pervasive in public education and has been for decades.

1.6.3 Returns to Experience

Education researchers also criticize the common practice of linking teacher salaries to years of service in a particular public school district. In many public school districts, teacher salaries are almost completely determined by whether or not a given teacher has a master's degree and how many years the teacher has taught in the district, but the education production literature provides little evidence that teaching experience improves teacher performance after five years of teaching experience.[26]

On the surface, this policy seems to mirror the practice of granting raises for teachers who acquire master's degrees. Public schools are paying teachers with 15 years of service more than their peers with 10 years of service even though, in expectation, these more senior teachers are not better teachers. However, there is one important difference. Raises linked to master's degrees are payments for spending time and money on activities outside school, but raises linked to seniority are payments for time spent teaching.

The fact that teacher salaries in public schools apparently continue rising with experience long after teacher productivity stops rising with experience is not prima facie evidence that public schools are wasting resources. A large literature in personnel economics demonstrates that firms may back-load compensation to encourage workers not to shirk.[27] Older workers are less likely to reduce effort as they near retirement if they know that being fired will cause them to forfeit their highest earning years and a noteworthy portion of their pension benefits. Nonetheless, many public school teachers work under contracts that offer extraordinary levels of employment protection and mandate few consequential performance reviews. In this setting, the pay scales that back-load teacher compensation may do little to solve agency problems between teachers and schools.

1.6.4 Unions

Public discussions of education policy often proceed as if the questionable aspects of personnel policies in public schools result directly from the activities of teachers' unions. However, rigid salary schedules, work rules, and robust employment protections feature prominently in the civil service systems that govern employment in many nonunion school districts. Further, Lovenheim (2009) examines data from union certification elections and reports that, over several decades, districts in three midwestern states did not experience important increases in costs per student following successful union efforts to organize teachers.

On the other hand, Hoxby (1996) reports quite different results from a study that employs a similar research design but a different measure of unionization. Using data from a national panel of school districts, she finds that active union representation for teachers does increase school spending and reduce school efficiency.

Both of these studies avoid concerns that plague much cross-sectional work on educational production. Since both studies exploit variation in union status and outcomes within school districts over time, we know that neither set of results is driven by unmeasured characteristics of school districts where political support for unions tends to be strong or weak. However, both studies address narrow questions.

Lovenheim (2009) defines the effects of unionization as changes in outcomes that result when unions win representation elections. Hoxby (1996) reports effects of unionization that are best thought of as the effects of active union engagement in collective bargaining.[28] Yet neither paper is able to examine the potential efficiency gains associated with moving to a system where many different private organizations operate publicly funded schools and compete with each other for both students and teachers, in part, by experimenting with new approaches to personnel policies that govern hiring, retention, promotion, and wage setting.

1.7 Class Size

We noted earlier that, during the past half century or more, public schools in the US have induced millions of teachers to acquire master's degrees in education by linking pay scales to this credential, even though there is no evidence that the training provided by master's courses in education improves classroom performance.

According to the 2013 Digest of Education Statistics (DES), another policy trend has contributed even more to rising per-pupil expenditure in recent decades (Snyder and Dillow 2015). The number of students per teacher declined dramatically over the period 1960 to 2000 and remained relatively constant during the period 2000 to 2010. In 1960, elementary and secondary schools in the US averaged just over 30 students per teacher, but in 2010, the comparable ratio was just over 15. Further, the 2013 DES reports that salary and benefits for instructional staff accounted for more than half of public school expenditures in the 2010–2011 school year. Taken together, these data imply that, since 1960, public school systems in the US have aggressively pursued a policy of reducing the number of students per teacher and that this policy shift alone is likely responsible for a noteworthy portion of the dramatic increase in spending per pupil that occurred over the same period.[29]

Given these facts, a large literature examines the effects of class size on student outcomes.[30] Table 1.4 (at the end of this chapter) summarizes some key results. We will not attempt to review the entire literature here. Instead, we review two bodies of work that provide the most compelling evidence about the effects of changes in class size on student achievement.

The first examines outcomes for children who participated in the Tennessee Student/Teacher Achievement Ratio experiment, also known as Project STAR. In 1985, Project STAR randomly assigned kindergarten students and teachers from 80 schools to one of three groups: small classes of 13–17 students, regular classes of 22–25 students, and regular classes of 22–25 students that contained a full-time teacher's aide. Each school had at least one of each of these three class types, and teachers and students were randomly assigned within schools. The experiment continued as this cohort of students moved from kindergarten to third grade, and most students who were assigned to small classes in kindergarten also attended small classes in grades 1–3.

Krueger (1999) explores the many ways that pressure from parents, attrition, and other factors compromised the experimental design of Project STAR. He concludes that, even though these flaws exist, the data provide strong support for the claim that small class sizes in kindergarten boost achievement and that these gains are larger for minority students and those who receive free lunch.[31]

Over the past fifteen years, scholars have returned to this data to measure long-term outcomes for the treatment and control groups in the Project STAR experiment. Results in Krueger and Whitmore (2001), Dynarski et al. (2013), and Chetty et al. (2011) provide evidence that the Project STAR students assigned to small classes did enjoy long-term benefits. These students earned higher test scores in elementary school, took college entrance exams more often, attended college at higher rates, and enjoy higher socioeconomic status as young adults. In all cases, these gains are larger among minority students than whites.

The second body of work exploits variation in class sizes induced by administrative rules that dictate maximum allowable class sizes in given school systems. In these studies, researchers exploit the fact that demographic variation in cohort sizes over time and among attendance zones may generate significant differences in class sizes among classes that serve otherwise similar students.

Angrist and Lavy (1999) pioneered this approach. They used a legal cap on maximum class size in Israeli schools to explore the effects of variation in class sizes induced by the interaction between this cap and fluctuations in grade-specific enrollment for elementary schools. Maimonides' rule requires classes to be less than 40, so a school with 85 students in a given grade will have three classes while one with 78 students may have only two. Angrist and Lavy (1999) employ regression discontinuity methods to explore the effects of class-size variation induced by this rule on student achievement. They find that smaller classes improve academic performance in fourth and fifth grade but not in third grade.

Fredriksson et al. (2012) examine the impacts of class size on student outcomes using Swedish data that cover cohorts born in 1962, 1972, 1977, and 1982. Since Sweden also imposes an enrollment cap on primary school classrooms, the authors employ a fuzzy regression discontinuity design similar to that of Angrist and Lavy (1999). They find that, among students ages 10–13, smaller classes improve measures of cognitive and noncognitive skills, increase future educational attainment, and increase adult wages and earnings between ages 27 and 42.

Urquiola (2006) examines data on third-graders in Bolivia. He employs standard instrumental variable methods as well as a regression discontinuity model that mirrors the Angrist and Lavy (1999) approach. He reports that class-size reductions generate large achievement gains. Hoxby (2000) exploits variation in elementary school class sizes in Connecticut that reflects both random changes in student populations and their interactions with state rules about maximum and minimum class sizes. In contrast to the related literature, she does not find evidence of important causal links between class size and student achievement.

Urquiola and Verhoogen (2009) argue that the assumptions researchers use to justify regression discontinuity studies of class-size effects may be problematic. They argue that parents care about class size because it affects school quality, that families have different demands for school quality, and that these differences in demand may be correlated with unmeasured determinants of student achievement. Thus, if some schools compete for students by taking actions to manipulate class size, endogenous sorting patterns should affect the distributions of measured and unmeasured student characteristics around class-size discontinuities.

Urquiola and Verhoogen (2009) provide evidence of this type of endogenous sorting in Chile, but it is not clear that these sorting patterns are present in other countries. Chile runs a large-scale voucher system that grants families great freedom in choosing schools for their children. More work is needed to assess the extent to which endogenous sorting patterns compromise regression discontinuity studies of class-size effects given data from traditional public school systems.

Spending on both master's degrees in education and smaller classes has increased dramatically in the US over the past half century or more. Most evidence suggests that the practice of linking teacher salaries to master's degrees in education serves no educational purpose. In contrast, the existing evidence indicates that smaller class sizes improve learning outcomes. Further, there is evidence that minority students and economically disadvantaged students enjoy the most noteworthy gains from placement in smaller classes.

1.8 Evidence from Developing Countries

Early in your economics training, you encountered the Law of Diminishing Marginal Returns. This law applies to settings where at least one factor of production is fixed. It states that as producers increase their use of variable factors of production, the marginal returns to these variable factors must begin to decline at some point. Since all students have only twenty-four hours per day available for learning and face biological constraints that limit the attention and energy they can devote to learning during a given day, each student is a fixed factor in the production of her own human capital, and the Law of Diminishing Marginal Returns tells us that the returns to additional educational resources in the production of student skill must diminish at some point.

So far, we have focused on the relationship between changes in inputs and learning outcomes within public school systems in the US and a few other developed countries. Because baseline school spending levels in developing countries are much lower, you may expect that, in these countries, the marginal student learning gains that follow improvements in school resources are much larger. However, in many instances, this is not the case.

Several recent articles survey existing research on how changes in public school funding and resources impact student outcomes in developing countries. These articles cover a voluminous literature that we do not have time to review fully.[32] However, two findings from this literature help motivate our explorations of alternatives to the traditional public school model.

First, in many developing countries, public school teachers are often absent, and even when they are present at school, they are often not in their classes teaching. Further, in these same countries, teachers rarely face sanctions for being absent or negligent.[33] Bruns et al. (2011) discuss several results from the literature on teacher absences in developing countries. Teachers in many developing countries work less than four of five school days per week, and in some countries, actually engage with students in learning activities for only two-thirds or less of scheduled class time. Further, these patterns of teacher behavior are present even in some countries where teachers are highly qualified and highly paid. In India, public school teachers are civil servants who attain their jobs through a competitive civil service examination process, and their pay places them well above the median of the personal income distribution. Nonetheless, in rural schools, teachers are often absent, and they are often negligent when present.

Second, in many developing countries, corrupt public officials divert substantial resources away from classroom activities toward their own agendas. Bruns et al. (2011) review results from a number of studies that trace the use of grant money designated for classroom programs. They describe results from eight studies from eight different countries in Africa and South America. Researchers typically find that less than 50 cents of every dollar designated for classroom programs is actually spent on classroom activities. The appendix material at the end of this chapter shows that education officials in the US also divert funds allocated to education for their own purposes. However, when expressed as a fraction of total education spending, corruption activities in developing countries likely impose much larger taxes on schools.

The available evidence suggests that public school systems in many developing countries may be quite inefficient. Muralidharan and Sundararaman (2015) report results from a recent experiment in the Andhra Pradesh province in India. The authors collected data from 180 villages. The authors collected voucher applications from all 180 villages but only implemented their voucher program in a random sample of 90 villages. Within treatment villages, the authors assigned vouchers to a random sample of applicants and allowed these students to use these vouchers to attend private schools. This design allows the authors to examine treatment at the village level and at the student level within treated villages.

In India, private schools spend far less per pupil than public schools, in part, because they hire less qualified teachers at lower wages. However, teachers in private schools do not have the civil service employment protections that public school teachers enjoy. As a result, they are less likely to be absent and more likely to engage with students when present.[34]

The results of the experiment show that private schools produce the same or slightly better learning outcomes while spending roughly one-third as much per student as public schools. This outcome directly establishes the inefficiency of rural public schools in Andhra Pradesh. In the treatment villages, the voucher system created by Muralidharan and Sundararaman (2015) achieved the same or better overall learning outcomes observed in control villages at significantly lower per-pupil cost.[35]

In Chapter 5, we review evidence from voucher experiments in the United States that often produce similar results. Voucher schools in the US typically produce learning outcomes that are comparable to those in nearby public schools while spending roughly half as much money per student. However, these US experiments involve relatively small and select samples of students who applied for the program and were then randomly assigned to vouchers or a control group. It is not clear that policy makers could scale up these US voucher programs without spending more per student. In contrast, Muralidharan and Sundararaman (2015) demonstrated that offering vouchers at the village level in India may well reduce public expenditures significantly without harming learning outcomes.

1.9 Approaches to Education Reform

In both developed and developing countries, traditional public schools often appear wasteful or inefficient. Given this reality, few scholars or policy makers advocate more spending on public schools as a simple strategy for improving student learning. Even those who favor more spending often bundle calls for increased spending with calls for specific changes in how schools operate: for example, smaller class sizes, better teacher training, better curricula, or improvements in information technologies.

Many education policy debates center on the specifics of such recommendations, and much research on education seeks to inform these debates. For more than a decade, the Institute for Education Sciences (IES) has promoted research designed to discover best practices in education. The What Works Clearinghouse (WWC) is part of this approach. Its website provides access to reviews of more than 10,000 education production studies that examine the efficacy of particular education practices and policies. These studies cover programs that address teacher training, pedagogy, school management, curriculum choices, etc., and the WWC provides reviews that assess the design of various studies and the credibility of related findings.

Knowledge is a public good, and if we assume that the WWC provides accurate summaries of lessons learned from research on education practices, we must conclude that its dissemination efforts are potentially quite valuable. Nonetheless, these debates are not our primary concern, since economists have no special expertise concerning how to operate schools.

As economists, we want to understand how to design systems that motivate educators to learn what the best available practices are and then implement them. Many papers in personnel economics and organizational economics remind us that both for-profit and nonprofit organizations can struggle to implement best practices, even when these practices are well known and understood,[36] and this observation clearly applies to public schools as well.

Public schools do not continue to grant pay raises to teachers who acquire master's degrees because principals and superintendents fail to understand that the training provided by these master's programs fails to improve classroom performance. Further, civil service teachers in India, Kenya, Uganda and elsewhere in the developing world understand that their students would learn more if they came to school every school day and taught their classes. Whatever the state of knowledge concerning pedagogy, school management, or the potential value of various types of school resources, effective education policy requires a set of mechanisms that create clear incentives for administrators and educators to serve their students and not their own agendas.

Nonetheless, it is important to recognize that even the best procurement policies and incentive systems will not guarantee that all publicly funded schools never make mistakes. The literature on management practices and productivity measurement in the private sector documents that, at any point in time, many plants in highly competitive industries are much less efficient than the most productive plants in the same industries, and this is also true among plants owned by the same firm.[37] Further, this result should come as no surprise. In any line of work, producers are constantly experimenting and trying to learn how to improve their performance, but due to differences in talent, luck, and other factors, realized productivity always varies among existing producers.

Nonetheless, public education differs from private industry in one important dimension. As a rule, inefficient producers in private industries either improve their performance or lose market share, and those that perform poorly on a consistent basis are much more likely to close.[38] In contrast, inefficient personnel policies and other forms of waste appear to be permanent components of many public school systems.

For this reason, many calls for education reform in recent decades began with the assertion that public school administrators and teachers who did not serve their students well had no reason to fear that they would lose their jobs or see their pay diminished. Given this starting point, various policy proposals offered assessment-based accountability systems, voucher systems, and charter schools as tools for placing performance pressures on public educators that would induce either improvement or exit.

For the remainder of our book, we shall devote most of our attention to the effects of such policies. However, we will not dive deeply into the large literature on best education practices. As economists, we are not interested in detailed arguments about the best ways to run a school or a school system. Rather, we seek to understand what policies are most likely to ensure that those who operate publicly funded schools actually implement these best practices.

1.10 Appendix: Tables Concerning Scandals and Class-Size Effects

Table 1.3 provides additional information about corruption scandals in several urban school systems in the US. Table 1.4 provides a summary of important results from studies that examine how changes in class-size impact the current achievement and future outcomes of students. These studies draw on data from the US, Israel, and Sweden.

Table 1.3 Corruption Scandals in US Urban School Districts

Chicago

2015	Chicago Public Schools CEO Barbara Byrd-Bennett took kickbacks from vendors in exchange for fraudulently granting them $23 million in no-bid teacher training contracts. (Peters 2015)
2014	Five men stole more than $870,000 from Chicago Public Schools through fraudulent purchasing and reimbursement requests. (Perez and Gormer 2015)
2011	A high school technology coordinator defrauded the school district of $400,000 through fake vendors. He then fled the country and was found dead in Tijuana, Mexico. (Eng 2014)
1995	A former Chicago Public Schools Facilities Director took $200,000 in kickbacks in return for directing $20 million in contracts to companies owned by his former employees. (Heard and O'Connor 1995)

Dallas

2008	The Chief Technology Officer of the Dallas Independent School District took over $1 million in kickbacks from a Houston businessman in exchange for two technology services contracts worth $120 million. (United States Attorney's Office 2008)
2001	The FBI concluded an investigation of Dallas Independent School District, finding that a roofing contractor swindled over $380,000 from district funds and several employees stole millions of dollars in overtime fraud. (Kim 2001)
1998	Roofing contractors conspired to defraud the Dallas school district by paying $100,000 in kickbacks to school officials in exchange for nearly $400,000 in fraudulent roofing contracts. (United Press International 1998)
1997	Seven employees, including high-level administrators, were suspended for overtime fraud totaling over $2 million in unearned compensation. (Keller 1997)
1997	Media and prosecutors allege that top school officials took over $1 million in bribes in return for fixing the terms of a $50 million energy contract. (*D Magazine* 1998)

Detroit

2013	A former Detroit Public Schools accountant defrauded the 2013 school district of $530,000 via fictitious payments to a shell corporation. (Dixon 2013)
2009	Barbara Byrd-Bennett, who was later prosecuted for corruption as CEO of Chicago Public Schools, directed a $40 million contract to her former and future employer while working for Detroit Public Schools. (Siedel et al. 2015)
2005	A senior administrator took kickbacks in return for approving $3.32 million in fraudulent invoices for a school district vendor. (United States Attorney's Office 2011)
2002	A *Detroit Free Press* report found over $305,000 missing in annual school funding. (Mackinac Center for Public Policy 2002)
1999	Detroit schools wasted a substantial portion of the funding for a $1.5 billion school construction project. (Bradsher 1999)

Table 1.3 *(continued)*

Los Angeles	
2015	Eight people in Los Angeles and surrounding communities stole $50 million through false invoices from a program designed to offer substance abuse treatment to students. (United States Attorney's Office 2015)
2014	Two men and an L.A. Unified School District employee fraudulently charged the Los Angeles school district with $5.4 million by submitting fake invoices for irrigation clocks. (County of Los Angeles District Attorney 2014)
1999	In the course of building the $200 million Belmont Learning Complex, contractors overbilled the Los Angeles school system by $2 million. (Smith 2000)
New York	
2005	School custodian engineers worked with a vendor to fraudulently acquire $529,000 in contracts in exchange for $329,000 in kickbacks. (Nardoza 2005)
2000	The Queens superintendent of schools was charged for taking over $900,000 in kickbacks in return for rigging $6 million in contracts to install computers in 19 schools. (Wyatt 2000)
San Francisco	
2013	Six employees embezzled more than $15 million from the San Francisco school district by moving money into nonprofits under their personal control. (Winegarner 2013)
Washington, D.C.	
2014	A compliance officer in the District of Columbia school district directed more than $460,000 in fraudulent payments to a transportation company which he owned and operated. (United States Attorney's Office 2014)
2008	The Federal Government fined District of Columbia Public Schools $1.75 million for fictitiously claiming immigrant students in order to acquire federal funds. (Taylor 2008)
2007	The District of Columbia head of charter school oversight was charged for stealing more than $200,000 of public funds through fraudulent invoices and awarding no-bid school contracts in return for $180,000 in kickbacks. (Taylor 2008)
1998	The founder of a D.C. school for emotionally troubled children stole more than $200,000 from the city to pay for luxury cars, a party, and other personal expenses. (Miller 1998)

Table 1.4 Experimental and Quasi-experimental Estimates of the Impact of Class Size on Educational Achievement and Life Outcomes

Sample	Study	Class Size Metric	Outcome Metric(s)	Results
US				
Project STAR (Tennessee)	Krueger (1999)	Assignment to small class in grades K–3	Average percentile score on Stanford Achievement Tests across three subjects (grades K–3)	0.22σ [a]
	Krueger and Whitmore (2001)	(same as above)	Propensity to take either SAT or ACT by 12th grade	3.7 percentage points [a]
			ACT or ACT-equivalent scores	0.13σ [a]
	Chetty et al. (2011)	(same as above)	Propensity to be enrolled in college at age 20	1.8 percentage points [a]
			Earnings at age 27	Not statistically significant
			Summary outcome index (home ownership, 401(k) savings, etc.)	0.05σ [a]
	Dynarski et al. (2013)	(same as above)	Propensity for attending college	2.7 percentage points [a]
			Propensity for on-time enrollment in college	2.4 percentage points
			Propensity for earning college degree	1.6 percentage points [a]
			Propensity for earning STEM, business, or economics degree	1.3 percentage points [a]
US				
Connecticut school data	Hoxby (2000)	Average class size in grades 1–3 and 1–5	4th and 6th grade class average math, reading, and writing scores	Not statistically significant

Table 1.4 (continued)

Sample	Study	Class Size Metric	Outcome Metric(s)	Results
US				
Florida school data	Chingos (2012)	District- and school-level class-size measures	Florida's Comprehensive Achievement Test scores; Stanford Achievement Test	Not statistically significant
Israel				
Israeli public schools	Angrist and Lavy (1999)	Number of students in 4th grade class	4th grade class average reading comprehension score	Not statistically significant
			4th grade class average math score	Not statistically significant
		Number of students in 5th grade class	5th grade class average reading comprehension score	-0.08σ [a] to -0.03σ [a]
			5th grade class average math score	-0.05σ [a] to -0.03σ [a]
Sweden				
Swedish students from one-school districts in ETF project's sample	Fredriksson et al. (2012)	Average class size in grades 4–6	Cognitive ability at age 13	-0.03σ [a]
			Non-cognitive ability at age 13	-0.03σ [a]
			Academic achievement at age 16	-0.02σ [a]
			Years of schooling at age 27–42	-0.02σ [a]
			Propensity to earn college degree at age 27–42	-0.8 percentage points [a]

a. The result is statistically significant. All are significant at the .08 level. Almost all are significant at the .05 level.
σ = a standard deviation in the outcome; e.g., for Krueger (1999), this is a standard deviation in the distribution of student achievement, and for Angrist and Lavy (1999), this is a standard deviation in the distribution of average scores at the classroom level.

EXERCISES

▶ Consider the following data-generating process: $Y_i = \beta_0 + \beta_1 * X_{1,i} + \beta_2 * X_{2,i} + \epsilon_i$ where Y_i is a test score, $X_{1,i}$ is the observed class size, $X_{2,i}$ is an unobserved variable measuring the extent to which a student's parents are helicopter parents (higher values imply more parental attention), and ϵ_i is a random shock to test scores (like weather). In particular, $\text{cov}(\epsilon_i, X_{1,i}) = \text{cov}(\epsilon_i, X_{2,i}) = E[\epsilon_i] = 0$.

- Calculate the bias in the asymptotic estimate of β_1 derived from an OLS regression of Y_i on $X_{1,i}$.
- Is there bias if $\text{cov}(X_{1,i}, X_{2,i}) = 0$?
- Assume that the vector $(X_{1,i}, X_{2,i}, \epsilon_i)$ is i.i.d. and drawn from a trivariate normal distribution with covariance matrix:

$$\begin{pmatrix} X_{1,i} \\ X_{2,i} \\ \epsilon_i \end{pmatrix} \sim N \left[\begin{pmatrix} 20 \\ 0 \\ 0 \end{pmatrix}, \begin{pmatrix} 4 & 5 & 0 \\ 5 & 10 & 0 \\ 0 & 0 & 1 \end{pmatrix} \right]$$

Also assume that $\beta_0 = 3$, $\beta_1 = -5$, and $\beta_2 = 7$.

Use your favorite statistical programming language (preferably R) to simulate samples from this distribution. First, fix the seed of the random number generator to make your results replicable. Then draw $N = 500$ students from this distribution, calculate the Y_i, and calculate numerically in R the amount of bias in the OLS regression from part 1.

- Repeat the simulation in part 3 (drawing 500 students) 500 times. Calculate the standard deviation and mean bias from each of your simulations and plot a histogram of the bias from each simulation. Interpret the histogram.
- Repeat parts 3 and 4 for $N = 10$, $N = 100$, and $N = 1,000$ students. What does your result tell you? Can you explain mathematically why the standard deviation of the bias changes for different values of N?

▶ Now assume that we observe $X_{2,i}^* = X_{2,i} + v_i$, with $\text{cov}(v_i, \epsilon_i) = \text{cov}(v_i, X_{1,i}) = \text{cov}(v_i, X_{2,i}) = E[v_i] = 0$.

- Calculate the bias in the asymptotic estimates of β_1 and β_2 derived from an OLS regression of Y_i on $X_{1,i}$ and $X_{2,i}^*$. Under what assumption is the bias zero for each coefficient?

- Assume that the vector $(X_{1,i}, X_{2,i}, \epsilon_i, v_i)$ is i.i.d. and drawn from a quadvariate normal distribution with covariance matrix:

$$\begin{pmatrix} X_{1,i} \\ X_{2,i} \\ \epsilon_i \\ v_i \end{pmatrix} \sim N \left[\begin{pmatrix} 20 \\ 0 \\ 0 \\ 0 \end{pmatrix}, \begin{pmatrix} 4 & 5 & 0 & 0 \\ 5 & 10 & 0 & 0 \\ 0 & 0 & 1 & 0 \\ 0 & 0 & 0 & 1 \end{pmatrix} \right]$$

Also assume that $\beta_0 = 3$, $\beta_1 = -5$, and $\beta_2 = 7$.

Set a seed. Then draw $N = 500$ students from this distribution, calculate the Y_i, and calculate numerically in R the amount of bias in the OLS regression from part 1.

- Repeat the simulation (drawing 500 students) 500 times. Calculate the standard deviation and mean bias from each of your simulations and plot a histogram of the bias from each simulation.

▶ Now assume that in addition to observing $X_{2,i}^* = X_{2,i} + v_i$, we also observe $\tilde{X}_{2,i} = X_{2,i} + u_i$ with $\text{cov}(v_i, \epsilon_i) = \text{cov}(v_i, X_{1,i}) = \text{cov}(v_i, X_{2,i}) = E[v_i] = 0$ and $\text{cov}(u_i, \epsilon_i) = \text{cov}(u_i, X_{1,i}) = \text{cov}(u_i, X_{2,i}) = \text{cov}(u_i, v_i) = E[u_i] = 0$.

- Assume that the vector $(X_{1,i}, X_{2,i}, \epsilon_i, v_i, u_i)$ is i.i.d. and drawn from a quintvariate normal distribution with covariance matrix:

$$\begin{pmatrix} X_{1,i} \\ X_{2,i} \\ \epsilon_i \\ v_i \\ u_i \end{pmatrix} \sim N \left[\begin{pmatrix} 20 \\ 0 \\ 0 \\ 0 \\ 0 \end{pmatrix}, \begin{pmatrix} 4 & 5 & 0 & 0 & 0 \\ 5 & 10 & 0 & 0 & 0 \\ 0 & 0 & 1 & 0 & 0 \\ 0 & 0 & 0 & 1 & 0 \\ 0 & 0 & 0 & 0 & 1 \end{pmatrix} \right]$$

Also assume that $\beta_0 = 3$, $\beta_1 = -5$, and $\beta_2 = 7$.

Can we consistently estimate β_1 and β_2? If so, prove it mathematically and show that your estimator works in the simulated data. If not, explain carefully why not.

TWO

Assessment-Based Incentives

Chapter 1 demonstrates that, at the margin, infusions of additional resources may improve learning outcomes in some traditional public school systems, but the chapter also shows that public school systems often waste resources and that public schools routinely adopt personnel policies that appear wasteful. Given this evidence, numerous scholars and policy makers have proposed various reforms that augment or replace traditional public school systems. In the balance of this book, we examine these proposals. As we do so, it is important to remember that we are not addressing what the level of government spending on education should be, or how governments should raise the funds they devote to education. These questions are important, but it would take a second book to address them.

We take education spending per student as given, and we seek to understand how different ways of authorizing, compensating and regulating publicly funded schools influence the total value of the skills they create. We are interested in optimal procurement policy. Taking per-student government expenditure levels as given, what tools can policy makers use to maximize the returns on these investments in children?

In this chapter, we examine assessment-based incentive (ABI) systems. In Chapter 3, we explore the potential gains from allowing students greater flexibility to choose which traditional public school they attend. Then, in Chapters 4 and 5, we examine the potential benefits of allowing parents to send their children and some portion of the public funds allocated for their children's education to publicly funded charter or voucher schools instead of traditional public schools. The idea behind these market-based reforms is to create incentives for educators to perform well by giving an army of performance monitors—specifically, parents—the power to punish poor performance and reward excellent performance.

In contrast, ABI systems are not market-based reforms. ABI systems are an alternative form of bureaucracy. In the traditional public school model, public educators are accountable to public administrators appointed by elected officials. In ABI systems, public educators are accountable to rules created by public administrators, and these rules assign rewards or punishments to educators based on how their students perform on standardized assessments. Advocates of ABI systems argue that by relying on rules rather than administrator discretion, these systems increase the chances that public administrators will actually dismiss principals or teachers who perform poorly.

To fully appreciate the public demand for some tool that forces public administrators to sanction or dismiss weak performers, we must take a step back and explore one more topic in the education production function literature. This body of work contains a large number of papers on performance differences among teachers in public schools, and this "teacher effects" literature has produced three important stylized facts about the determinants of student test scores.

- Consider a population of students in a given grade who have similar records of past achievement and attend schools with comparable resources. Expected test scores for these students differ systematically among classrooms. Further, this is true even among classrooms in the same school.
- One can predict much of these classroom differences in expected test scores based on the past performances of students taught previously by the teachers assigned to each classroom. That is, if a given teacher's previous students have scored better on end-of-year exams than other students who began the year at comparable achievement levels, her current students are more likely to do so again this year.
- Researchers have not identified observed characteristics of new teachers that allow them to reliably predict which new teachers will excel at fostering achievement among their students.

Jackson et al. (2014) provide a recent survey of this literature, and Appendix 2.12 explores the econometric details. Yet the many statistical controversies in this literature are not our main concern. We are interested in the tension between these findings and personnel practices in traditional public schools.

The teacher effects literature tells us that particular teachers have predictable influence on student achievement. However, there is no way to accurately predict these effects ex ante using observed characteristics of potential teachers. It takes time to learn which teachers consistently promote high rates of achievement growth and which teachers do not. In such an environment, school personnel practices should have important impacts on student learning outcomes.

Weak teachers may lack motivation, skill, or both. Thus, administrators enhance student learning when they motivate teachers not only to give their best efforts to their current students but also to continue to improve their teaching skills. In addition, administrators do a great service to students when they replace teachers who are either not able or not willing to teach well.

Yet public school administrators in traditional public school systems often face weak incentives to sanction weak educators, and administrators who are highly motivated by their own commitment to public education may find that they are not allowed to sanction weak performers. Public schools conduct tenure reviews early in teachers' careers, and once tenured, public school teachers enjoy robust employment protections.[1] Administrators in public schools find it costly to dismiss an experienced teacher, even if the teacher's students consistently perform less well than comparable students assigned to other teachers.

School principals and other administrators face these constraints for a reason. Civil service employment systems as well as the employment protections negotiated by public sector unions are efforts to guard against the possibility that public administrators may treat workers differently for reasons that have nothing to do with job performance. In contrast to private business owners, public administrators do not lose their own money when they promote or reward someone based on nepotism or political affiliation rather than merit. Thus, it is not surprising that government employees seek robust employment protections and rigid salary schedules that constrain the actions of their supervisors.[2]

In sum, education policy makers face a trade-off between the potential gains that public schools could achieve by treating different teachers differently and the concern that some public school administrators would abuse the opportunity to exercise additional discretion over teacher pay and retention. Given this dilemma, proponents of ABI systems argue that, by linking rewards and punishments for educators to objective performance measures derived from student achievement results, it is possible to reward excellent educators and remove weak ones without creating opportunities for their supervisors to make distinctions among them based on nepotism or favoritism. In the balance of this chapter, we seek to understand what policy makers have and have not accomplished with these systems. We also discuss how policy makers could improve their design.[3]

2.1 Defining Terms

Before we go further, let us define ABI systems more carefully:

> An assessment-based incentive (ABI) system is a set of rules that creates a mapping between the test scores of particular sets of students and the rewards or punishments that the educators responsible for educating these sets of students receive.[4]

Examples of the sets of students in question include: the students taught by a given teacher, the students in a particular school, or the students in a specific school district. Given our definition, actual and proposed ABI schemes take many forms. Report card systems generate negative or positive publicity for schools as a function of whether or not their students perform well or poorly on specific achievement tests. The No Child Left Behind Act (NCLB) of 2001 authorized the largest-scale ABI system in history. This system contained threats to close or reorganize public schools if the students in these schools continually failed to meet fixed proficiency standards on achievement tests. Some researchers have proposed ABI rules that would mandate termination for individual teachers if specific performance metrics derived from their students' test scores were to drop below specific thresholds, and others have proposed compensation formulas for teachers based on the test performance of their students.[5]

You may conjecture that ABI systems are effective policy tools. If we take existing curricula as given and we assess student skills relative to the standards in these curricula, the assessment results may allow us to measure how well educators are helping their students acquire the skills spelled out in the their curricula. Given this information, we should be able to improve educator performance by attaching rewards or punishments to these measurements.

2.2 An Empirical Regularity

Yet, for more than four decades, literatures in business, economics, and other social sciences have documented many cases where organizational attempts to reward workers based on statistical proxies for their measured output produced poor results.[6] Our first goal is to understand the causes of this empirical regularity. Given this understanding, we will explore the optimal design of ABI systems.

We begin by reviewing a case study of one city's effort to improve the performance of its police department. By the middle of the twentieth century, "clearance rates" had become a common statistic that police departments and the Federal Bureau of Investigation created to keep track of the rate at which police were able to solve reported crimes. Skolnick (1966) provides a detailed assessment of one police department's attempt to improve police effectiveness by holding detectives accountable for the clearance rates of particular crimes.

Detectives responded to the department's focus on clearance rates in many ways that city officials may not have intended or anticipated. First, detectives manipulated the recording of offenses. Given a report of an incident to police, detectives bear the responsibility to judge whether the incident actually occurred and whether or not the incident involved a crime. Skolnick observed that, after the department began placing more emphasis on clearance rates, detectives began using their discretion to reduce the number of reported crimes that needed to be cleared. They became more likely to classify reported incidents under the heading "suspicious circumstances" rather than recording that an actual crime occurred. Reports of sexual assault became suspicious disputes between partners, and reports of stolen property became suspicious cases of missing property.[7]

In addition, detectives entered into plea deals with arrested defendants that amounted to the department trading leniency in exchange for higher clearance rates. If defendants were willing to confess to multiple crimes,[8] the department would charge them with only one crime, usually a lesser one. Every confessed crime counted as a case cleared, but later, when these perpetrators came up for parole, parole boards had no way to know about the confessions that did not result in charges. Thus, they made their decisions based on criminal histories that were often abridged.

Several features of this account are noteworthy. To begin, before the department began directing greater attention to clearance rates, differences

in clearance rates over time may have been highly correlated with differences in the true effectiveness of policing. All else equal, when departments resolve more cases faster, they are likely doing better work. However,
clearance rates likely became less informative as measures of police performance after the department placed more emphasis on them. Finally, the
social harm created by making detectives directly accountable for changes
in clearance rates went well beyond the contamination of the information
conveyed in public reports on clearance rates. As outlined above, detectives chose to disregard certain incident reports rather than record them
as crimes and investigate them. Further, because detectives took additional
confessions without filing charges, parole boards granted early release to
many felons based on incomplete records of their criminal history.

It is not possible to judge the net effects of this department's decision to
place greater emphasis on clearance rates. Although detectives clearly manipulated the system, they also may have worked harder to solve real crimes.
Nonetheless, the account does demonstrate that gaming behaviors may do
more than inflate statistics. In this case, some of the actions detectives took
to manipulate clearance rates actually harmed public safety.

Campbell (1979) reviews numerous other case studies that document
the results of similar attempts to build government accountability and incentive systems around statistics, and each study documents the same pattern. A government agency creates statistics that track noteworthy social
outcomes. Then, political leaders or government administrators decide to
hold government employees accountable for changes in these statistics. In
response, these employees take actions that inflate the statistics in question without actually furthering the missions of their agencies, and some of
these actions harm the citizens that these employees are supposed to serve.

Campbell summarized his findings in a statement now known as
Campbell's Law:

> I come to the following pessimistic laws (at least for the U.S. scene): The
> more any quantitative social indicator is used for social decision-making,
> the more subject it will be to corruption pressures and the more apt it will
> be to distort and corrupt the social processes it is intended to monitor.[9]

2.3 Economic Theory and Campbell's Law

Twelve years after Campbell (1979), Holmstrom and Milgrom (1991) produced an economic model that identifies the mechanisms at work in the
episodes that Campbell chronicles. Interested readers can turn to Appen-

dix 2.13 for a detailed presentation of this model. Here, I describe the model setup, state key results, and discuss their applications.

In Holmstrom and Milgrom (1991), a principal (owner) must contract with an agent (worker) who will perform work that creates output. The agent may allocate effort to several different tasks, and the vector of tasks completed by the agent determines total output. Holmstrom and Milgrom follow the convention of assuming that the principal is risk neutral and that the agent is risk averse.[10]

Holmstrom and Milgrom make three key assumptions about information. First, they assume that the principal cannot observe the agent's actions. If the principal could observe the agent's actions, she would simply tell the agent how to allocate his time to different tasks, and then pay him for following her instructions. Such an arrangement is called a forcing contract because the principal implicitly forces the agent to follow all of her instructions by offering a contract that pays zero if the agent violates any instruction and an amount greater than the agent's total effort costs if he follows every instruction.

Second, Holmstrom and Milgrom assume that the principal and agent cannot enter into a contract that specifies the agent's compensation as a function of the actual output he produces. This means that the principal cannot write contracts that involve piece-rate payments, output quotas, or any mechanisms that require output verification. This assumption captures the idea that many workers produce output that is difficult to measure and impossible to verify in court.[11]

Third, the principal does observe a statistical proxy for output, and the principal can link the agent's compensation to realizations of this proxy. The expected value of this proxy may be influenced by the entire set of tasks that the agent performs. Further, shocks that are beyond the control of both the principal and agent may affect the actual value of this proxy.

In many environments with these features, the principal must adopt some form of incentive pay to induce agents to produce output. However, in one section of their 1991 paper, Holmstrom and Milgrom incorporate an assumption about effort costs that is not standard in the related literature: They assume that agents have personal effort norms. Norms may reflect personal pride, a commitment to the mission of an organization, or both. The key is that agents suffer a utility loss if they do not put forth enough effort to satisfy their own norms. This means that the principal does not need to provide incentive pay to induce the agent to produce positive output. As long as the principal offers a base salary great enough to get the agent to take the job, the agent's desire to satisfy his own norms causes him to produce positive output.

2.4 Parallels to Education

These key features of the Holmstrom and Milgrom (1991) production environment apply to the work environments in many of the case studies reviewed by Campbell (1979), and Holmstrom and Milgrom note that their model also applies to schools.

In schools, forcing contracts are not feasible. Teachers work alone in classrooms with students. Further, even if administrators placed cameras in classrooms, it would be quite expensive to carefully review exactly how teachers are teaching each of their classes.

In addition, school systems cannot readily implement piece-rate schemes that link teacher pay to the monetary value of the output they produce. Teachers help students acquire a broad range of skills. Many of these skills are quite difficult to assess, and as Appendix 2.12 demonstrates, it is difficult to isolate the contribution of any given teacher to the skill growth of her students. Further, it is almost impossible to price all aspects of teacher output. For example, high school science and computer teachers are now covering material that did not exist when many working adults were in high school. Thus, no panel data exists that could allow researchers to figure out how mastering this material now will impact the adult life outcomes of today's high school students.

Nonetheless, many policy makers and researchers have proposed ways to use student test scores to create proxies for school or teacher output. As in Holmstrom and Milgrom (1991), these proxies reflect not only teacher efforts but also random shocks beyond the control of teachers, since measurement error impacts all test scores and many factors that impact student learning are beyond the control of teachers (e.g., shocks to student health).

Finally, norms play an important role in education. For many teachers and principals, education is a mission activity. These teachers put significant effort and energy into their teaching without regard to the personnel practices or incentive systems they face.[12]

2.5 Optimal Incentive Design

Holmstrom and Milgrom (1991) describe the contract that maximizes the surplus generated by the relationship between a principal and an agent. The key components of the contract are a base salary that the principal pays the agent regardless of any outcomes and a bonus payment that increases linearly with the realized value of an output proxy. The slope of the relationship between the bonus payment and the output proxy is the bonus rate. Many incentive contracts are more complex than this one, but it is pedagogically useful to work in an environment where one parameter, the bonus rate, determines the strength of incentives.

Holmstrom and Milgrom spell out several factors that determine the optimal bonus rate:

Proxy Alignment   If agents can take actions that significantly improve the value of the output proxy while not improving or even harming true output, we say that the output proxy is weakly aligned with true output. In this case, strong incentives are less desirable because they induce agents to allocate time to the wrong tasks.

Effort Substitution   Incentive contracts based on output proxies almost always create some alignment problems. However, these concerns may be less serious in settings where the provision of incentives causes agents to allocate additional effort to less productive tasks but does not cause them to reduce the effort they allocate to the most productive tasks. Alignment concerns are likely more pressing in environments where agents respond to misaligned incentives by allocating both more time to less productive or even harmful tasks, and less time to the most productive tasks.

Proxy Noise   If the shock process is such that the value of the output proxy varies greatly, even among agents who choose the same effort levels, then ABI schemes are less desirable since they impose sizable costs on risk-averse agents.[13]

We seek to understand how these considerations shape the optimal design of ABI schemes for educators. In the next few sections, we focus on ABI schemes that reward or punish a given set of educators. Here, and in Appendix 2.13, we discuss how alignment concerns and potential patterns of effort substitution shape our thinking about the design of optimal ABI schemes. In this discussion, we ignore the income risks that proxy noise imposes on educators because the results we discuss hold even when workers are risk neutral.[14]

We then turn to ABI schemes that not only provide performance incentives but also dictate school closures or individual termination decisions whenever measured performance at the school or teacher level falls below certain thresholds. Under these ABI schemes, proxy noise and worker attitudes toward risk are important since a few bad measurement shocks may end an educator's career.

2.6 Alignment Problems

When a principal attaches incentives to a poorly aligned performance metric, agents take hidden actions that improve their measured performance without generating commensurate improvements in their actual performance. Observers often say that those who engage in such hidden actions are "gaming the system." Here, we explore the links between specific design features of ABI systems and various actions that educators take to game these systems.

2.6.1 Corruption

ABI schemes involve a number of steps. Students take tests. Testing agencies grade and score these tests. Education authorities use student test results to create performance statistics for educators, and based on these statistics, education officials assign rewards or sanctions to educators.

There is considerable empirical evidence that some educators or groups of educators respond to ABI schemes by manipulating the initial data-gathering steps in ABI systems. These educators take actions that corrupt the administration, grading, or scoring of student exams.

In large-scale ABI systems, high-stakes tests are almost never administered by independent proctors. Instead, most high-stakes exams are administered by the educators that ABI systems seek to incentivize. Thus, it is not surprising that researchers and journalists have documented instances where educators allowed their students to cheat on high-stakes assessments or changed their students' answers after collecting their exams.

In the late 1990s, the Chicago Public Schools (CPS) implemented a district-level accountability system tied to student assessment results. Jacob and Levitt (2003) present clear evidence that some teachers in Chicago responded to this system by changing blank answers to correct answers before turning their students' exams in to the district.

Under NCLB, a 2011 report filed by investigators working for the Office of the Governor in Georgia reported that roughly 180 teachers and two dozen principals in the Atlanta Public Schools conspired to change student answer sheets on state accountability exams before delivering the exams to the state agency in charge of grading them. In April 2015, eleven of these teachers were convicted of racketeering and related crimes.[15]

Kingdon (2007) reports even more striking evidence of cheating on high-stakes exams taken by high school students in the Indian state of Uttar Pradesh. Kingdon writes,

> While the true levels of learning achievements in secondary education are generally hidden, fortuitously they became visible one year in Uttar Pradesh . . . when the Kalyan Singh government brought in an anti-cheating rule and installed police at all examination centres in 1992 to prevent the mass-cheating that routinely takes place at board examinations in Uttar Pradesh, the pass rate in the high school exam fell from 57 per cent in 1991 to a pitiful 14.7 per cent in 1992.[16]

These scandals in Chicago, Atlanta, and India document crude and blatant forms of cheating. However, many ABI systems invite more subtle forms of cheating. The testing agencies that create annual exams for ABI systems and also determine grading and scoring protocols for each exam are often politically linked to the schools or school districts that these systems seek to monitor and incentivize. These political connections can corrupt the grading and scoring of exams in ways that inflate student test scores.

For example, although NCLB was a federal law, it did not mandate national testing. Rather, NCLB instructed states to develop their own assessment systems and their own definitions of student proficiency, and state education departments oversaw the development of each set of annual assessments.[17] Cronin et al. (2007) examine data from a large collection of states during the first four years of NCLB. They compare results from a series of low-stakes assessments that students took in many states to parallel results from the high-stakes NCLB tests administered in the same states. They conclude that, in many states, much of the reported rise in proficiency rates from 2003 to 2006 came about because states made exams easier over time without making appropriate adjustments to the scaling and scoring of exam results.[18]

In Neal (2010), I present compelling evidence that, in 2006, the state of Illinois did compromise the proficiency standard for eighth-grade math. During the first several years of NCLB, proficiency rates in most grades for most subjects rose by at most a few percentage points. However, between

2005 and 2006, the fraction of students deemed proficient in eighth-grade math rose from 54 to 78 percent. Nothing in the history of education research suggests that improved teaching could create an increase this large in one year given a fixed proficiency standard. So how did this proficiency rate jump so much in one year?

Between 2005 and 2006, Illinois made significant changes to its assessment system and then commissioned a consulting firm to conduct an equating study that developed the scoring rules and the proficiency standards for the new exams. The striking jumps in proficiency rates suggest that these consultants compromised the proficiency standards by proposing lenient scoring rules.[19]

2.6.2 Coaching

These accounts of cheating and scale manipulation are sensational. However, the literature on high-stakes testing devotes relatively little attention to blatant corruption. Instead, the literature focuses much more attention on coaching.

Teachers coach rather than teach if they devote class time to activities that are not ideal for building lasting subject mastery but do raise expected student scores on particular exams. The following example should make the distinction between coaching and teaching clear. Shepard and Dougherty (1991) report that elementary schools in two Arizona districts responded to an assessment-based accountability program by reducing the number of writing assignments and increasing the number of assignments where students were asked to find grammar mistakes in prewritten passages. This change is difficult to defend as a strategy for making students better writers, but it works well as a strategy for raising test scores on certain standardized grammar assessments.[20]

Many of you paid for coaching when you were preparing to take the SAT or ACT, and you may soon pay for coaching services again if you plan to take the GRE, GMAT, MCAT, or a host of other exams that professional and graduate school admissions departments require. Some may argue that since many higher education institutions consider results from coachable tests in their admissions processes, policy makers should not be terribly concerned about the use of coachable tests in ABI schemes. However, such arguments fail to recognize that there is no such thing as a good or bad assessment system. Assessment systems are measurement tools, and tools must be matched with tasks. Judgments about the use of any particular assessment system must focus on whether or not the system serves the mission of the organization that uses it.

The SAT, ACT, GRE, etc. are all screening devices. They produce information about the talents that applicants possess, and if almost all students receive some coaching for these exams, the presence of coaching may do little to distort how students rank relative to one another on these exams. Universities do not care per se that the time and money students spend mastering test-taking strategies may not build any lasting skills. They simply demand a way to rank students on a common scale, and no single university may be able to devise screening mechanisms that provide better information without imposing equal or greater costs on students.

In contrast, the primary goal of ABI systems is not to select elite students for selective programs but rather to induce educators to teach well. So, whenever an ABI scheme induces an educator to devote class time to coaching that could be allocated to excellent teaching, the scheme is working against its intended purpose. This observation is key because many empirical studies document evidence that educators coach rather than teach in response to ABI systems.[21]

Advocates of the ABI approach have argued that coaching is not a problem, per se. These proponents argue that teaching to the test is desirable if teaching to the test amounts to good teaching, and this idea greatly influenced education policy during the Obama administration. In 2009, the administration announced their Race to the Top Assessment Program that established a competitive grant program to develop national standards and assessments designed to help ensure that future generations of students would be prepared for both college and modern work environments.[22]

Using these funds, two consortia of states developed two new assessment systems. The Smarter Balanced Assessment Consortium (SBAC) and the Partnership for Assessment of Readiness for College and Careers (PARCC) developed assessment systems aligned to the new Common Core State Standards. SBAC and PARCC sought to limit the opportunities for state-level manipulation of standards by creating consortia of states that would both adopt common standards and also agree to employ a common assessment system. Further, many features of the SBAC and PARCC systems appear to be attempts to make coaching more difficult.[23]

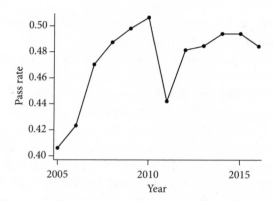

Figure 2.1 Uniform CPA examination's REG section pass rates, 2005–2016.
Data source: The American Institute of CPA (AICPA) released reports on cumulative annual Uniform CPA Examination pass rates. In 2011, the AICPA changed the format of the exam. However, the content of the REG section did not change. The AICPA did not make major changes to the exam's REG section during 2012–2016.

These assessments minimize the use of multiple choice items and require students to convey information in a variety of contexts and formats. The SBAC also employs computer-adaptive testing that presents students with more challenging questions if they perform well early in the exam. It is too early to know how coachable these exams are.[24] However, we can make an educated guess by examining results from other high-stakes exams that share these same features.

The American Institute for Certified Public Accountants (AICPA) administers the Uniform CPA Examination and awards the certified public accountant (CPA) credential to accounting students based on the results. In 2004, the AICPA began a transition to a computer-based format for the Uniform CPA Examination that employs the advanced features of the SBAC and PARCC systems. The first full year of testing under this new system was 2005. Figure 2.1 presents pass rates on the regulation exam (REG) starting in 2005. Pass rates rose steadily until 2010. Then the pass rate dropped about eight percentage points in one year before starting to rise again.

The AICPA claims that the testing experts they employ make sure that the standard for passing the REG exam does not vary from year to year. However, the results presented in Figure 2.1 raise questions about this claim. What could cause pass rates to rise from just over 40 percent to over

50 percent between 2005 and 2010? And what could cause pass rates to fall so sharply in 2011?

There is no evidence of a change in the composition of test takers, and the curriculum for this exam did not change. Further, these patterns are not sampling error. Well over 20,000 students take the exam each year.

The most likely explanation is that even sophisticated modern assessment systems are quite coachable. Between 2010 and 2011, the test developers employed by the AICPA did change the computer interface that students used to take the exam. Before the end of 2011, a prominent test-preparation service responded to this change by advertising that their team of experts had developed new simulation software that "mirrored exactly the new exam's functionality and replicated the exam-day experience for students." Pass rates rose over the next several years.[25]

In a technical sense, the AICPA is holding their standard for passing fixed over time. However, aspiring accountants are more likely to meet that standard if they develop test-taking skills that are specific to a particular exam format, and it is hard to believe that these test-taking skills help new CPAs do better work as accountants.

We return to this topic below. It is ironic but true that the AICPA's desire to create a fixed passing standard is likely a key reason that passing rates become inflated over time. The assessment features that facilitate efforts to link and equate scores on multiple assessment forms make assessments predictable and therefore coachable.

2.6.3 Triage

When teachers coach, they devote too much time to activities that do more to improve test scores than to enhance actual learning. When teachers engage in educational triage, they allocate too much time to students whose learning gains are most likely to improve their own measured performance as educators, and as a result, devote too little attention to other students who need additional help.

In Neal and Schanzenbach (2010), Diane Whitmore Schanzenbach and I provide evidence that two different ABI schemes based on proficiency levels induced Chicago teachers to devote less attention to their lowest-performing students.[26] In both systems, Chicago teachers were held accountable for the number of their students who scored above predetermined proficiency levels. When these ABI schemes began, the bottom twenty percent of Chicago elementary school students had almost no chance of becoming proficient regardless of the efforts of their teachers. Thus, teachers found it in their interest to focus their attention on students who were not yet proficient but had a better chance of becoming proficient. Among these students, measured achievement growth between third and fifth grade improved significantly following the introduction of both ABI systems, while among students in the bottom twenty percent, scores remained flat or fell.[27] These triage practices appear to have been widespread under NCLB. Software companies even developed products that helped schools identify which students to ignore and which students to give extra attention.[28]

ABI schemes built around proficiency levels may also create an indirect form of triage by distorting the allocation of teachers to students. Such schemes penalize educators who teach students who are far below grade level. These educators must work harder than other educators to avoid sanctions, and Clotfelter et al. (2004) provide evidence that, when ABI systems employ performance metrics built around proficiency scores, able teachers become more likely to leave schools that serve disadvantaged students.

2.7 Solutions to Alignment Problems

Given the evidence that existing ABI schemes often induce cheating, coaching, and triage, let us consider how policy makers can design ABI systems that avoid these problems.

2.7.1 Remove Opportunities for Obvious Forms of Corruption

Education authorities can eliminate much of the cheating that ABI schemes induce by having external agencies administer and proctor high-stakes exams. External administration would raise the cost of high-stakes testing, but in developed countries, this cost increase would represent a trivial fraction of current per-student expenditure in publicly funded schools.

In addition, the testing agencies that develop high-stakes assessments should not be linked in any way to the educators who work under ABI systems. Policy makers promote the SBAC and PARCC assessment systems, in part, as ways to address the inherent conflict-of-interest problems that arise when state employees in one agency develop assessments that are used to produce accountability measures for public administrators and educators in the same state. As we note above, comparisons between state-specific trends in proficiency rates under NCLB and other measures of state-specific achievement trends suggest that these conflicts of interest are important policy concerns.

2.7.2 Abandon Standards

Education authorities must not link performance statistics for educators to learning standards for students. This claim surely sounds heretical to many policy makers and education researchers, but those who insist that accountability measures must be defined relative to learning standards fail to appreciate an important design principle. Explicit incentive systems should be built around performance metrics that are easy to verify and therefore hard to corrupt. However, measures of student subject mastery relative to learning standards are hard to verify and therefore easy to corrupt.

Assume that a school district purchases 500 textbooks from a publisher, and the publisher delivers five large containers of books. The district can examine each book while counting the number of books in each container and easily verify whether or not the publishing company delivered the 500 books that the district ordered. However, if the district develops learning standards for its students, and then informs its teachers and principals that they will be rewarded or punished based on how many of their students meet various learning standards, the district cannot easily verify whether or not particular students in the district actually met these standards.

In the textbook example, the district can verify delivery by using a simple and legally recognized measurement technology: counting. Yet, when a district develops a set of learning standards, it cannot employ an established measurement technology to determine whether or not students have met these standards. Rather, the district must employ assessment developers who then create the tools that the district uses to measure student learning relative to its standards.

Since there is no fixed, verifiable protocol for creating these assessment systems, developers must make many judgment calls concerning how to develop items, how to pretest and select items, and how to set the performance levels associated with various learning standards. Because different developers could make different calls even when they are both using their best judgment, the district may find it difficult, if not impossible, to audit the work of any assessment developer it hires.

This implies that ABI systems built around reports concerning whether or not students have met certain learning standards invite malfeasance that education officials may not be able to detect or deter. In any setting where educators or their political representatives are able to convince testing agencies to implement lenient standards, education authorities are not likely to be able to prove that the developers failed to act in good faith. This may help explain why federal education officials did not challenge state reports of proficiency rates under NCLB even though researchers have shown that many of these reports were quite suspect.[29]

2.7.3 Report Only Ranks

Policy makers can avoid these verification problems by asking testing agencies to report only how the achievement levels of various students rank relative to each other on high-stakes assessments. Testing agencies can manipulate the development and scoring of assessments in ways that inflate the number of students deemed proficient or excellent according to a given set of learning standards. However, reports of percentile ranks cannot be inflated in this manner. In any given student population, only one percent of students can earn scores in the top one percent of the achievement distribution, and only half can score above the median. Further, a testing agency cannot inflate the percentile rank of one student without decreasing the percentile rank of other students. This implies that, if education officials collect only ordinal ranks from the testing agencies that conduct assessments for ABI systems, educators, as a group, cannot gain from applying collective pressure on testing agencies.

2.7.4 Develop New Assessment Systems

Designers of ABI schemes not only want to avoid corruption, they also want to induce educators to teach well. Thus, policy makers should design ABI schemes that reward educators for helping students develop subject mastery but not for coaching students on test-taking strategies that are tailored to a particular assessment system. To achieve this objective, policy makers must develop new assessment systems that require students to demonstrate subject mastery while removing the coaching opportunities that most modern assessment systems create.

Koretz and Béguin (2010) propose the development of self-monitoring assessments that would contain audit tests as subtests within otherwise standard assessments. It is possible that policy makers could design penalty functions that eliminate coaching responses to high-stakes assessments by penalizing educators whose students consistently perform less well on audit questions than other questions. However, no existing research has spelled out what this penalty function would be, given other parameters of a particular ABI system.

In Neal (2013), I argue that, in order to design high-stakes assessment systems that do not create opportunities for coaching, policy makers must abandon many principles that shape the development of most modern assessments. Modern assessment systems are not designed to gather data on how well educators teach. They are designed to produce exam forms and scoring rules that produce measurements of student achievement that are comparable even though the various forms are given to different populations of students at different points in time. This goal requires assessment developers to create links between assessments and to impose restrictions on how question-writers develop items. Thus, the literature on assessment development documents the following:

- Often, between 20 and 30 percent of the items on a given assessment form have been used on previous forms.
- The professionals who write questions for each assessment form must adhere to strict item-development guidelines that govern the format, framing, and wording of questions.
- Developers pretest potential questions to make sure that they satisfy what are known as invariance requirements. These requirements arise because the Item Response Theory (IRT) model that dominates modern assessment development assumes that both student achievement and question difficulty are one-dimensional constructs. Thus, if Betty is more likely than Joe to get question five correct, Betty must also be more likely than Joe to get any other given question correct. Likewise, if Betty is less likely to get question five correct than question six, the same must be true for Joe. Developers only retain collections of questions that exhibit these invariance properties.

All of these features make it easier for developers to accurately place results for different exam forms on a common scale, but these features also create exams that are quite predictable given access to previous test forms from the same assessment series. Therefore, when policy makers employ these exams within high-stakes testing systems, they induce educators to coach rather than teach.[30] As discussed in Section 2.6.2, the Uniform CPA Examination is a sophisticated modern assessment system that is designed to establish a passing standard that is fixed over time. Yet the results in Figure 2.1 suggest that the features of the exam that are supposed to ensure a fixed passing standard actually create the very opportunities for coaching that the exam-preparation services exploit. Further, as these services perfect their coaching methods, exam scores become inflated measures of the candidates' true mastery of accounting.

Some of you may be thinking that, if policy makers were to require developers to create assessments that are less predictable, testing agencies would find it difficult, if not impossible, to place results from different annual assessments on a common scale.[31] This is true, but it may not be a problem. Section 2.8 shows that, if testing agencies can simply rank students according to their achievement levels at a point in time, they can build useful performance metrics for educators. Further, we will see in Section 2.9 that policy makers can produce better information about differences in distributions of achievement for student populations defined by time and demographic characteristics if they administer traditional assessments in no-stakes settings.

2.7.5 Make All Achievement Matter

ABI systems should adopt performance metrics for educators that vary positively and continuously with the achievement gains of all students. Educators who know they will be rewarded for the progress that each of their students makes will devote additional attention to each of their students.

Yet knowing that the progress of all students should matter when measuring educator performance does not tell us how the progress of each student should matter. The existing literature contains many proposed methods for transforming information on the achievement growth of a group of students into a measure of overall performance for the educators who teach this group of students. However, as Jacob and Rothstein (2016) note, these approaches all rest on arbitrary assumptions about the interpretation of the achievement scales produced by modern assessment systems.

Consider two teachers who each work with two students. Teacher A teaches Joe and Sue. Joe began the year with a 150 scale score and earned a 160 on the final assessment at the end of the spring semester. Sue began with a score of 250 and earned a final score of 265. Teacher B teaches Bob and Carol. Bob, like Joe, began the year with a 150 but earned a 155 on the final assessment. Carol, like Sue, began with a 250 but earned a 270 on the final.

Given these outcomes, who performed better overall, teacher A or teacher B? And by how much? Both teachers had one student outperform their peer in the other class by five points, but is there any reason to believe that the value of skills gained among students moving from 155 to 160 on this scale is the same as the value of skills gained among those moving from 265 to 270? Since psychometric scales are not designed to measure the economic value of skill stocks, the answer is no, and this same reasoning indicts most attempts to create aggregate performance metrics for teams of teachers or entire schools. Nonetheless, education researchers and policy makers keep proposing arbitrary ways to combine the test-score outcomes of all students in a given class, grade, or school to create aggregate performance metrics that allegedly allow them to compare the aggregate performance of any two sets of educators that teach the same curricula.

Reliance on these metrics is not only problematic but also unnecessary. There are ways to provide incentives for workers without measuring the total value of their own output directly or creating statistical proxies for their aggregate performance. So, in Gadi Barlevy and Neal 2012, we argue that policy makers should admit defeat and go in a new direction. They should design contests among educators and offer rewards to educators based on their overall record of wins and losses in these contests. By taking this alternative path, education authorities may be able to simultaneously deter corruption, coaching, and educational triage.

2.8 Pay for Percentile

In Barlevy and Neal (2012), we propose an ABI scheme that minimizes scale corruption, coaching, and triage. The system is called Pay for Percentile (PFP). It relies only on achievement reports about how students rank relative to one another, so PFP creates no opportunities for scale corruption. Further, since there is no need to scale high-stakes assessment results, education officials can employ new exams that are much less predictable and therefore less coachable than most modern assessments. Finally, PFP weights the academic progress of each student in a given classroom or school equally, so educators have clear incentives to devote extra attention to all of their students.

To see how PFP works, consider a population of sixth-grade math students in a state. In early September, place each of these students in a league that contains other students with similar past records of academic achievement, common family environments, and similar peers. Then, in late May, test all students and give each student a percentile score that describes the fraction of students in his league that performed less well than he did. Next, take the average of these percentile scores over all the sixth-grade math students in a given classroom or school. This average is the percentile performance index (PPI) for the teacher or team of teachers that educates these students. Finally, pay bonuses to teachers that are proportional to their PPI scores.

School systems that implement PFP should structure contests so that teachers do not compete against other teachers who work in the same school. Within-school competition could hamper cooperation or even create sabotage. In some settings, it may even be optimal to pay group bonuses to teachers based on the PPI scores of teams of teachers who teach in the same school or who teach the same subject in a given school.

Under PFP, testing agencies only report ordinal measures of student achievement, such as a student's percentile rank in math within her contest group. Therefore, a PPI score is not a statistical measure of aggregate educator performance.[32] Rather, it is a winning percentage that tells us how often students in a given educational unit perform better than students in other units who began the year at the same achievement levels. A PPI score tells us nothing about the value of the learning created by an educator's efforts, and PPI score differences among educators tell us nothing about differences in the values of the skills created by their efforts. Yet PPI scores are useful for incentive provision.

Lazear and Rosen (1981) were the first to study the use of contests as incentive mechanisms. To understand their seminal result, consider an educational tutoring company that seeks to provide incentives for two tutors. To keep things simple, assume that each tutor works with only one student. Further, assume that each of these students begins the school year at the same achievement level. Now, consider the following contest between the tutors: Let both students take the same end-of-year assessment and pay a prize to the tutor who works with the student who earns the highest score. Lazear and Rosen derive the prize, P^*, that induces optimal teacher effort in this two-tutor, two-student contest.

The Lazear and Rosen (1981) contest is important because it shows that employers do not need to create statistical measures of total worker output in order to provide incentives for workers. In our example, the tutoring company only observes which student won. It does not need to know anything about the margin of victory.

In Barlevy and Neal (2012), we show how PFP generalizes the Lazear and Rosen (1981) result to settings where many workers (e.g., teachers in a district or state) produce many different types of output simultaneously (e.g., learning gains for many different students). Lazear and Rosen specify a prize for the winner of one contest. PPI scores are just average winning percentages for educators or teams of educators who compete in many contests at once,[33] and the constant that transforms PPI scores into bonus payments is P^*, the Lazear and Rosen (1981) prize for a comparable two-tutor, two-student contest.[34]

Under certain conditions, PFP induces all educators to choose efficient levels of effort for all tasks that promote learning for all their students. The most important condition is that each teacher must believe that she is competing in a properly seeded contest, that is, she must believe that the teachers she competes against have the same talent and resources. If not, she will not choose efficient effort in response to PFP. Teachers who believe that they have a clear advantage over their competitors will tend to coast, and those who believe that they are competing with the deck stacked against them will be tempted to give up. As a result, policy makers need to implement PFP by placing teachers in leagues defined not only by the baseline achievement levels of their students but also by their own levels of experience and the resources available in their schools.

2.8.1 Experimental Results

PFP is a relatively new mechanism, but several researchers have already tested PFP in field experiments. Loyalka et al. (2016) ran a large-scale randomized control trial in rural China. The experiment involved six treatment groups and one control group. In each of the six treatment groups, sixth-grade teachers had the opportunity to earn either generous or modest bonus payments according to one of three different ABI schemes. The first linked bonuses to average-level scores among students. The second linked bonuses to the average score gains among students. The final scheme implemented a form of PFP. Loyalka et al. report that PFP clearly outperformed the two simple, scale-dependent schemes, which produced small and mostly insignificant changes in student achievement. They report that, on average, the introduction of PFP raised student achievement by roughly

.15 standard deviations.[35] Further, estimated treatment effects on measures of the amount and types of material covered by teachers indicate that PFP did elicit more effort from teachers. Finally, PFP generated improvements in student learning for students at all baseline achievement levels. There is no evidence that PFP induced any form of educational triage.

Gilligan et al. (2017) report preliminary results from a similar field experiment in rural Uganda that I have been involved with over the past several years. This experiment involved 302 schools: 151 treatment, 151 control. In the 151 treatment schools, we offered sixth-grade math teachers a PFP bonus scheme. The results differ from those that Loyalka et al. report in rural China. In rural Uganda, PFP did not generate learning gains for all students. Students in treated classes who were far below grade level at baseline did not experience learning gains relative to their peers in the control schools. However, among students in the top half of the baseline achievement distribution, those who attended a treatment school that provides textbooks enjoyed achievement gains that were slightly greater than those that Loyalka et al. document in rural China. Further, all students who attended a PFP school with books were more likely to remain in the school during the following academic year.

In rural Uganda, many sixth-grade students begin the school year at a second- or third-grade level in math. So teachers in this experiment worked with students who differed greatly in their baseline math skills. These teachers may have found it difficult, if not impossible, to deliver lessons that raised achievement for the highest and lowest achieving students in these diverse classes. Given that the system of leaving exams in Uganda focuses public attention on the highest-achieving students, it may not be surprising, ex post, to learn that PFP only produced learning gains for students who were near grade level.

The fact that PFP was not effective in schools without books suggests that policies that provide schools with better resources should not be always be seen as alternatives to policies that provide better incentives for educators. Policies that improve school resources may make policies that improve educator incentives more effective.

Fryer et al. (2013) report the results of a PFP field experiment in an economically disadvantaged suburb of Chicago. They provided PFP incentives to elementary school teachers in two different ways. The first treatment was a standard PFP scheme. The second treatment paid teachers the average bonus payment up-front, but required teachers who performed below average to return the difference between the PFP bonus associated with their performance and the up-front average payment. Those who performed above average received an additional bonus payment at the end of the year to bring their total bonus up to their total PFP payment.

The Fryer et al. (2013) design was more complex than most because some teachers in this district worked with more than one homeroom class of students. As a result, some treatment teachers worked with students whose scores did not count toward their PPI scores. Thus, these students did not belong in the treatment group because their scores did not affect PFP payments, but they could not serve as clean controls because their teachers were treated. In analyses that removed these partially treated students from control groups, PFP raised mean achievement growth during the year by .185 standard deviations.[36] Further, the treatment that involved paying average bonuses up-front and then imposing fines at the end of year based on PPI scores produced an even greater gain of .338 standard deviations.

In Fryer et al. (2013), the average bonus paid was $4,000. Chetty et al. (2014b) examine the relationship between future adult earnings and improvements in elementary school achievement associated with better teacher quality. Their calculations imply that the present discounted value of the .185 standard deviation average gain generated by the standard PFP treatment is much greater than $4,000, which suggests that PFP may improve efficiency.

Existing experimental results suggest that well-designed contests may work well as incentive schemes for educators. However, it is too early to conclude that PFP represents a simple, cost-effective tool for raising student achievement. Further, it is difficult to anticipate how educators would attempt to game PFP if a large school system adopted it permanently. Any school system that implemented PFP on a permanent basis would need to develop new assessment systems that exploit the capacity of PFP to reward educators based on results from assessments that are not scaled and therefore less predictable. Further, it would need to establish rules that determine how teachers are grouped into leagues to create well-seeded contests. These and other design choices would likely have significant impacts on the long-run social returns from implementing PFP permanently on a large scale.

2.9 Two Tasks Require Two Measurement Systems

PFP eliminates scale corruption because it asks testing agencies to report only ranks of student achievement; hence there is no scale to corrupt. PFP deters coaching by avoiding predictable exams. PFP discourages triage because PPI scores weight the winning percentage of each student in a classroom or school equally.

Yet PFP does not achieve a stated goal of many policy makers. Because the assessment system employed in PFP does not produce scaled achievement scores, it provides no information about secular trends in student achievement. Thus, it produces no information that allows policy makers to know whether or not current cohorts of students are performing better or worse than students from previous cohorts.

To some, this feature of PFP represents a significant failure. However, PFP solves the alignment problems that plague other ABI systems precisely because it does not attempt to produce scaled measures of student achievement. Policy makers want both to provide incentives for educators to teach well and to track trends in student outcomes, but as we note above, Neal (2011) and Neal (2013) present much evidence that existing ABI systems often fail to do either task well, precisely because they are trying to accomplish two separate tasks using only one assessment system.

"Two for the price of one" is a nice ad slogan, but the results from the Uniform CPA Examination demonstrate that even the most sophisticated modern assessment systems cannot produce scaled scores that have comparable meaning over time without creating opportunities for test takers to improve their scores through coaching activities that build little subject mastery. Further, Neal (2011) reviews clear evidence that, when policy makers attach high stakes to student scores on modern assessments, teachers and their students find ways to exploit these opportunities.

To bring this point closer to home, consider the final exams you have taken in different college classes. Your professors are each only allowed to give you one final exam, and they do not attempt to create exams that both provide optimal incentives for you and allow them to create consistent grading scales over time. Instead, they take one of two approaches. Some recycle old exam questions, and each year, they give exams that are quite similar to exams from previous years. In these classes, teaching assistants find that it is relatively easy to grade and score the exams so that the standard for an A or B in the class is the same each year. However, students do not prepare for these exams by exploring the material deeply. Instead, they retrieve copies of old exams from test banks that different student organizations maintain, and they study these old exams. They memorize the answers to old questions, and play around with possible variations on these questions that may appear on this year's exam.

In other classes, professors give exams that vary greatly from year to year. They never repeat questions, and they experiment with new formats for questions. The teaching assistants for these classes hate grading these exams because they have no similar exams or answer keys from previous years to use as references. Further, these teaching assistants cannot hope to grade these exams so that the standard for earning an A remains constant across years. However, students do not study for these exams by memorizing answers from past exams. Rather, they attempt to dig deeply into the material and master it. If they do review old exams, they do so only because they believe that working through the questions may help them understand the material better.

Your own professors must pick a lane. They can develop exams that allow their teaching assistants to produce grades that reflect fixed grading standards over time but induce students to allocate time to test-prep activities that crowd out real learning, or they can test in ways that induce students to probe the material more deeply and grade on a curve each year. But no professor can employ one set of exams and grading rubrics that both induces students to probe the material deeply and allows teaching assistants to maintain fixed absolute grading standards over time.[37]

2.9.1 A Better Way to Measure Achievement Trends

Please note that I am not suggesting that policy makers employ only one assessment system that produces no scale scores and is designed to minimize incentives for educators to engage in coaching and other gaming behaviors. Policy makers need tools that create proper incentives for educators, but they also need tools that help them track trends in student achievement. Therefore, educational standards and modern assessment systems that produce measures of student achievement relative to fixed standards are vital. However, these assessments should be administered in no-stakes settings.

Policy makers should administer and manage the Common Core assessments, or something like them,[38] in a manner similar to how the federal government currently runs the National Assessment of Educational

Progress (NAEP) assessments. NAEP does not report results for individual students or schools. Rather, it reports trends for groups of students defined by state of residence, gender, race, and other demographic traits.

In the first decade of NCLB, many researchers used the trends in the NAEP assessments to assess the credibility of observed trends in state-level NCLB exam results. The appeal of this method rests on the observation that no individual student or educator is or ever could be rewarded or punished based on their NAEP performance. As a result, researchers do not worry that coaching, cheating, and other gaming behaviors contaminate NAEP results.

Educational standards are necessary. They define goals for educators and anchor public reporting about secular trends in achievement. However, our discussion of PFP shows that reports concerning scaled achievement levels of individual students or collections of students in particular schools are not a necessary component of ABI systems. Further, much research indicates that attempts to use one assessment system to both track secular trends in achievement levels and provide proper incentives for educators often fail to accomplish either objective.[39]

2.10 Who Teaches

To this point, we have discussed how ABI systems affect the actions of a fixed set of educators. However, some scholars have argued that policy makers should make retention and tenure decisions based on measures of educator performance derived from student achievement outcomes.

2.10.1 Optimal Promotion and Retention Rules

Gordon et al. (2008), Staiger and Rockoff (2010), and Chetty et al. (2014b) all conduct policy simulations that attempt to measure the social gains that policy makers could generate by adopting firing rules that mandate termination for teachers whose measured performance falls below some percentile in the overall distribution of measured teacher performance.

The Chetty et al. (2014b) paper is unique because the authors used data on adult outcomes (e.g., adult earnings) to link VAM measures of educator performance and monetary measures of future benefits for students.[40] The Staiger and Rockoff (2010) paper is interesting because it attempts to determine the optimal firing rules for public school teachers given different assumptions about the length of tenure clocks.

Neal (2011) shows that the conclusions in Staiger and Rockoff (2010) are somewhat sensitive to the modeling choices they make. Nonetheless, taken at face value, the results in all of these papers imply that policy makers would produce significant learning gains for many students by adopting firing rules that remove a significant fraction of each new cohort of teachers during their first five years of service, even if these termination decisions were to be based solely on the test score performance of their students.

However, this conclusion rests on a maintained hypothesis that teacher performance is determined entirely by fixed teacher traits that teachers cannot alter through training, preparation, or increased effort. The popularity of this approach stems from the fact that measured differences in teacher performance tend to persist over time. This evidence of persistence has led some researchers to treat measures of performance for a given teacher as measures of teacher quality (i.e., measures of teacher talent), rather than as measures of the quality of the teacher's teaching, which should reflect not only the innate talent of the teacher but also decisions that she makes concerning training, preparation, and effort in the classroom.

Yet researchers typically estimate VAM models using data on test scores from students who attend schools where teachers face fairly weak performance incentives and enjoy robust employment protections. Given the policies that govern employment and pay in most public school systems, differences among teachers in their personal commitments to the mission of the school could be important determinants of differences in measured teacher performance, and if differences in effort norms drive a significant portion of observed differences in teacher performance, the simulation results in Staiger and Rockoff (2010) likely tell us little about optimal policy. Any policy that mandates termination for lower-performing teachers would likely improve and compress the entire distribution of teacher performance.[41] Thus, any "optimal" firing rules derived from the properties of the current distribution of measured teacher effectiveness could not actually be optimal.

Rothstein (2015) justifies the assumption that individual teachers cannot improve their own performance by pointing to results from two performance pay experiments that report no measured changes in student performance following the introduction of assessment-based performance pay for teachers. However, in Neal (2011), I point out that these two studies are exceptions and not the rule. In both the developed and developing world, teachers typically respond to assessment-based incentive systems that impact their pay or job security. In some cases, they respond by engaging in coaching and cheating behaviors that are not desirable, but they do respond, and student test scores typically rise.[42] Further, more recent experimental evidence suggests that teachers do respond to PFP. Finally, I note that the exceptions to this pattern reported in Goodman and Turner (2013), Fryer Jr. (2013), and Springer et al. (2011) may well reflect design flaws in the two performance-pay schemes that they studied.[43]

2.10.2 The Supply of Teachers

To this point, we have ignored the risks that ABI schemes impose on educators. Yet any ABI schemes that require school systems to terminate teachers with low measured performance impose significant risks on teachers. In many states, the certification process requires new teachers to invest significantly in skills and training that have little value outside teaching, and existing evidence suggests that new teachers may not be able to accurately forecast their own performance as teachers. Further, as we discuss more in Appendix 2.12, even among teachers who have been teaching for several years, the best predictors of future teacher performance contain significant noise. So any scheme that would link teacher retention decisions to educator performance metrics derived from student test scores would lead to the dismissal of some good teachers whose students performed below expectations in a year or two for reasons beyond these teachers' control.

Many workers are loathe to accept jobs where there is a significant risk that they will be involuntarily terminated in the future for reasons beyond their control. Thus, Rothstein (2015) argues that ABI systems that require schools to dismiss young teachers who have two or three bad years would reduce the supply of people who are willing to enter teaching and would force schools to either raise base salaries or see the average quality of new teachers fall. Using a simulation model, Rothstein concludes that even though assessment-based firing rules would require increases in teacher salaries, these policies could still be welfare improving. However, key parameters that affect his simulation results are difficult, if not impossible, to estimate directly. To date, no large-scale ABI experiments have imposed immediate risks of dismissal on teachers. More work is needed before economists can make confident predictions about the likely effects of such policies or make recommendations about the optimal design of such systems.

2.11 The Limits of ABI Systems

Even if future research allows researchers to greatly improve the design of ABI systems, such systems alone cannot accomplish all the objectives of education policy makers. Well-designed ABI systems may lead to gains in student math and reading skills or other skills that test developers know how to assess, but policy makers and many parents want schools to produce more than academic skills. Educators interact with their students for five or six hours per day, and they have many opportunities to foster important skills and character traits that testing experts may not know how to measure.

Most adults believe that children should learn to be honest, intellectually curious, hardworking, kind, and empathetic. Further, society benefits whenever schools find ways to minimize the nonmonetary costs that children pay to attend schools. In schools where children feel safe, respected, supported, and encouraged, attending school is less of a burden, and it is reasonable to expect such children to persist longer and graduate more often.

We have already mentioned the seminal contributions of Campbell (1979) and Holmstrom and Milgrom (1991) to the social science literature on incentive design. Kerr (1975) made an important and related contribution to management science by noting that organizations should not reward A while hoping for B. ABI systems reward educators for developing the academic skills of their students, and it is foolish to think that educators will devote sufficient attention to the emotional and social development of their students if ABI systems alone determine the incentives they face.

This brings us to two obvious questions. How can policy makers acquire information about these nonacademic aspects of school performance, and how should they reward them? Current policy debates address two approaches. First, school choice reforms make educators accountable to parents by linking school budgets to enrollment levels and then allowing parents to choose which school their child attends. Many parents may not know the answers to their child's trigonometry homework, but they do know whether or not their child feels safe at school and whether or not their child is becoming more mature and responsible. School choice proposals allow parents to punish schools that perform poorly on these dimensions and reward schools that perform well.

Yet parental choice may not be enough. We began this book by arguing that public investment in the schooling of children is warranted because many children have parents who are not both wealthy enough and altruistic enough to invest in them efficiently. Further, we noted that schooling is mandatory in most developed countries because, if governments simply gave per-child education stipends to parents, some parents would not allocate all of these resources to their children's education. Thus, we must entertain the possibility that, given complete freedom to choose their child's school, some parents would make choices that do not serve their child well, either because they are poorly informed or because they are motivated by concerns other than their child's development.

This observation may help us understand the ubiquity of a second approach. All public education authorities make some provision for school inspections, and in some education systems, these inspections are quite detailed and consequential.[44] In Neal (2011), I argue that the optimal accountability system for public educators likely involves some combination of ABI provisions, school choice, and school inspections, and in the final chapter, we return to the task of combining these elements into a coherent system.

Although much of the education literature treats ABI systems, school choice programs, and school inspection systems as policy alternatives, these policies are complements. Any policy that rewards educators for only one aspect of their performance may well induce them to allocate effort among tasks inefficiently. A multifaceted approach is needed to hold educators responsible for all aspects of their performance.

2.12 Appendix: Empirical Work on Educator Quality

This appendix describes basic facts about how researchers create VAM measures of teacher quality. We explore a special case of the most general model in order to simplify the presentation. Once we understand the basic method, we will discuss how to interpret VAM measures of teacher quality.

Take the VAM model in equation (1.3) and add dummy variables that denote the identities of the teachers assigned to each of the students.

$$a_i = a_i^- \alpha + \tilde{x}_i \beta + d'_{ij}\theta + v_i \qquad (2.1)$$

where $i = 1, 2, \ldots, N$ indexes students and $j = 1, 2, \ldots, J$ indexes teachers. Further,

- a_i is a measure of achievement for student i.
- a_i^- is a measure of prior achievement for student i.
- $\tilde{x}_i$ is a vector of demographic characteristics that describe student i or her family. These may include race, gender, parental education, family income, etc.
- d_{ij} is a $J x 1$ vector where the jth element equals 1 if teacher j teaches student i and 0 else.
- θ is a $J x 1$ vector of teacher quality effects.
- v_i captures unmeasured factors that influence the growth of measured achievement for student i.

In our example, the researcher has data on one class of students taught by each teacher, and the data include a lagged measure of achievement as well as demographic characteristics of each student. Many studies in this literature have access to data from multiple classes taught by the same teacher, and in some cases, multiple collections of classes taught by the same teacher in different years. The methods used in these studies require more calculations, but they rest on the same principles that we explore in our simpler setting.

We consider the case where $[a_i, a_i^-, \tilde{x}_i]$ are all measured in deviations from sample means. Further, we normalize our concept of teacher quality so that $\mu_\theta = 0$; that is, if the quality of teacher j equals the average quality in the population of all teachers, $\theta_j = 0$.

Thus, as a first step, we take the elements of the vector $\hat{\theta}_{ols}$ produced by running OLS on equation (2.1) and re-center these elements around the sample mean of the elements of this vector. This transformation guarantees that the sample mean of teacher quality equals zero.

Let $\tilde{\theta}$ denote this re-centered vector. We can think about the elements of this vector as signals concerning the quality of each teacher, and for each teacher j, we may write

$$\tilde{\theta}_j = \theta_j + e_j \qquad (2.2)$$

which says that our VAM estimate of the quality of teacher j can be decomposed into teacher j's true quality θ_j and an estimation error e_j. If we assume that $E(v_i | a_i^-, \tilde{x}_i, D_{ij}) = 0 \; \forall i$, our VAM estimator is unbiased; that is, $E(\tilde{\theta}_j) = \theta_j$ for all j, and we have $E(e_j | \theta_j) = 0$ for all j.

However, even in VAM studies where researchers are willing to defend the assumption $E(v_i | a_i^-, \tilde{x}_i, D_{ij}) = 0 \; \forall i$, researchers often do not employ $\tilde{\theta}$ as their estimator of teacher-quality effects. Rather, they employ a shrinkage estimator that takes the form

$$\bar{\theta}_j = \frac{\hat{\sigma}_\theta^2}{\hat{\sigma}_\theta^2 + \hat{\sigma}_{e_j}^2} \tilde{\theta}_j$$

$$\hat{\sigma}_\theta^2 = \sum_j \frac{\tilde{\theta}_j^2}{J}$$

$$\hat{\sigma}_{e_j}^2 = \frac{\sum_i \frac{\hat{v}_i^2}{N}}{S_j}$$

where S_j is the number of students in teacher j's class. In educational statistics, $\bar{\theta}_j$ is known as an empirical-Bayes shrinkage estimator.

To understand the appeal of this estimator, note that even if $E(\tilde{\theta}_j) = \theta_j$ for all j, $\tilde{\theta}_j$ is not our best linear predictor of θ_j. Given the data-generating process in equation (2.2), the coefficient from a population regression of true teacher quality, θ, on measured teacher quality, $\tilde{\theta}$, is always less than one because $E(e | \tilde{\theta}) \neq 0$. Large absolute values of $\tilde{\theta}_j$ are correlated, by construction, with large absolute estimation errors, e_j. Thus, even when we assume $E(\tilde{\theta}_j) = \theta_j$, our best forecast of θ_j given $\tilde{\theta}_j$ is less than $\tilde{\theta}_j$ in absolute value, i.e, $E(\theta_j | \tilde{\theta}_j) \neq \tilde{\theta}_j$. In fact, if we assume that, for all $j = 1, 2, \ldots, J$, both θ_j and e_j in equation (2.2) are i.i.d. draws from normal distributions with zero means, the following well-known result holds exactly:

$$E(\theta_j | \tilde{\theta}_j) = \frac{\sigma_\theta^2}{\sigma_\theta^2 + \sigma_{e_j}^2} \tilde{\theta}_j$$

Recall that $\sigma_{e_j}^2$ is the variance of the estimation error in $\tilde{\theta}_j$ given a class size of S_j. Thus, as S_j increases, $\sigma_{e_j}^2$ decreases, and there is less need to shrink $\tilde{\theta}_j$ toward our normalized mean of zero. In more complicated sampling designs, the precision of $\tilde{\theta}_j$ is determined by the number of years of data available, the number of classes teacher j teaches each year, and the sizes of the classes she teaches. Yet the principle remains the same. Education researchers shrink estimates of teacher quality toward a common mean because the estimates contain noise. Thus, more data means less noise and less shrinkage.

We motivated our shrinkage equation under the maintained assumption that $E(v_i | a_i^-, \tilde{x}_i, D_{ij}) = 0$ $\forall i$, or $E(\tilde{\theta}_j) = \theta_j$ for all j, but as you would expect given our discussion in Section 1.5, a significant literature debates whether or not $\tilde{\theta}$ is an unbiased estimator of θ, given the different data-generating processes that produce data for education research. Most researchers agree that $\tilde{\theta}$ is typically biased to some extent, at least in observational studies,[45] but many empirical papers have shown that shrinkage estimators derived from $\tilde{\theta}$ are nonetheless useful for predicting how the students of particular teachers will perform in the future.

Kane et al. (2013) estimate measures of teacher effectiveness using observational data and a shrinkage estimator similar to the one described above. Then they randomly assign teachers to classrooms in the following year and investigate whether or not they can predict future achievement differences among students based on the random assignment of teachers to classes. They find that average student scores in a classroom increase roughly one for one with movements in expected average scores derived from measures of how effective various teachers were in previous years.

Shrinkage estimators of teacher quality derived from VAM regression results are not unbiased, but they are useful as predictors of how the assignment of teachers to classrooms should affect average student performance in the future. This property of these estimators has led some researchers and policy makers to argue that education authorities should develop accountability or incentive systems around these predictors of future performance. However, as Kane et al. (2013) acknowledge, best predictors are not always good predictors. In many cases, predictions regarding the average performance of students in a particular teacher's classroom often miss the mark badly.

These prediction errors may be minor concerns in schemes that attach bonus pay to VAM measures of teacher performance. In any given year, a specific teacher may win a larger or smaller bonus than she deserves, but these discrepancies should tend to average out over time. However, if policy makers were to create firing rules that dictate termination for teachers with low VAM scores, such rules would possibly lead to dismissals of many competent teachers. As discussed earlier, Rothstein (2015) notes that education authorities would need to compensate new teachers for bearing the risks associated with these unwarranted dismissals.

Further, while we know little about how the predictive value of VAM measures of teacher quality would change if teachers knew that their pay and job security were linked to these measures, Campbell's Law gives us reason to conjecture that attaching high stakes to these measures would diminish their value as predictors of future teacher quality.

2.13 Appendix: Multitasking for Beginners

Here, we consider a particular case of the Holmstrom and Milgrom (1991) multitasking model. This presentation also borrows from lecture notes prepared by Robert S. Gibbons.[46]

A risk-neutral principal hires a risk-averse agent to create a payoff $B(t)$ for the principal, where $t = (t_1, t_2)$ is a vector that describes how the agent allocates his time among two different tasks. The principal cannot observe $t = (t_1, t_2)$ or $B(t)$. However, the principal does observe a noisy signal $x(t)$, which is verifiable:

$$x(t) = \mu(t) + \varepsilon$$

where $\varepsilon \sim N(0, \sigma^2)$ and $\mu : \mathbb{R}^2 \to \mathbb{R}$ is concave in each component.

The agent's utility function is

$$U(w, t) = - \exp \left[-r \left(w - C(t) \right) \right]$$

where w is the payment the agent receives from the principal, r is the interest rate, and $C(t)$ captures disutility from effort. Since $x(t)$ is verifiable, the principal can make payments to the agent that are contingent on $x(t)$, i.e., $w[x(t)]$. So let us specify the utility for an agent who works under a given contract, $w[x(t)]$, as

$$U(w[x(t)], t) = - \exp \left[-r \left(w[x(t)] - C(t) \right) \right]$$

Our goal is to characterize the contract that maximizes the total surplus generated by the principal-agent relationship. The principal's payoff $B(t)$ is a monetary payoff. Thus, to characterize the joint surplus in the relationship, we need to express the agent's expected payoffs in monetary terms as well. Contracts that take the form $w[x(t)]$ typically impose risk on the agent because the shocks to $x(t)$ generate random variation in $w[x(t)]$ holding t

fixed. Yet the principal could offer the agent a constant fixed payment, z, that did not depend on t. In this scenario, the agent would incur no effort costs because he would respond by exerting just enough effort to satisfy his own effort norms, and his utility would be

$$- \exp[-rz]$$

Given any contract $w[x(t)]$ that contains incentive provisions, we say that a fixed payment z is the "certainty equivalent" of $w[x(t)]$ if

$$- \exp(-rz) = E\left[- \exp\left[-r\left(w[x(\hat{t})] - C(\hat{t})\right)\right]\right]$$

Here, we are taking expectations over realizations of ε, the shock to the signal process. $\hat{t}$ is the agent's optimal vector of effort choices when the principal offers contract $w[x(t)]$. We follow Holmstrom and Milgrom (1991) and consider only linear contracts that take the form

$$w(x) = s + bx$$

where s is the base salary and b is the bonus rate. Given this restriction, you should be able to show that, for all combinations (s, b), the certainty equivalent is[47]

$$z = s + b\mu(\hat{t}) - C(\hat{t}) - \frac{rb^2\sigma^2}{2}$$

The final term is the cost of risk induced by the contract. It increases in magnitude with the strength of incentives and the variance of the shocks to the performance signal.

The certainty equivalent z allows us to express the value of a particular contract to the agent in monetary terms. The principal's expected monetary payoff is $B(\hat{t}) - E\left\{w[x(\hat{t})]\right\}$, which, given a linear contract, becomes $B(\hat{t}) - s - b\mu(\hat{t})$. Thus, the total surplus in the relationship is

$$TS = B(\hat{t}) - C(\hat{t}) - \frac{rb^2\sigma^2}{2}$$

Note that the base salary and the expected bonus payment are not part of total surplus since these are transfers between the principal and the agent. The surplus equals the benefit created for the principal minus the effort and risk costs that the agent bears to create these benefits.

2.13.1 Optimal Contract

The optimal contract maximizes TS given $\hat{t} = \hat{t}(b, s)$, the function that gives the agent's optimal response to any contract that the principal chooses, subject to the constraint that both the principal and the agent are willing to participate in the relationship. To economize on notation, we normalize the outside options for both principal and agent to zero.

We solve for the optimal contract in two steps. First, we solve the agent's problem to recover $\hat{t} = \hat{t}(b, s)$. Then we solve the following maximization problem:

$$\max_{b,s} B(\hat{t}(b, s)) - C(\hat{t}(b, s)) - \frac{rb^2\sigma^2}{2}$$

$$\text{s.t.} \quad s + b\mu(\hat{t}) - C(\hat{t}) - \frac{rb^2\sigma^2}{2} > 0$$

$$B(\hat{t}) - s - b\mu(\hat{t}) > 0$$

If the potential surplus is positive, $B(t)$ is concave, and $C(t)$ is strictly convex, a solution to this problem exists but is not generically unique. The base salary is simply a tool for dividing the surplus between the principal and the agent, so many different optimal base salaries are possible. However, the optimal bonus rate, $\hat{b}$, is unique.

To make sure you understand the model, work through a parametric example. Assume

- $B(t) = f_1 t_1 + f_2 t_2$
- $\mu(t) = p_1 t_1 + p_2 t_2$
- $C(t) = \frac{1}{2}(t_1 - \bar{t})^2 + \frac{1}{2}t_2^2$

Here, $\bar{t}$ is an effort norm. With a little work, you should be able to show that the optimal bonus rate is:

$$\hat{b} = \frac{f_1 p_1 + f_2 p_2}{p_1^2 + p_2^2 + r\sigma^2}$$

This optimal bonus formula teaches two key lessons about optimal incentives.

1. Holding other factors constant, there is a trade-off between risk and incentives. If agents are more risk averse ($\uparrow r$) or the signal has more noise ($\uparrow \sigma^2$), the optimal bonus rate should be lower ($\hat{b} \downarrow$). This

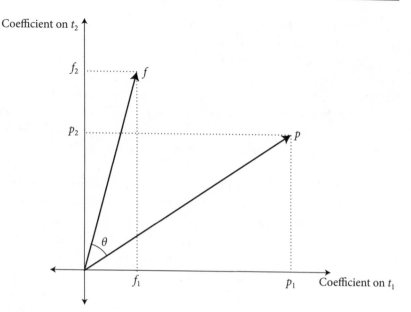

Figure 2.2 Multitasking.

makes sense because stronger incentives amplify the link between the signal shock, ε, and the agent's realized earnings.

2. Putting risk to the side, the strength of incentives is determined by the alignment of $x(t)$ relative to $B(t)$. If $\frac{p_1}{p_2} \approx \frac{f_1}{f_2}$, then $x(t)$ is well aligned with $B(t)$ since the relative productivity of the two tasks in generating signals approximates the relative productivity of the two tasks in generating real benefits.

To see point 2 more clearly, set $\sigma^2 = 0$, and take a moment to show that, in this case,

$$\hat{b} = \frac{f_1 p_1 + f_2 p_2}{p_1^2 + p_2^2} = \frac{||f||}{||p||} \cos \theta \tag{2.3}$$

where θ is the angle between the vectors f and p. This formula tells us that, when risk plays no role, the optimal bonus rate reflects two factors: scaling and alignment. See Figure 2.2.

The scaling function is just an accounting consideration. The ratio of the length of the two coefficient vectors converts the scale of the performance metric into dollars. The $\cos \theta$ term determines how the alignment between the performance metric and $B(t)$ shapes optimal incentives.

To see how the bonus rate scales the signal, x, in units of benefit, $B(t)$, consider a farmer who hires someone to pick his tomatoes. Let x equal the pounds of tomatoes picked, and $B(t)$ equal the market value of the tomatoes picked. Here, $\theta = 0$, $\cos \theta = 1$, and $\hat{b} = \frac{\|f\|}{\|p\|} = $ the market price of tomatoes per pound. This is the case of "perfect alignment," and the bonus rate is just an accounting tool. It converts a pound of tomatoes into dollars.[48]

Next, consider a signal $x(t)$ that is scaled correctly but not well aligned with $B(t)$. Let $p_2 = f_1$, $p_2 > p_1 = 0$ but $f_1 > f_2 = 0$. In this case, $\frac{\|f\|}{\|p\|} = 1$, so scaling is not an issue, but there is a serious alignment problem. Note that $f \cdot p = 0$. Thus, $\hat{b} = \cos 90 = 0$. Here, the productive action does not improve the signal, and the action that improves the signal is not productive, so $\hat{b} = 0$ and the maximum TS equals $B(\hat{t}_1 = \bar{t}, \hat{t}_2 = 0)$. In this case, the optimal contract pays the agent a fixed salary, and the principal accepts the benefit that the agent's effort norm produces. The agent bears no effort costs in this case, and she bears no salary risk either.[49]

The optimal bonus formula in equation (2.3) may give the false impression that most optimal contracts should involve some incentive pay, i.e., $\hat{b} > 0$, since $f \cdot p = 0$ may be a rare case. However, the solution expressed in equation (2.3) hinges on our assumptions about the shape of $C(t_1, t_2)$. In Neal (2011), I point out that when t_1 and t_2 are substitutes and the agent's effort norm is defined in terms of total tasks completed, e.g.,

$$C(t) = \frac{1}{2}(t_1 + t_2 - \bar{t})^2$$

it is easy to construct examples where the optimal contract involves a fixed salary and $\hat{b} = 0$. Assume that, given no performance incentives, the agent satisfies his norm for total effort by allocating effort to the task that generates the greater benefit for the principal. Further, assume that the performance signal is not perfectly aligned with B. In this case, any incentive scheme, $\hat{b} > 0$, diverts effort away from the more productive task. Thus, it may be optimal to accept the output that the agent would produce to satisfy his norm, and pay him a fixed salary in return.

This insight is at once trivial and central. Incentive schemes are least attractive in settings where they induce agents to divert effort away from productive tasks that they would have completed in the absence of any incentives. Thus, the potential value of ABI schemes in education hinges on the norms that exist ex ante among educators in a given school and the patterns of task substitution that ABI systems induce.

There are only about 300 minutes of potential instruction time in most school days. If teachers are already devoting most of these 300 minutes to quality instruction, ABI schemes are likely not desirable. Given strong ex ante norms, ABI schemes may simply induce teachers to substitute test-prep activities for lessons that would have created greater long-term value for students. However, in settings where teachers are wasting half of the instruction time available to them, introducing ABI systems makes more sense. As long as the test-prep sessions build at least some lasting skills, filling wasted time with test-prep sessions may improve welfare.

EXERCISES

▶ Consider the following parametric version of the Holmstrom-Milgrom principal-agent model. Let the agent make a one-time choice of a two-dimensional vector of efforts

$$t = [t_1, t_2]$$

The agent pays personal cost $C(t) = \frac{1}{2}t_1^2 + \frac{1}{2}t_2^2$ for exerting effort. The efforts t lead to expected gross benefits of $B(t) = 0.9t_1 + 0.1t_2$, which accrue directly to the principal. The agent's efforts also generate a scalar performance signal:

$$x = \mu(t) + \epsilon$$

where $\mu(t) = 0.1t_1 + 0.9t_2$ and $\epsilon \sim N(0, \sigma^2)$. Let the wage contract be linear:

$$w(x) = \alpha x + \beta$$

where α is the bonus rate and β is the fixed payment from the principal to the agent. Assume both the principal and the agent are risk neutral, so the expected utility for the agent is:

$$E[U] = E[w(x) - C(t)]$$

- Solve for the efficient bonus rate (α^*) and a fixed payment (β^*) that satisifies both participation constraints.
- Are the efficient bonus rate and fixed payment unique?
- What value(s) of α^* and β^* maximize principal surplus?
- What value(s) of α^* and β^* maximize agent surplus?

► Now, we solve for the optimal prize in a simple tournament between two teachers.

Consider the following tournament environment: There are two teachers, each assigned to teach one student. Both students have identical baseline achievement/ability. The teacher of the student who receives the highest end-of-year score earns a prize. The testing authority only reports ranks (i.e., teacher j either won or lost; there is no measure of the margin of victory or defeat). Let the test score (s_j) for the student of teacher j depend on teacher j effort, e_j, in the following way:

$$s_j = e_j + \epsilon_j$$

where $\epsilon_j \sim N(0, \sigma_j^2)$ and $\sigma_j = \sigma_k = \sigma$ for both teachers. Also, assume that σ is sufficiently large for a Nash equilibrium to exist.

Let the winning teacher receive W_1 and the losing teacher receive W_2, with $W_1 > W_2$; i.e., W_2 is the base salary, and $W_1 - W_2$ is the prize.

Suppose effort is costly to the teachers with cost function $C(e_j)$, where C', $C'' > 0$. Each teacher is risk neutral and has an outside option of zero. Teachers select their effort level e_j to maximize their expected utility:

$$E[U] = E[W_j - C(e_j)]$$

where W_j is the prize for teacher j. The school is risk neutral and produces

$$(s_j + s_k)V$$

where V is a constant. Assume there is free entry of schools. Also remember that only the relative ranks of s_j and s_k are observed.

- Find the value of $W_1 - W_2$ that maximizes the difference between the expected value of the skills that teachers create and their total effort costs.
- What would W_2 be in a world where schools compete actively for teachers and where teachers get all the surplus from production?

THREE

Letting Parents Choose

Advocates of ABI schemes offer them as mechanisms for placing competitive pressures on schools. However, ABI schemes are not mechanisms for creating market competition. ABI schemes, even ones built around contests, are another form of bureaucracy. Traditional bureaucracy revolves around rules that both guide and constrain the decisions public administrators make concerning resource allocation, and many of these rules govern the employment and pay of public employees. ABI schemes simply replace traditional bureaucratic rules with new rules that require public administrators to make certain decisions based on the realizations of statistical performance metrics. These systems may make it easier for the public to verify that education authorities are actually monitoring public educators, but effective authority and control still rest with the public officials who design the performance metrics and the data collection systems used to create them.

In this chapter and the two that follow, we discuss policies that grant parents more control over the publicly funded education of their children. We begin by examining the most benign form of school choice: centralized school assignment mechanisms. Many school districts no longer assign students to schools but instead employ school assignment mechanisms that allow parents to express their preferences over different schools in their districts. These systems produce information, and they may improve welfare by allowing parents to find schools that their children enjoy.[1] However, these mechanisms alone create no penalties for educators who perform poorly or rewards for those who perform well and thus create no incentives for schools to improve. Further, these mechanisms do not force bad schools to close or provide opportunities for better schools to open.

In Chapter 4, we discuss charter schools. Charter schools receive public funds, but independent organizations operate these schools. Charter systems create competition for students. Charter schools receive more funding if they enroll more students, and part of these funds come from reductions in funding for the traditional public schools that see their students leave to attend charter schools.

In some locations, charter systems create rather limited competition. These systems place caps on the number of charter schools or allow local public school systems to veto charter applications. Nonetheless, even these charter systems foster experimentation in organizational and educational practice because most charter schools are not bound by the bureaucratic constraints on personnel policy and school operation that exist in traditional public schools.

Chapter 5 explores voucher systems. Voucher systems often place few restrictions on school entry, and many voucher systems fund both traditional public schools and private schools according to a common per-pupil formula, which means that parental choice allocates public funds to schools. Nonetheless, most voucher systems contain noteworthy regulations. Several countries in Europe have voucher systems that require all publicly funded schools to follow a common national curriculum. Further, in some cases, these systems require voucher schools to follow the personnel policies set by national union contracts. These systems allow schools to compete for students, but regulations limit the ways that schools are allowed to compete.[2]

We end Chapter 5 by discussing policies that determine the extent to which voucher schools are allowed to control their own admission priorities. For example, education authorities that run voucher systems must decide whether or not schools can require families to pay more than the nominal voucher amount in tuition and whether they can deny students entry based on their prior academic achievement, their family background, their religion, etc. These policy choices are among the most controversial that education officials confront and also involve many questions about education production that existing research has not yet settled.

3.1 Attendance Zones

In this chapter, we examine different mechanisms that a school district could use to allocate students to schools. We start by examining attendance zone systems because many public school systems have historically assigned students to public schools based on their place of residence. Once we have described this approach and explored the potential inefficiencies it creates, we examine alternative mechanisms that allow families to express their preferences over schools.

Consider a school district with J schools that we index with $j = 1$, $2, \ldots, J$. To keep things simple, assume that each school serves grades K–12. Further, assume that each school has a maximum enrollment capacity of κ_j. Next, assume that N families live in the district, and again for simplicity, assume that each family has one child. We assume that no one school can serve the whole district, but together, all schools in the district provide an enrollment capacity greater than the number of students in the district.

In attendance zone systems, each home or apartment in a given district belongs to an attendance zone associated with a specific school, and students who live in the attendance zone for school j attend school j. Such systems use the real estate market to allocate available seats in different public schools. Rents and home prices in a given attendance zone therefore reflect, in part, the willingness of families to pay for the right to send their child to the school in that zone.

Attendance zone systems create inefficiencies because they force families to choose their school and their residence as a bundle. Thus, when choosing a school, a family also chooses many attributes of their home, such as its location, the quality of the surrounding houses, the demographics of the families who live there, etc. Ex post, there may exist pairs of families who would find it in their mutual interests to trade their school assignments. Yet these trades do not take place because the two families are not also willing to trade houses.

Consider two families, A and B. Family A is quite wealthy, and their child excels in leadership activities like student government but is not that motivated academically. They live in the attendance zone associated with the best academic program for gifted students, school j. This school is not a great match for their child, but the parents in family A like nice houses, and the attendance zone for school j is the most upscale attendance zone in the district.

The child in family B is academically gifted but not interested in student government or other extracurricular leadership opportunities. Family B enjoys a modest income and cares little about the extra features that come with the best homes in the best neighborhoods. Yet family B does care greatly about finding an excellent gifted program for their child. For every hour that family A spends watching *Million Dollar Listing*, family B spends two hours watching documentaries on PBS.

Family B lives in the attendance zone for school j', which has an acceptable program for gifted students but really excels at providing excellent extracurricular programs (e.g., student government, student newspaper, model UN, etc.). Families A and B would gladly trade their school assignments if they could do so without moving, but family B cannot afford a home in the attendance zone for school j, and family A cannot imagine living in one of the modest homes that populate the attendance zone for school j'.

Attendance zone systems may not only harm allocative efficiency; they may also perpetuate inequality. In our example, family B has a child who is particularly well suited to the gifted program in school j, but given their lack of income, wealthier students who are less well matched will populate this program instead.

Similar results may apply to racial inequality. Suppose that for reasons related to past discrimination, the best public schools are in attendance zones where few or no minority families live. Further, suppose that all families prefer to live in neighborhoods where a nontrivial fraction of other families share their racial or ethnic background. In this environment, attendance zone systems may perpetuate racial differences in school quality by requiring minority families to choose between sending their kids to the best schools and living in neighborhoods where they are not racially isolated.

At one time, attendance zone systems were ubiquitous in developed countries, but in recent decades, many school districts throughout the developed world have adopted centralized assignment mechanisms that grant students the opportunity to seek entrance to schools throughout their districts.[3] In the balance of this chapter, we discuss these alternative mechanisms and their properties.

3.2 Deferred Acceptance

In recent decades, many school districts, especially urban school districts, have expanded the number of schools that do not restrict enrollment to students who live within specific attendance zones. These programs fall broadly under the heading of public school choice programs. As long as all teachers in a district work under a common union contract and education authorities do not rely on the information produced by the choices parents make among public schools when determining school budgets or making school closing decisions, public school choice programs should have limited impacts on how public schools perform. However, these programs can improve allocative efficiency by placing students in public schools where they feel better matched with the prevailing educational practices or school culture. Students may learn more and become more likely to finish school if they find a school where they have a sense of belonging rather than alienation.

3.2.1 Match Making

We noted above that attendance zone allocation rules may well generate inefficient allocations of students to schools. An alternative mechanism, known as the deferred acceptance (DA) algorithm, may prove useful as a tool for mitigating some of the inefficiencies and inequities created by attendance zone systems. Gale and Shapley (1962) first proposed this algorithm in a paper, entitled "College Admissions and the Stability of Marriage," that analyzed the problem of assigning students to colleges and then dealt with the problem of assigning men and women to marriages. We will proceed by examining the marriage problem first, and then turn to the problem of assigning students to schools.

Suppose that you have a set of men, $M = \{m_1, m_2, \ldots, m_n\}$, and a set of women, $W = \{w_1, w_2, \ldots, w_p\}$, that occupy a common marriage market. Further, suppose you want to analyze the possible collections of marriages that could exist in this market.

It is useful to start by considering a function μ that maps the set $M \cup W$ into itself. We say the μ is a matching if it satisfies the following conditions: given the identity of any man, μ returns either a specific woman or the man in question; given the identity of any woman, μ returns either the identity of a specific man or the women in question; μ never matches more than one woman with the same man, and also never matches more than one man with the same woman.

For example, given $n = 4$ and $p = 3$, the following diagram represents a matching:

m_1	m_2	m_3	m_4
w_3	w_1	m_3	w_2

Here, m_1 is matched with w_3, m_2 is matched with w_1, m_3 is single, and m_4 is matched with w_2. To make sure you understand what a matching is, take a moment to confirm that there are 73 possible matchings in this marriage market.

Given that 73 matchings are possible, which matchings could we actually expect to observe? Economists usually restrict their attention to the set of stable matchings. The set of stable matchings contains all of the matchings such that it is impossible to propose an affair that would dissolve an existing marriage. Put differently, for each woman, the men whom she prefers to her current match do not prefer her to their current matches, and for each man, the women whom he prefers to his current match do not prefer him to their current matches.

Before we consider ways to identify stable matchings, note that, in this example and others that follow, preference orderings are strict. We assume that no man finds any two women equally suitable, and no woman finds any two men equally attractive.

Given this framework, consider the following algorithm. Have each man, who is willing to marry, propose to his favorite woman. Next, have each woman who received proposals select her favorite man from her set of acceptable suitors and have her reject the rest. Then, have each rejected man propose to his favorite woman among the set of women that satisfy two criteria. He must be willing to marry them, and none of them have already rejected him. Once again, have each woman select her favorite man from her set of suitors and have her reject the rest. Repeat these steps as long as unmatched men remain who have not proposed to all the women whom they are willing to marry. Then, match each woman with the last suitor she retained.

This procedure is the DA algorithm presented in Gale and Shapley (1962). This algorithm not only produces a stable matching but also produces the stable matching that is best for men and worst for women. By best for men, we mean that if we were to replace this matching with another stable matching, each married man would either be married to the same woman, married to a woman he finds less desirable, or single, and each single man would remain single. By worst for women, we mean that, in every other stable matching, each woman enjoys the same match or is matched to a man she likes better.[4]

3.2.2 Assigning Students to Schools

These results are quite striking. Yet you may wonder what they have to do with the problem of assigning students to schools. To see the connection, consider the set of schools in a district, and assume that each school contains a set of lockers for students. Next, assume that there are a fixed number of students in the district and that this number is less than the total number of lockers in the district. Also, assume that each student must submit a strict preference ranking over all schools in the district, from her most preferred to her least preferred, and that each student adopts an arbitrary procedure that allows her to also rank the lockers within any given school.[5] Further, assume that each school has a set of criteria that allow it to rank any collection of potential students from most desirable to least desirable. This set might include measures of student achievement or demographics, such as commuting distance to the school, family income, or prior test scores. We also assume that the district assigns a random number to each student in the district, and each school uses these random numbers to create a strict priority ranking over all students (i.e., to break ties whenever two students are identical with respect to all other school-specific ranking criteria). Finally, require each locker in each school to adopt its school's priority ranking over all students, and then run a student-proposing deferred acceptance algorithm, where students propose to schools by proposing to the lockers in schools.

Because students propose, this mechanism yields the stable matching between students and schools that is optimal for students, *given the ranking criteria that the district assigns to each school.* These criteria may include random numbers that districts assign to students for the purpose of breaking ties.

In our context, stability implies that no student possesses *justifiable envy*. If any student wants to transfer from school A to school B, it must be true that school B ranks this potential transfer student at or below all of its current students. If this were not the case, we would say that the student's envy of those who attend school B is justifiable.

To make the parallel with marriage easier to follow, I have described a one-to-one matching between lockers and students. In practice, when school systems employ DA, students propose to schools, and schools consider all proposals. In any round, each school that has received fewer total proposals than its capacity retains all students associated with these proposals, and each school that has received more proposals than its capacity rations seats by retaining students with the highest priorities and rejecting the rest. In each round, any student may propose to any school that has not rejected her. The mechanism stops when each student has been retained by some school.[6]

3.2.3 Honesty Is the Best Policy

The DA mechanism is also strategy-proof for students. If a school system assigns students to schools using a strategy-proof mechanism, it is in the interest of each student to rank schools according to her true preferences and to make proposals accordingly, regardless of what the student believes about the strategies that other students follow when submitting their own rankings. Put differently, if a school assignment mechanism is strategy-proof, honesty really is always the best policy for each student.

To see why DA is strategy-proof, recall that all students must submit a complete ranking over all schools in the district. Thus, a student never gains an advantage by having any school consider her proposal in a particular round. If we take any given school, the algorithm never stops until each student has been either rejected by this school, retained by this school, or retained by a school that she deems even better than this school. Thus, no student can shape the competition they face for placement in any school by trying to manipulate the round in which any school considers her. Further, because a student who proposes truthfully is able to keep making proposals to her favorite school, among the set of schools that have not already rejected her, regardless of how many times she has been rejected, a student who reports her preferences truthfully never forfeits the opportunity to be considered by a school.

However, consider a student who, at some point in the algorithm, proposes to a school that is not her favorite among the set of schools that have not yet rejected her. If this school retains her, she may end up being matched with this school permanently and forfeit the opportunity to ever propose to her true favorite. Thus, any student who, at any step, proposes to a school that is not her favorite among her remaining options cannot improve and may harm the quality of her final match.

The same principle holds in our marriage market example. Whenever a man proposes to a woman, she will either reject the proposal or retain the man. If she rejects the proposal, the man is allowed to make another proposal. However, if the woman retains him, she may eventually marry him without ever allowing him to propose to anyone else. So, at each stage, it is in the man's interest to propose only to his true favorite, among those who have not rejected him.

3.2.4 Efficiency

So far, we have learned that the DA mechanism creates incentives for families to truthfully report their preferences among schools and produces a matching between students and schools that, from the perspective of students, is the best matching among the set of all stable matchings. Thus, you may be surprised to learn that DA does not always produce matchings that are Pareto efficient. If a school district uses a DA mechanism to assign students to schools, then ex post, there may exist two students who would both benefit by trading assignments.

The most expedient way to see this is to return to our attendance zone system above. We have already noted that the allocations produced by attendance zone systems are likely not to be Pareto efficient, and it turns out that we can implement the attendance zone allocation of students to schools using DA, if we choose a particular set of *ranking criteria for schools*.

Suppose each school deems all students who live outside its attendance zone as unqualified, and then ranks all students within its attendance zone alphabetically. You should be able to show that, in this environment, DA will produce the same allocation of students to schools produced by an attendance zone system. The key here is that DA allows schools to reject students. So, if the priorities for each school dictate that students who live outside the attendance zone of any school are rejected by that school, DA creates the same allocation of students to schools produced by an attendance zone system. Taking the schools' ranking criteria as given, this assignment of students to schools is stable but likely inefficient for reasons we have already discussed.

3.2.5 An Important Difference

Let us return to our marriage market example. If both men and women report their true preferences, DA produces a matching that is stable and Pareto efficient. However, given truthful reporting by both students and schools, student-proposing DA mechanisms may still produce matchings such that, ex post, some students would benefit from trading school assignments. These results are not in conflict. Given any matching produced by a student-proposing DA mechanism, ex post trades that benefit students must involve forcing schools to accept students with lower priority than those they release. We do not consider comparable trades in our marriage example because women would not accept trades that yield inferior matches.[7]

Although DA respects the priorities of schools as if they were the preferences of a person, another well-known mechanism, Top Trading Cycles (TTC), treats school priorities differently. TTC was first proposed by Shapley and Scarf (1974) as a mechanism for allocating indivisible commodities (e.g., houses) among consumers. Thus, when applied to education, TTC treats the right to attend a given school as a property right that a student may trade to another student for the right to attend a different school. In a TTC school assignment system, school priorities determine how initial claims on seats in various schools are assigned to various students, but do not constrain how families may trade these claims.

3.3 Top Trading Cycles

To understand how the TTC mechanism works, let us consider a different problem. Consider a freshman dorm that has only single rooms. There are six students assigned to this dorm and six rooms in the dorm. Now, assume that when students arrive on campus, the college uses a random number generator to assign a room to each of the six students.

Some schools would choose to stop the room assignment process here. However, the college may be able to do better by implementing the TTC mechanism. Consider Figure 3.1 below. The names next to the room numbers display the outcomes of the computer program that generated the initial room assignments; for example, the computer assigned room #5 to Sue and room #2 to Carol. The solid arrows indicate first choices (e.g., Russell likes room #3 the best, and Carol likes room #1 best).

In this diagram, a cycle is a sequence of endowments and desires that form a closed loop. For example, the computer endows Carol with room #2, and Carol desires room #1. The computer endows Min with room #1, and Min desires room #2. The presence of this cycle implies gains from trade. If we let Carol and Min trade room assignments, both are better off, and no other student is harmed.

Cycles need not imply bilateral trade. It would be easy to create another configuration of preferences and initial room assignments such that three students involved in a cycle would benefit from trade: for instance, the first student would give her assignment to a second student who would give her assignment to a third student who would give her assignment to the first student in the cycle. These exchanges would result in each of the three students receiving her most preferred room assignment while leaving other room assignments unchanged.

Finally, not all cycles involve trade. The other cycle in our diagram involves room #6 and José. The computer initially assigns room #6 to José, and room #6 is José's first choice. So, it is clearly optimal for José to keep his initial assignment.

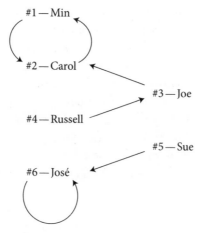

Figure 3.1 Top trading cycles.

Now that you know what a cycle is, consider the following algorithm for assigning rooms.

1. Let the computer make initial room assignments.
2. Ask each freshman to point to his or her favorite room. (See arrows in Figure 3.1)
3. Identify all of the cycles in the implied diagram and make final assignments to the rooms involved in these cycles. In our diagram, Carol and Min achieve final assignments by swapping initial assignments, and José claims his initial assignment as his final assignment.
4. Hand out room keys to students who have final assignments and remove their rooms from consideration.
5. If all students have keys, STOP.
6. If not, have each remaining student point to his or her favorite room among the rooms that remain. (If a student's previous favorite was removed in the last round, draw a new line to identify the student's favorite remaining option.)
7. Go back to step 3.

This algorithm is the TTC mechanism. You should take time now to convince yourself that, at each step in this algorithm, at least one cycle does exist, and that no two cycles intersect (i.e., no single room is involved in two cycles). Because these two claims are true, we know that the TTC mechanism does not leave any rooms unassigned and never assigns two students to the same room.

By construction, the final room assignments that result from the TTC mechanism are Pareto efficient. Consider a case involving N students and rooms numbered $n = 1, 2, \ldots, N$. At each step in the algorithm, freshmen who receive final room assignments receive the key to their *favorite* room among those that remain. Thus, if a given student receives room #n in a given round of the TTC algorithm, we know two things. First, this student prefers room #n to all of the rooms assigned in this round or later. Second, all of the students who received their keys in earlier rounds prefer their room to room #n. Taken together, these results imply that, after the TTC produces a final set of room assignments, no Pareto-improving room swaps are possible.[8]

TTC is also strategy-proof. Roth (1982) proves this result using two insights. First, at any stage of the mechanism, a given student knows that there are a collection of people who are directly or indirectly, through a cycle, pointing to her room, and none of these people can point at another room or leave the mechanism before she leaves.[9] Second, when this student does exit the mechanism, she leaves with the room to which she is pointing. Taken together, these observations imply that she can never harm herself by pointing truthfully. In any round, if she points truthfully, she may get her first choice, and if she does not, she still retains all of the other persons who are now pointing to her as options for trade in the future.

3.3.1 Lockers Instead of Rooms

To apply TTC to the school assignment problem, once again endow every locker in every school with a strict priority ranking over all of the students in a district. Further, require that all lockers in the same school adopt the same priorities. Again, assume that each student has a strict preference ranking over schools and also assume that each student ranks lockers within schools according to the numbers on the lockers.

As before, let κ_j equal the enrollment capacity for school j, where $j = 1, 2, \ldots, J$. Here, we assume that κ_j also denotes the total number of lockers in school j, and we again assume that there are more total lockers in the district than students.

TTC works as follows. Let n_j denote enrollment at school j. Set $n_j = 0$ for all $j = 1, 2, \ldots, J$. So, when the algorithm starts, all schools have zero enrollment, and no school has given a locker key to any student. Given these initial conditions, follow these steps:

1. If $n_j < \kappa_j$ and school j does not have a locker key in circulation, let school j give the key to locker #$(n_j + 1)$ to its favorite non-enrolled student. If $n_j \geq \kappa_j$, remove school j from the mechanism.
2. Have each student who holds at least one key point to her favorite school, *among the schools that remain in the mechanism*.
3. Based on a diagram that parallels Figure 3.1, identify all cycles. Execute the key exchanges implied by these cycles.
4. After these exchanges, enroll any student who now holds a key to a locker in her favorite school, *among the schools that remain in the mechanism*. Tell her to keep the key to her locker.
5. Have any enrolled students who hold extra keys to lockers in other schools return the keys to the appropriate schools.
6. If non-enrolled students remain in the mechanism, go back to step 1. If not, STOP.

Given the parallels to the room assignment problem above, we know that TTC produces a matching between schools and students that is Pareto efficient for students. Thus, in contrast to our DA example, school districts cannot implement the attendance zone allocation using a TTC mechanism. Even if each school gives priority to students within its attendance zone according to the inverse of the distances from the school to their homes and also refuses to issue keys to any students who live outside its attendance zone, there is no guarantee that any school will enroll only or even mostly students from its surrounding neighborhood. When school systems use TTC, school priorities determine the order in which schools endow different students with keys, but nothing in TTC prevents students from trading these keys in any manner they deem mutually beneficial.

Nonetheless, endowments do matter. In exchange economies, many feasible allocations are Pareto efficient. Yet, for each initial set of endowments, there is only one Pareto efficient allocation that agents can reach through voluntary exchange. Likewise, in a given school district, the TTC algorithm could produce many different Pareto efficient allocations of students to schools, but holding student preferences constant, the priorities that schools use to determine which efficient allocation TTC actually produces.

3.4 DA vs. TTC

Abdulkadiroğlu and Sönmez (2003) introduced the school assignment problem to the modern mechanism design literature. They argued that DA and TTC were both obvious alternatives to the flawed mechanisms that several urban school systems employed as part of their public school choice plans. Abdulkadiroğlu and Sönmez (2003) frame the choice between DA and TTC as a choice between equity and efficiency. DA produces outcomes that respect public school priorities and therefore avoid justifiable envy, but these outcomes may not be efficient from the perspective of students and families. TTC produces outcomes that are efficient because families are allowed to freely trade their initial school assignments. However, TTC does not respect school priorities and therefore may produce outcomes that do create justifiable envy.

It seems that whether policy makers prefer DA or TTC likely hinges on the weight that policy makers give to the school priorities that schools use to rank potential students. Suppose that a district conducted an extensive study that allowed them to estimate the expected value of the skill growth that would occur if any given student were to attend any particular school in the district. Based on the results of such a study, each school could prioritize students based on the expected values of the skills that different students would acquire if they enrolled in that school. Given such priorities, policy makers might view DA as more attractive than TTC because any ex post trades of assignments that violate school priorities would lower the total expected value of the skills created in the school system.

In practice, school priorities often place students in groups based on where they live and whether or not they have an older sibling who already attends the school. Schools then break ties within these groups using lottery numbers. You may wonder why policy makers want to respect coarse priorities based on criteria like residential location or the presence of an older sibling in a school, but these priorities may well reflect political realities that limit acceptable ex post trades of school assignments among families.

Consider the following scenario. School A is an excellent school that excels in language arts and ranks potential students in coarse groups based on whether these students live less than one, one to two, two to three, or more than three miles from school A. School B is an excellent school that excels in math and science education, and it ranks students based, in part, on residential location but primarily on whether or not an applicant has an older sibling who already attends the school.

Now, assume that Sue, who is an only child, has high priority at school A because she lives in the expensive neighborhood that surrounds the school, and she got a good random number draw. Jim lives far from school A in an area where houses are relatively cheap, but he has high priority at school B because his older sister attends the school.

In addition, assume that a student-proposing DA mechanism assigns Sue to A and Jim to B, but Sue's family and Jim's family wish to trade assignments. Jim has a strong interest in language arts and does not get along well with his sister. Further, Jim is quite happy to commute to school A using public transportation. Sue's parents want her to be an engineer and fear that she will end up being an unemployed writer if she attends school A.

This hypothetical trade would create a Pareto improvement for these two families. However, families who are not involved in this trade would possibly raise quite a fuss. Families who live in Sue's neighborhood but failed to get into school A because they got a bad random number draw would likely feel cheated, especially if they chose their neighborhood in order to gain higher priority for school A. Families who already have a child enrolled in school B may feel cheated if their younger child does not get into school B while Sue, who is an only child, enters school B from a different neighborhood.

Rules that govern priorities shape perceptions of fairness and equity. Table 3.1 lists some of the cities that have adopted DA systems in recent years. Although a few cities have used TTC systems for short periods of time, DA systems appear to be more popular reform tools. The coarse priorities that shape how schools rank potential students in DA systems may reflect binding political constraints.

3.4.1 A Third Way

If we stipulate that education authorities may have good reasons to adopt assignment mechanisms that respect coarse school priorities, how should we think about the strict priorities created by differences in lottery numbers among students in the same coarse priority groups? Erdil and Ergin (2008) propose a two-step algorithm that respects the coarse priorities of schools but does not respect priorities created by random numbers. The mechanism works as follows. First, implement DA using random numbers to breaks ties. Then, starting with the resulting DA allocation, allow students to trade their school assignments as long as the trades respect the coarse priorities of the system. Thus, Jim could trade his assignment in school B to Sue for her assignment in school A, as long as there is no other student in the system that prefers A to her current school and has higher

Table 3.1 Selected Adoptions of School Choice Mechanisms in US School Districts

City	School Type	Year of Adoption	School Choice Mechanism Adopted [a]
Boston School District	Elementary, middle, and high schools (public)	2005	DA
Denver Public Schools	Elementary, middle, and high schools (public and charter)	2012	DA
New Orleans' Recovery School District	Elementary, middle, and high schools (public and charter)	2012	DA[b]
New York City Department of Education	High schools (public)	2003	DA
Seattle Public Schools	Elementary, middle, and high schools (public)	2009	Boston [c]

a. Boston = Boston School District's mechanism prior to adopting deferred acceptance in 2005 (see Section 3.6 for more information); DA = deferred acceptance; TTC = top trading cycles.

b. New Orleans' Recovery School District adopted TTC in 2011 for one year before adopting DA in 2012. See Abdulkadiroğlu et al. (2017) for more information.

c. Seattle Public Schools had DA in place for nearly a decade before reverting to the Boston mechanism, which had been in place before 1999. See Pathak and Sönmez (2013) for more information.

For examples of school choice mechanisms beyond the US, see Pathak and Sönmez (2013), Table 1.

coarse priority than Jim for school A, and there is no student in the system who prefers school B to her current school and has higher coarse priority than Sue for school B.

This two-step approach is quite appealing. It allows policy makers to respect broad priorities while allowing families to make trades ex post that result in final allocations that Pareto dominate the allocations produced by DA with random tiebreaking. However, this two-step mechanism is not strategy-proof. Further, a key result in Abdulkadiroğlu et al. (2009) implies that any mechanism that follows this two-step approach—that is, allows families to conduct trades that Pareto improve initial allocations that result from DA with random tiebreaking—will not be strategy-proof.[10]

3.5 The Importance of Being Earnest

Some may argue that, if education authorities can eliminate the ex post inefficiencies that arise from using lottery numbers to create strict priorities within groups of students who have the same true priority, then the creation of incentives for strategic behavior is a small price to pay for these welfare improvements. However, it is not obvious that education authorities should willingly pay this price. Over the past several decades, a number of school systems have replaced school matching procedures that were not strategy-proof with DA mechanisms. These policy changes made sense, in part, because education authorities have good reasons to prefer strategy-proof assignment mechanisms.

3.5.1 Burning Money

If a school assignment mechanism is not strategy-proof, many parents may devote considerable time and money toward devising the optimal strategy for misrepresenting their preferences in school assignment mechanisms. Available data do not allow researchers to measure these costs perfectly, but anecdotal evidence suggests that, when school assignment mechanisms invite strategic play, some parents spend considerable time and effort trying to devise optimal strategies.[11]

It is possible that these investments in strategy formation are quite wasteful from a social perspective. These expenditures do not change the number of seats in each school, and there is no guarantee that the presence of these gaming behaviors improves the quality of the final matching between students and schools.

3.5.2 Enhancing Inequality

Further, mechanisms that invite strategic play likely exacerbate inequality. If the quality of a given student's school assignment is influenced by how well her parents learn to play the school assignment game relative to other parents, then the children of parents who are less motivated or have fewer resources may well see their school assignment improve if their district adopts a strategy-proof mechanism. If parents who invest heavily in learning how to game school assignment mechanisms are the parents who also invest heavily in creating other valuable opportunities for their children, the presence of assignment mechanisms that invite strategic behavior could amplify inequality of opportunities among children.

In 2005, Boston adopted a DA mechanism to replace an existing school assignment mechanism that was not strategy-proof. This previous mechanism, now known as the Boston mechanism, asks students to list schools from most preferred to least preferred. In the first round, each school considers applications from all students who list it first. Each school accepts as many of these students as it can, given its capacity. If a school faces excess demand in the first round, it rations seats using its priority ranking over students.[12] In the second round, each school with remaining capacity considers students who listed it as their second choice and accepts as many as it can. A school that faces excess demand in the second round rations seats using its priority ranking over students. In the third round, a school with remaining capacity considers students who listed it as their third choice, and so on.

The fact that some schools exit the mechanism in early rounds may create incentives for students to submit preference orderings that do not represent their true preferences. Imagine a student whose true first two choices are schools A and B. Further, suppose that the student only prefers A slightly to B, but views both A and B as vastly superior to all the remaining schools in the district. Also, assume that both schools A and B have long histories of being oversubscribed, and finally assume that the student in question has high priority at school B because he lives in the attendance zone for school B. We expect this student to submit a preference ordering that lists B as his first choice, even though B is not his favorite school.

This false-reporting strategy guarantees that the student receives a seat in one of the two schools that he deems best; that is, school B. In contrast, if he reported his true preferences, he could easily fail to get a seat in either A or B. Given his lower priority at A, he might not get in during round one, and if school B were to reach its capacity during round one, he would not be considered by school B during round two.

Abdulkadiroğlu et al. (2006) report that, prior to 2005, some but not all Boston parents appear to have engaged in this type of strategic misreporting of preferences. Further, Pathak and Sönmez (2008) present theoretical results that support the contention that students whose parents engaged in this strategic behavior often benefited at the expense of students whose parents did not. Thus, Pathak and Sönmez conjecture that many parents who expressed political opposition to the 2005 switch to a DA mechanism were acting in their own self-interest. Since DA is strategy-proof, parents who understood the best ways to game the original Boston mechanism had reason to worry that moving to a strategy-proof mechanism would eliminate the strategic advantages they enjoyed under the status quo.

3.5.3 Wasted Information

School assignment mechanisms that are not strategy-proof also waste information. Assume that parents learn things about schools that district administrators do not know; for example, how nurturing different school environments are, how well teachers prevent bullying, or how creative teachers are in planning learning activities and field trips. Then, the preferences submitted by parents in a strategy-proof school assignment mechanism provide education authorities with valuable information. For example, if the preference orderings submitted to a strategy-proof mechanism reveal that even families who live quite close to school A actually do not want their children to attend school A, the education authority should attempt to learn why.

On the other hand, education authorities may learn little from the preference orderings that parents submit to mechanisms that are not strategy-proof. Suppose that an education authority uses the Boston mechanism, and further assume that school A is known by parents to be a pretty good school. Yet also assume that parents know that school A's capacity is much larger than the total school-age population in all of its surrounding neighborhoods. In this situation, we could see no families rank school A as their first choice simply because they do not want to "waste" their first choice on a school that will certainly be available in round 2, since it will not reach its capacity in the first round. However, in this scenario, the education authority would have no way to know the reason that no parents list school A as their first choice.

3.5.4 Transparency

We have already noted that more school systems have adopted DA mechanisms than TTC mechanisms, even though both mechanisms are strategy-proof. Pathak (2016) points out that Boston school officials adopted DA, in part, because they believed that DA is easier to explain to parents than TTC. Further, because DA is easier for parents to understand, parents in a DA system are more likely to believe that truthful reporting is really their best strategy. These advantages are important, and they may help us understand the greater popularity of DA.[13]

If a school assignment mechanism is both strategy-proof and easy to understand, parents are more likely to believe that no parents are engaging in strategic behavior. Thus, all parents are more likely to believe that no one is gaming the system at their expense.

Fairness is a fuzzy but important concern when education authorities choose school assignment mechanisms. Any system will face political opposition if significant numbers of parents worry that the mechanism is just a game and that some other group of parents better understands how to play the game.

3.6 Recent Empirical Work

Following the publication of Abdulkadiroğlu and Sönmez (2003), Boston and New York were among the first US cities to adopt centralized, strategy-proof school assignment mechanisms, and since then, many other cities have moved in similar directions.[14] The Institute for Innovation in Public School Choice (IIPSC) reports that it has worked or is working with 16 other US cities to implement or improve centralized school assignment mechanisms.[15] IIPSC stresses the importance of implementing mechanisms that are both strategy-proof and transparent, and argues that a number of cities have benefited from adopting such assignment systems.

To this point, we have explored many reasons why education authorities should welcome the opportunity to adopt transparent, strategy-proof mechanisms. Nonetheless, a recent and growing literature argues that variants of the Boston mechanism may be desirable because the strategic behavior that these mechanisms induce reveals something about the intensity of preferences.[16]

Consider two students, Jack and Jill, who live in a district that uses the Boston mechanism to assign students to one of three schools, schools A, B, and C. Jack and Jill have the same preference ordering over schools. School A is their favorite, school B is their second favorite, and school C is their least favorite. However, they differ in the intensity of their preferences. While they both agree that school B is much better than school C, they do not agree concerning how much better school A is compared to B. Even though both students come from families with similar incomes, Jack's family would pay a great deal to have Jack attend school A rather than school B, while Jill's family has only a slight preference for school A over school B.

Both Jack and Jill have high priority for school B and are almost certain to get a seat in school B if they rank it first. However, their district has used the Boston mechanism for a long time, and school B always reaches its capacity in round one. Therefore, if they do not rank B first, they have no chance to enroll in B. Neither Jack nor Jill have high priority in school A, but school A has a large capacity. So, if they rank school A first, they have a roughly 70 percent chance of getting into school A.

Given this scenario, it is reasonable to expect that Jill would rank B first to make sure that she gets one of her two first choices, but Jack might rank A first in an effort to get the school he really wants. In contrast, if their school district were to operate a DA mechanism, both students would rank A first, B second, and C last.

Defenders of the Boston mechanism argue that the strategic play in the Boston mechanism is valuable because it allows Jack to signal how much he likes school A, and this may allow the mechanism to place more students in schools that they have a strong desire to attend. Note that, under DA, students like Jack may have much more competition for slots in school A, and many of these competitors may have only a slight preference for school A over their next best choice.

Several recent working papers attempt to recover the willingness to pay of different students for placement in different schools and then use these estimated preference parameters to calculate the utility gains that different students would expect if their school districts moved from a Boston-style mechanism to DA or from DA to some version of the Boston mechanism. Calsamiglia et al. (2014) study school assignment in Barcelona. Hwang (2016) investigates school assignment in Seoul, while He (2016) explores the school assignment process in Beijing. Agarwal and Somaini (2014) study school assignment in Cambridge, MA, and Kapor et al. (2017) examine school assignment in New Haven, CT.

The results in these papers are mixed, but several authors conclude that, on average, students fare better under some variant of the Boston mechanism than DA. Calsamiglia et al. (2014) and Hwang (2016) conclude that average student welfare is greater under versions of the Boston mechanism than it would be under DA. Agarwal and Somaini (2014) find a similar qualitative result, but the implied average loss associated with using DA rather than the Boston mechanism is small.

He (2016) reports several results that imply higher welfare under Boston than DA, but he finds that naive parents are more likely to benefit from the switch to DA, and the results from his policy simulations vary notably as he varies the assumed fraction of naive parents in the population.

Kapor et al. (2017) conducted a survey to determine how well parents in New Haven understand the mechanism that New Haven uses, which shares some features of the Boston mechanism and is not strategy-proof. They found that less than 20 percent of families understand exactly how the mechanism works and that parents' beliefs about their chances of getting into different schools are often quite different from their true chances. Kapor et al. determine that, if parents understood the New Haven mechanism and possessed correct beliefs about their chances of getting into different schools, then a switch from the existing New Haven mechanism to DA would lead to a modest reduction in average welfare. However, results from simulations that incorporate the actual information and beliefs of parents imply that switching to DA would significantly improve welfare in New Haven.

The empirical results in this growing literature are mixed, and the existing empirical methods require strong assumptions.[17] It is difficult to predict what the future consensus may be, if one emerges, but however this empirical literature evolves, DA will remain strategy-proof and transparent, and these properties will remain important considerations for policy makers.

3.7 Rearranging the Deck Chairs on the Titanic

We have noted that strategy-proof mechanisms are useful because they provide a credible way to gather information concerning how different types of families actually view different schools. Yet existing public school choice programs rarely use the information contained in the rankings that parents submit. Few districts punish or close schools because large numbers of parents rank them poorly, and few districts reward schools because most parents rank them highly. Absent such feedback mechanisms, improvements in the design of school assignment mechanisms can only accomplish so much.

Imagine a small city where there are ten excellent schools that differ only in their approach to nonacademic programs. Assume that all schools provide excellent basic education during the first five periods of the day, but each school devotes the last period of each day to different extracurricular activities. Some schools focus on music, others focus on art, others focus on physical fitness, and others focus on academic competitions like debate. Finally, assume that all of these schools are located close together in the center of the city, so there is no reason for schools to establish priorities based on location or the presence of older siblings. In such a city, a TTC assignment mechanism that employed priorities determined by a single lottery could produce a matching of students and schools that is not only Pareto efficient for students but also close to the allocation that maximizes the total surplus generated by the school system as a whole. If all schools were providing excellent basic education, then creating a mechanism that allows children to match well with the other activities offered by the school would come close to ensuring that the school system as a whole produces the greatest possible value for families.

On the other hand, imagine a larger city where there are ten schools that provide great basic education and ninety schools that provide poor basic education. If all schools are the same size, and the system has little excess capacity as a whole, then close to 90 percent of students must attend a bad school, and no changes in school assignment mechanisms can change this outcome. Different assignment mechanisms may change the identities of the students who end up in these bad schools, but these assignment mechanisms cannot change the fact that there are not enough good schools to go around.

In the next two chapters, we explore policies that change the menu of school options that parents face. These policies seek to improve efficiency by forcing schools that receive public funds to compete for funding by competing for students.

EXERCISES

▶ Throughout this question, assume that we have four students and four schools. Each school has a capacity of one student. All students and schools prefer being matched to being unmatched.

Students' preferences for schools are:

- Student 1 has strict preferences for schools in this order: $1 > 2 > 3 > 4$.
- Student 2 has strict preferences for schools in this order: $2 > 1 > 3 > 4$.
- Student 3 has strict preferences for schools in this order: $3 > 1 > 2 > 4$.
- Student 4 has strict preferences for schools in this order: $1 > 4 > 3 > 2$.

Schools' preferences for students are:

- School 1 has strict preferences for students in this order:
  $3 > 2 > 1 > 4$.
- School 2 has strict preferences for students in this order:
  $3 > 2 > 1 > 4$.
- School 3 has strict preferences for students in this order:
  $2 > 4 > 1 > 3$.
- School 4 has strict preferences for students in this order:
  $1 > 3 > 2 > 4$.

(a) How many potential matchings of students to schools are there in this example? Take into account the fact that each student and school could, hypothetically, be unmatched.

(b) Implement the following four mechanisms by hand and state the final allocations:
  - Student-proposing deferred acceptance
  - School-proposing deferred acceptance
  - The Boston mechanism
  - Top Trading Cycles

(c) If we consider only the preferences of the students, does one mechanism dominate the other mechanisms?

▶ How many potential matchings are there in a world with M students and W schools? Each school has a capacity of one. Students and schools have strict preferences over each other and over the possibility of remaining unmatched.

FOUR

Charter Schools

The next two chapters explore systems that provide public funds to schools that are not operated by government employees. All of these systems fall under the broad heading of school choice programs. We follow the convention of dividing this topic into a discussion of charter school systems and voucher systems, but this distinction is not always illuminating. Both charter and voucher systems grant parents more control over the public funds that pay for the education of their child, and both types of systems place some restrictions on the schooling options available to parents and on how schools that receive public money may operate. In this chapter, we focus mainly on studies of charter schools in the US. Thus, we define charter schools in terms that reflect common policies among the forty-three states that have passed charter school laws.

Charter schools are publicly funded schools that government education officials or their appointees authorize but do not operate. Organizations that wish to operate charter schools submit charter applications to authorizing agencies.[1] These applications explain the missions of the proposed schools and the organizational practices that will support these missions. When an authorizing agency approves one of these applications, it establishes a charter that dictates how education authorities fund and monitor the school. Further, these charters typically spell out performance targets for new schools as well as provisions for closing schools that do not meet these targets.

Most charter schools operate as independent nonprofit organizations. However, some belong to networks of nonprofit charter schools. These networks are called Charter Management Organizations (CMOs). For-profit charter networks, known as Educational Management Organizations (EMOs), also exist. Although charter systems have much in common with voucher systems, many charter systems share three features that are typically not present in most voucher systems.

First, charter systems routinely impose significant barriers to entry. In many systems, the total number of available charters is fixed ex ante. An organization that is applying for a charter may have a long history of operating successful schools but still fail to obtain a charter if the statutory limit on the number of charters binds. Many states do not place caps on the total number of charter schools in operation, but a number of large states do—for example, California, Illinois, New York, and Texas. In Illinois, state law caps the total number of charters at 120, and in recent negotiations with the Chicago Teachers Union, the Chicago Public Schools agreed to stop granting new charters.[2]

Second, charter schools are not allowed to charge tuition. Some voucher systems allow a family to use a voucher to purchase education for their child at a private school even if its tuition exceeds the face value of the voucher. However, charter schools receive funding from governments based on fixed formulas that often specify per-student spending in charter schools as a function of per-student spending in public schools within the same district. Epple et al. (2016) explain that the ratio of charter school spending per student to local public school spending per student varies greatly among the forty-three states that allow charters, but in the vast majority of states, charter schools receive significantly less funding per pupil than traditional public schools.

Finally, charter schools are not allowed to implement selective admission policies. In some voucher systems, schools that receive vouchers are allowed to determine whether or not they wish to accept individual voucher applicants, but charter schools never have this freedom. Charter schools must announce ex ante how many students they are willing to accept for a given school year, and if the number of applicants to a given school exceeds its announced capacity, the charter school in question must conduct a lottery to assign admission status among its applicants.

This operational feature of charter systems not only shapes how these systems serve students but also generates experimental data that researchers employ to evaluate charter schools. Admission lotteries at oversubscribed charter schools create social experiments. Among a population of students who want to leave their current school and enter a given charter school, some randomly receive this opportunity and others do not. By following lottery winners and losers over time, researchers have learned a great deal about the effects of gaining access to charter schools.

Most charter systems impact the traditional public schools that operate in the same area because at least a portion of the funds that charter schools receive comes from reductions in funding for local public schools that lose students to charter schools. The details of the rules that govern how much money public schools lose when they lose students differs from state to state. Still, if we assume that enrollment and funding reductions make staffing reductions more likely, the expansion of charter schools may create performance pressures for educators in traditional public schools. These pressures should be weak in systems where traditional public schools are already oversubscribed and barriers to charter entry are high, but charter systems do create direct competition among schools for students.

In the US, charter schools often compete for students by adopting organizational and educational practices that are not allowed in traditional public schools. Charter schools usually have significant freedom to deviate from the curriculum employed in the neighboring public schools, and charter schools do not have to follow the personnel policies employed in local public schools. Charter school teachers are not public employees, and most charter schools do not employ unionized teachers. Thus, the work rules that characterize civil service systems or union contracts for public employees are often absent in charter schools.

In sum, charter schools blend bureaucratic control and market competition. Public school systems or authorizing agencies appointed by these systems grant and renew the charters that allow charter schools to operate,[3] but charter schools are also accountable to parents since enrollment levels determine their budgets. Charter schools that cannot attract steady demand cannot provide steady incomes and stable employment for their teachers.

Educators in charter schools know that they must please both their authorizing agencies and parents in order to keep their jobs and maintain their incomes. Since preferences for specific school attributes differ considerably among parents, it is not surprising that charter schools are quite heterogeneous. Charter schools often adopt and advertise specific educational philosophies and practices in order to attract parents who value them.

Below, we review evidence on the effects of charter school attendance on students. With regard to any specific student outcome, there is no such thing as "an effect" of attending a charter school. The benefits that a given student derives from gaining access to a charter school vary greatly with the practices of the charter school in question and the quality of the student's fallback option in the public sector.

We also explore how the introduction of charter schools affects the performance of local public schools. The results in this literature are mixed, and it is not yet clear how to interpret them.

4.1 Lottery Results

The empirical literature on the performance of charter schools relative to traditional public schools is voluminous. Epple et al. (2016) provide a recent survey of this literature. So, we will not review all of it here, but instead focus on only a few segments of it.

Table 4.1 reviews results from a set of studies that all employ similar research designs. In each study, the authors examine outcomes from samples of applicants to charter schools, and all of these charter schools have more applicants than capacity. By law, such schools must use lotteries to randomly assign their available seats among the students in their applicant pools. Because these assignments are random, researchers can easily estimate how receiving an offer to attend a charter school affects expected future outcomes for a student in a given lottery.

Yet these lottery studies tell us nothing about the expected effects of taking a randomly selected group of public school students and forcing them to attend a charter school. All students in these lottery studies belong to families that took steps to place them in the lottery. Further, these charter schools face excess demand for seats in their classrooms. There is no reason, a priori, to expect similar results among students from families who were not willing to take the time to apply or who were simply not interested in these charter schools, or among students who attend charter schools with significant excess capacity.[4]

4.1.1 Methods

These lottery studies employ variations on a common empirical method. Before reviewing the results, let us review the principles behind this method. Assume that you have the following data on $i = 1, 2, 3, \ldots, N$ students who entered an admissions lottery for some charter school in a given district.

- Z_i an indicator variable equal to one if student i won admission through the lottery and zero else.
- D_i an indicator variable equal to one if student i attended a charter school that operates an admissions lottery and zero else.

Table 4.1 The Impact of Charter School Attendance on Achievement Estimated by Lottery Studies

Study	Sample	Grades	Results
Hoxby et al. (2009)	New York City	3–8	0.09σ math[a] 0.06σ ELA[a]
		9–12	0.19σ math[a] 0.18σ ELA[a]
Gleason et al. (2010)	National sample of charter middle schools	5–8	−0.08σ math[b] −0.08σ ELA[b]
	Subsample of free or reduced-price lunch	5–8	0.17σ math[a b] 0.05σ ELA[b]
Dobbie and Fryer Jr. (2011)	Harlem Children's Zone's Promise Academy Schools (New York City)	5–8	0.23σ math[a] 0.05σ ELA
Abdulkadiroğlu et al. (2011b)	Boston	5–8	0.36σ math[a] 0.20σ ELA[a]
		9–12	0.36σ math[a] 0.27σ ELA[a]
Angrist et al. (2012)	KIPP Academy Lynn (Massachusetts)	5–8	0.36σ math[a] 0.12σ ELA[a]
Angrist et al. (2013)	Urban schools in Massachusetts	5–8	0.32σ math[a] 0.15σ ELA[a]
		9–12	0.34σ math[a] 0.27σ ELA[a]
	Nonurban schools in Massachusetts	5–8	−0.12σ math[a] −0.14σ ELA[a]
		9–12	−0.02σ math −0.05σ ELA
Dobbie and Fryer Jr. (2013)	NYC charter schools	3–5	0.11σ math[a] 0.06σ ELA[a]
		5–8	0.13σ math[a] 0.05σ ELA
Curto and Fryer Jr. (2014)	SEED boarding schools (Washington, DC)	6–12	0.23σ math[a] 0.21σ reading[a]
Hassrick et al. (2017)	University of Chicago Charter Schools	3	0.40σ M&R[a b]
		4	0.58σ M&R[a b]
		5	0.51σ M&R[a b]
		6–8	0.96σ M&R[a b]

a. The result is statistically significant at the .05 level. In most cases, the result is also significant at the .01 level.

b. Instead of the per-year impact of being enrolled in a charter school, this represents the cumulative impact of being enrolled in a charter school. M&R = composite score for math and reading exams.

- Y_i some outcome for student i that is measured after the lottery (e.g., end-of-year test scores, high school completion, college enrollment, etc.).

Next, consider two models that describe the processes that generate our data:

$$Y_i = c_Y + \gamma_Y Z_i + e_i$$
$$D_i = c_D + \gamma_D Z_i + u_i$$

Both c_Y and c_D are constant terms. The two error terms, e_i and u_i, capture unobserved factors that influence outcomes and charter school attendance conditional on Z_i, the lottery outcome for student i. If officials conduct the lottery properly, random assignment implies that $E(e_i|Z_i) = 0$ and $E(u_i|Z_i) = 0$ for all i. Thus, taking expectations, we have the following results:

$$\gamma_Y = E(Y_i|Z_i = 1) - E(Y_i|Z_i = 0)$$
$$\gamma_D = E(D_i|Z_i = 1) - E(D_i|Z_i = 0)$$

The parameter γ_Y captures the intent to treat. It gives the expected outcome change associated with offering a student a lottery assignment in a charter school. The parameter γ_D is the change in the probability of attending a charter school associated with winning the lottery. The ratio of these two parameters (γ_Y/γ_D) gives the treatment on the treated (TOT), that is, the expected gain for lottery winners who attend charter schools.

To see why this ratio equals the TOT, consider the following special case. Assume that lottery losers cannot gain entrance to charter schools, i.e., $E(D_i|Z_i = 0) = 0$; then $\gamma_D = E(D_i|Z_i = 1)$ is the probability that student i attends a charter school given that student i is a lottery winner. Further, suppose $\gamma_Y = 1$, which implies that a particular outcome, Y, is greater by 1 in expected value among those who win admission lotteries compared to those who lose. Finally, suppose that $\gamma_D = .5$, so that, on average, one-half of lottery winners actually attend the charter school that offered them admission. If only half of the lottery winners received the treatment that produced the $\gamma_Y = 1$ outcome, the TOT among lottery winners must equal 2, or (1/.5).

When we discuss TOT, we are implicitly assuming that the expected values of the various effects of attending an oversubscribed charter school are the same for all students *who participate in the admissions lotteries*.[5] However, it is possible that some lottery participants can expect greater benefits from charter schooling than others. In this case, two-stage least squares (2SLS) estimates of the effects of charter school attendance cannot be interpreted as mean effects of charter schooling among the population of lottery participants, meaning the TOT impacts of charter schooling for lottery students. Instead, each 2SLS estimate in Table 4.1 must be interpreted as an estimate of the local average treatment effect (LATE) of charter school attendance on a given outcome. LATE is the average treatment effect among a group of students known as compliers. The compliers are the set of students in a charter school lottery who would choose to attend the charter if and only if they were to win the lottery, and there is no reason to believe that the average effect of charter schooling among this set of compliers should be the same as the average effect among all lottery applicants.[6]

Nonetheless, to facilitate exposition, we assume that the mean effect among compliers does equal the mean among all lottery participants, i.e., TOT = LATE, and we discuss the results in Table 4.1 as estimates of TOT effects. Appendix 4.5 explores settings where TOT and LATE may not be equal.

4.1.2 Achievement Results

The results in Table 4.1 describe effects of charter schooling on measured achievement. These studies typically examine both math scores and English language arts (ELA) scores. We discuss the effects of charter schooling on attainment and future life outcomes later.

The table contains results from only one nationwide study. In a study of twenty-eight charter lotteries that involved schools from many different states, Gleason et al. (2010) report that, in the population of lottery applicants, charter school attendance has no statistically significant effect on achievement in either math or language arts. Further, these insignificant estimated effects of charter schooling are both negative.

However, Gleason et al. (2010) do report statistically significant achievement gains in math among economically disadvantaged students who attend charters. This result appears to be driven by outcomes among disadvantaged students who attend urban charters, which makes sense given the results that Angrist et al. (2013) report. They find that, among lottery participants in Massachusetts, students who win lotteries and attend urban charters enjoy substantial achievement gains relative to their counterparts in public schools. Yet lottery winners who attend nonurban charters suffer achievement losses relative to lottery losers who remain in public schools.

Further, Angrist et al. (2013) show that this large urban/nonurban differential in the treatment effects associated with attending charter schools does not imply that students in urban charters are at the top of the achievement distribution in the state. Urban charters take students who are well below average achievement levels in the state and bring them up to the middle of the state achievement distribution. Nonurban students enter charter schools in MA with baseline achievement levels well above state averages and then see their achievement levels fall relative to their peers who remain in public schools.

Angrist et al. (2013) report that black and Hispanic students account for over 65 percent of urban charter school students but less than half of urban public school students, while in nonurban areas, more than 90 percent of students in both sectors are white. Further, within their urban sample, black and Hispanic students enjoy significantly larger achievement gains than white students.

We see a similar pattern in New York City. The results in Hoxby et al. (2009) and Dobbie and Fryer Jr. (2013) describe average treatment effects for all charter schools in New York City, and in math, these gains are much smaller than the gains that Dobbie and Fryer Jr. (2011) report in their study of charter lottery applicants in Harlem. The students who entered Promise Academy in the Harlem Children's Zone and enjoyed large achievement gains in math also had lower baseline achievement levels than the average student in New York's public schools. Charter schools appear to offer greater learning benefits to minority students who are not faring well in the traditional public schools that serve them.

Hassrick et al. (2017) study applicants to two charter schools operated by the University of Chicago. Almost all of these students are black, and many are economically disadvantaged. It is difficult to compare their results to those from other studies since most studies report gains per year of charter attendance while Hassrick et al. report gains from ever attending a charter school. Further, most studies report separate results for math and ELA achievement, while the Hassrick et al. (2017) results describe effects on a composite measure of math and reading. Nonetheless, the middle school results from this study are striking. These results suggest that, if one could replicate the success of these schools in other black communities around the country, it might be possible to completely eliminate the black-white test score gap in one generation.[7]

Finally, charter schools that adhere to the No Excuses model produce particularly impressive gains for students. Angrist et al. (2013) report that the large gains they observe for students in urban charters are primarily driven by positive outcomes for children who attend No Excuses schools. Further, most of the urban schools that Abdulkadiroğlu et al. (2011b) study, the school examined by Angrist et al. (2012), and Promise Academy, which Dobbie and Fryer Jr. (2011) study, also follow the No Excuses model. Fryer Jr. (2014) describes the No Excuses model in terms of five tenets, and the actions schools take to pursue each one:

Increase time devoted to learning   Implement longer school days, remove breaks from the school day, and hold classes and tutoring sessions on Saturday.

Human capital   Conduct extensive evaluations of potential principals and teachers. Hire only those with clear commitment to the school's mission and organizational practices. Evaluate teachers often and measure the achievement growth of each teacher's students. Offer high-quality professional development but retain only those who become and remain excellent educators. Do not grant tenure.

High-dosage tutoring   Provide individualized tutoring during and after school for students who are below grade level.

Data-Driven instruction   Assess often and adapt instruction to target areas where students most need to improve.

Culture of high expectations   Clearly define goals and expectations for all students and faculty. Require school representatives and parents to sign contracts pledging to set high expectations for students and to honor commitments to support student learning.

Table 4.1 shows that the most dramatic success stories in the charter school sector involve schools that employ some form of the No Excuses model in urban schools that serve communities with significant minority populations. The University of Chicago does not market its charter schools as adherents to the No Excuses model. However, according to Hassrick et al. (2017), these schools do follow the five principles that Fryer Jr. (2014) uses to define No Excuses.

Minority students who attend No Excuses charters in large cities often live in socially and economically disadvantaged communities, and these students often do not receive the academic investments and support that more advantaged children receive outside school. The education production function presented in Chapter 1 (see equation (1.1)) suggests that students from disadvantaged homes and communities must receive more educational investments in school in order to match the achievement levels of their more advantaged peers. No Excuses charters provide these additional investments by identifying faculty who are willing and able to provide more and better teaching than educators in the public sector without demanding higher pay.

4.1.3 Scaling Up the No Excuses Model

It is tempting to conclude that urban school systems should simply implement No Excuses in all or most of the traditional public schools that serve disadvantaged communities. However, the union contracts that govern the employment of public school teachers in most large cities would not permit public schools to fully implement the No Excuses model. Teachers' unions would not accept contracts that require their members to work after school and on weekends until all of their children reach certain learning targets. Further, the tenure systems and job security protections in most union contracts would make it difficult, if not impossible, for principals to make hiring and retention decisions that remain faithful to the No Excuses paradigm. Unions would never grant public school principals the control over hiring and retention decisions that principals now enjoy in No Excuses charter schools.[8]

There are good reasons for teachers' unions to oppose attempts to implement the No Excuses model in traditional public schools. As we note in Chapter 1, public school principals are also civil servants, and teachers in traditional public schools may have reason to fear that their principals would use enhanced discretion over hiring, firing, and work loads to grant favors or administer punishments to teachers based on personal or political considerations.

In contrast, many No Excuses charter schools belong to networks that seek to build a brand name in the education market. If the schools in these networks do not attract students and do not produce impressive learning results, the education leaders who run these networks can expect to lose prestige, income, and possibly their jobs. Thus, teachers in these networks have reasons to believe that principals in these networks are going to use their discretion to promote the educational missions and philosophies of their organizations.[9]

Fryer Jr. (2014) describes the results of attempts to implement the No Excuses model in traditional public schools in three different cities: Houston, Denver, and Chicago. He reports that the No Excuses approach produced learning gains in all three cities. These learning gains were concentrated in math. The estimated treatment effects in reading are smaller, and in some cases not statistically significant. He reports the largest and most impressive math gains in Houston. In Houston, Fryer had the political support required to fully implement the No Excuses model. Fryer had less control over the implementation in Denver, but the implementation was faithful to the No Excuses model on most dimensions, and the Denver intervention also produced noteworthy learning gains in math. In Chicago, the implementation was not as faithful. Treatment schools in Chicago did not lengthen the school day or add high-dose tutoring programs. Measured math gains in the Chicago treatment schools were statistically significant but were also far less than half the size of the reported gains in Houston.

Abdulkadiroğlu et al. (2011b) also present results that highlight the value of faithfully implementing the No Excuses approach. They draw comparisons between students who win lotteries for admission to charter schools in Boston and students who win assignments to attend Pilot schools within the Boston Public Schools.[10] Pilot schools function as charter schools that are operated by the Boston Public School system. These schools provide extra instructional hours for students, although not as much as typical No Excuses charter schools, and these schools enjoy additional freedom to set school policies concerning curriculum, student promotion, and graduation. However, Pilot school teachers belong to the Boston Teachers Union, and the district-wide contract between BTU and the district governs most aspects of their employment, pay, benefits, and working hours.

Abdulkadiroğlu et al. (2011b) report that students who list a given Pilot school as their first choice and win an assignment to the school experience no achievement gains relative to similar students who choose the same Pilot school as their first choice and lose. Yet, as Table 4.1 reports, Abdulkadiroğlu et al. (2011b) find that students who win charter school lotteries in their sample benefit greatly from attending these charters. Most of the charter schools in this sample adhere to key elements of the No Excuses model.

Thus, the authors interpret their results as suggestive evidence that the success of No Excuses charters may depend on the ability of charter schools to adopt personnel practices and job requirements that union contracts do not typically allow in public schools.

The results in Abdulkadiroğlu et al. (2011b), Angrist et al. (2013), and Fryer Jr. (2014) paint a consistent picture. No Excuses charters consistently take children who likely do not receive the same learning investments at home that more advantaged children receive and, over time, bring them close to grade level, at least in math. However, these schools do not close achievement gaps between advantaged and disadvantaged students simply by employing some secret pedagogical sauce. They close these gaps by investing additional time on focused instruction in core subjects. In essence, these schools take in students who may receive less-than-average levels of educational investments at home and give them above average levels of investment at school.

Existing No Excuses charters provide these additional investments while spending less per student than neighboring public schools, but it is not obvious that urban school districts could provide No Excuses charter schools for all disadvantaged students without increasing per-pupil expenditure. The educators who work in No Excuses charters must possess the talent and the energy required to follow the model, and existing research tells us little about the market salaries that would be needed to attract enough of these educators to serve all of the students who would benefit from the No Excuses model.

In recent work, Abdulkadiroğlu et al. (2016) do demonstrate that, in the New Orleans Recovery School District (RSD), a program that converted many low-performing public schools to No Excuses charter schools appears to have produced impressive gains for students who attended these schools before they were converted to charters.[11] Seats in these schools were not allocated by lottery, so the empirical methods that Abdulkadiroğlu et al. employ require strong assumptions. Nonetheless, these results suggest that the No Excuses model may be cheaper to implement at scale than some have feared.

4.1.4 Reading vs. Math

Overall, the urban charters that follow the No Excuses approach have produced noteworthy gains in measured achievement. However, in almost all cases, these schools produced greater learning gains in math than in reading or ELA. Further, Fryer's introduction of No Excuses in the Houston public schools produced much better results in math than in reading.

The Curto and Fryer Jr. (2014) study of the SEED boarding school in Washington, DC, appears to be an exception to this rule. However, the sample size for this study is small relative to most studies in the literature, and the authors note that in both math and reading, the measured achievement gains associated with SEED attendance reflect a combination of large measured gains among girls and no evidence of learning gains among boys.

Hassrick et al. (2017) is the most noteworthy exception to the rule that successful urban charters produce greater learning gains in math than reading. In fact, Hassrick et al. state that they report composite gains because their estimates of treatment effects from separate models of reading and math are so similar.[12] Because the Hassrick et al. (2017) results are not estimates of gains per year of attendance, it is difficult to compare their results to those reported in the rest of the literature. Nonetheless, the UCCS effects on reading achievement are impressive.

Most of the students in UCCS entered in kindergarten, and these schools place a strong emphasis on a particular approach to early reading instruction. In contrast, most of the lottery winners in the other studies reviewed in Table 4.1 entered charter schools in later grades, after falling behind national norms for their grade level. The UCCS success may reflect unique aspects of their reading instruction or the fact that the entry point for most students in these schools is kindergarten. More research is needed to pin down why the reported achievement effects in Hassrick et al. (2017) are so much larger in reading than those found in the rest of the literature.

4.1.5 Longer-Term Effects

In Chapter 2, we reviewed evidence that modern assessments are coachable. Because the Data-Driven Instruction component of the No Excuses model requires students to take assessments often and to receive tutoring in areas where they do not perform well, some may worry that the No Excuses model does not improve true subject mastery but simply improves performance on the exams that states use to create accountability measures that inform charter renewal decisions.

However, more recent follow-up work on these lottery samples demonstrates that the No Excuses model does produce long-term learning gains that generalize to other measures of attainment and achievement. Dobbie and Fryer Jr. (2015) report follow-up results for the Harlem students they examined in Dobbie and Fryer Jr. (2011), and they report that lottery winners who attended Promise Academy for middle school scored higher on the New York State's Regents exam in high school, were more likely to graduate on time from high school, more likely to enroll in college right after high school, and much more likely to enroll in a four-year college.[13] Dobbie and Fryer Jr. (2015) also administered low-stakes math and reading assessments to these students in an effort to gauge the extent to which the achievement gains reported in Dobbie and Fryer Jr. (2011) reflected coaching or real subject mastery. Promise Academy students scored .28 standard deviations higher in math and .12 standard deviations higher in reading, although the reading gain was not statistically significant. Finally, only 7 percent of girls who win lottery admission to Promise Academy became pregnant during their teen years, and the comparable rate among lottery losers is 17 percent. Among boys, almost no lottery winners were incarcerated even though almost one in twenty lottery losers were.

Angrist et al. (2016) find similar results in Boston. They find that lottery students who attend No Excuses charter high schools in Boston typically have higher SAT scores, are more likely to take Advanced Placement (AP) exams, score higher on AP exams, and are substantially more likely to attend four-year colleges.

In both Dobbie and Fryer Jr. (2015) and Angrist et al. (2016), charter attendance does not have noteworthy effects on the likelihood that students actually finish high school and attend some type of college. This may indicate that families who are willing to put forth the effort to apply to charter school lotteries are going to put significant pressure on their children to stay in school regardless of lottery outcomes. However, these lottery outcomes do matter. No Excuses charters have noteworthy impacts on the likelihood that students finish high school with strong academic records and enter four-year schools. Further, the results from Harlem show that simply attending a No Excuses middle school changes life trajectories for students in ways that make teen pregnancy and prison much less likely.

4.2 Studies without Lotteries

We do not have time to carefully review the large nonexperimental literature on charters. However, much of this literature presents estimates of the effects of charter schooling on achievement that broadly mirror the results in Gleason et al. (2010). Measured performance relative to local public school alternatives varies greatly among charter schools, and in samples drawn from a number of states, the average impacts of charter schools on achievement is often small and negative. However, there is also evidence that charter schools perform better after they have been open a few years, and comparisons between mature charters and traditional public schools are more likely to imply that charter schooling generates small, positive achievement effects.[14]

A recent report by the Center for Research on Education Outcomes, Cremata et al. (2013), argues that policy makers should devote more attention to policies that govern how charter schools are authorized and reauthorized. Both the experimental and nonexperimental literature conclude that many charters provide excellent options for students who are not pleased with their local public schools. The policy challenge is to design authorization and accountability systems that expand these options while eliminating charter schools that serve their students poorly.

This is a difficult design problem because Gleason et al. (2010) report that, on average, both urban and suburban charters generate significant improvements in student and parent satisfaction. Some families may make a conscious decision to send their children to charter schools knowing that their math and reading scores will not improve but also knowing that these schools offer opportunities that are not present in their local public schools. These opportunities may involve art, music, science experiments, community service projects, or many other participatory learning activities. Or these opportunities may simply involve the chance to attend a safer school that effectively discourages bullying and harassment.[15]

Data do not exist that would allow researchers to assess the value that charter schools provide by offering services that improve parent and student satisfaction without improving basic math and reading skills. Thus, we cannot determine whether or not particular groups of parents who send their children to a given collection of charters are making decisions that serve their children well.

Likewise, we cannot know for sure whether or not parents who decline opportunities to apply for openings in charter schools are serving their children well. In recent work on the demand for charters in Boston, Walters (2014) concludes that the students who are likely to receive the greatest achievement gains from attending No Excuses charter schools in Boston are not among the most likely to enter the application lotteries for these schools. As effective as these schools are for those who attend them, Walters concludes that they would produce greater academic benefits for students who are even less advantaged than the students who currently apply.[16] Yet, because Walters cannot measure many nonacademic outcomes, we cannot know for sure that these less-advantaged families should apply.

The charter literature and the voucher literature that we review in the next chapter both provide clear evidence that families who choose charters or voucher schools typically report high levels of satisfaction with their choices, even when they choose schools that do not foster measurable improvements in math or reading achievement. This pattern presents a challenge for policy makers. Parents know things that are not measured by standardized test scores, and children may benefit from systems that allow parents to choose schools based on this information. However, policy makers cannot directly discern what information or decision-making process is causing a given parent to choose a particular school for their child and therefore cannot directly evaluate the quality of a given parent's decision.

4.3 Competitive Pressures on Public Schools

In studies of charter school effectiveness, researchers attempt to measure the gains that some population of students does receive or could receive from attending a charter school instead of their next best option among the traditional public schools in their area. The empirical models employed in these studies almost always impose the assumption that the outcomes that any student would enjoy in the public school sector are not affected by the number of students who attend charter schools. However, both advocates and opponents of charter expansion often contend that this should not be the case.

Advocates of charter expansion claim that when students leave public schools and enter charter schools, the accompanying losses of revenue and increased public scrutiny provide incentives for public schools to improve. Opponents of charters counter that as charter schools expand enrollment, the resulting transfers of revenue from public schools to charter schools may leave public schools unable to cover their fixed costs without reducing per-student spending on instruction. Further, union rules and civil service employment protections that govern salary schedules and dismissals may also hamper the ability of public schools to respond effectively to competitive pressure since retention decisions and salaries may be determined by seniority rather than merit. In response, advocates of charters argue that, by providing even greater access to charters, policy makers can force public schools to abandon bureaucratic rules and personnel policies that raise fixed costs and prevent improvements in teacher quality.

To date, we do not have definitive evidence concerning how charter expansion impacts the quality of local public schools. Existing studies differ methodologically and do not always examine school systems in the same location.[17] Thus, you may not be surprised to learn the results from these studies also differ. Some imply that charter school competition improves public school performance, some imply that it harms public school performance, and others imply that it does not matter at all. However, the absolute magnitudes of these estimated effects are always quite modest. No results from this literature suggest that we should believe that the introduction of charter schools directly changes the quality of local public schools in ways that seriously impact the estimated gains or losses in existing work on charter school effectiveness.[18]

4.4 Competition Is Not a Magic Bullet

You may be noticing a theme. There is no simple formula for optimal education policy, and this should make sense given the material in the Introduction. Education authorities use public funds to purchase education for children because many children are born to parents who are not both willing and able to invest efficiently in their children's education, but a host of agency problems complicate this procurement problem.

Chapter 1 reviews considerable evidence that traditional public schools often waste resources. This outcome must, in part, reflect the fact that most educators work alone with their students performing complex, nuanced tasks, which means that even the most well-intentioned education authority may find it quite costly to verify that educators who receive public funds are actually providing quality education.

Suppose that a benevolent education czar hired professional evaluators to constantly monitor the performance of each educator. This approach would dramatically increase the cost of instruction, and it would not guarantee effective teaching. Well-intentioned evaluators would not necessarily assess teacher performance the same way, and less mission-minded evaluators would likely find it easy to collude with the educators under their supervision in ways that would lower effort costs and harm students.

When actions are difficult to monitor, employers often build incentives around output signals. Yet Chapter 2 shows that many attempts to build incentives around objective measures of educator output have created incentives for educators to invest in gaming efforts that waste resources and corrupt public information about student performance.

We learned that education authorities may do better by using seeded contests, such as PFP, as incentive schemes. However, PFP only provides incentives for educators to foster growth in assessed skills, and excellent educators do more than promote higher achievement in reading and math. They also foster emotional, social, and character development, and they do so while creating environments where children feel safe and encouraged to learn.

Parents possess considerable information about the social and emotional well-being of their children, and most parents are motivated to pursue their children's best interests. Chapter 3 stressed the importance of adopting school assignment mechanisms that give parents an incentive to truthfully report what they believe about the suitability of different schools for their child.

The charter systems discussed in this chapter and the voucher systems discussed in the next chapter embrace markets as procurement mechanisms. These policies elicit information from parents by giving parents the power to influence how resources are allocated among publicly funded providers of education.

To understand the appeal of these reforms, consider the following scenario. We began this book by arguing that credit market imperfection hampers investment in the education of children. Suppose a philanthropist started a program to subsidize computer purchases for economically disadvantaged college students because he felt that credit constraints forced these students to use old, unreliable computers that wasted time they could spend learning. Such a program might work as follows: each eligible student would receive a $1,000 debit card that she could use to purchase a computer at one of ten participating computer stores. These students would have a clear incentive to buy the laptop that would serve them best in their desired course of study, and the ten stores would actively compete for the business of program participants, as they compete for other customers. So our debit card plan would likely function as a cost-effective mechanism for delivering computing services to students who face binding credit constraints.[19]

As we work through the material in the final two chapters of the book, two features of this example are important. First, each person would be buying a computer for her own use, so she would have every incentive to buy the computer that would work best for her. Second, we were implicitly assuming that these students, with the help of the sales staff at the competing vendors, would make an informed computer choice.

In contrast, school choice programs grant parents the power to select a school on behalf of their child. So, we must address the possibility that some parents may knowingly choose schools that serve their interests rather than their child's interests. For example, some parents may choose a school known for weak academic performance simply because it is convenient. Further, we must also address the possibility that some parents do not possess the information they need to choose a school that serves their child well. These observations are key because existing empirical work on school choice reforms suggests that some parents make school choices that seem questionable.

Yet we must proceed with caution when interpreting such evidence. Choice systems rest on the premise that parents observe things that policy makers, and the researchers who advise policy makers, do not. So choices that seem questionable to researchers may, in fact, be sound choices that are based on information that researchers do not possess.

4.5 Appendix: Experimental Data and LATE for Beginners

In this chapter, we examined results from many experimental studies of charter school effectiveness. In recent decades, economists have devoted much effort to the task of discerning what can and cannot be learned from such experiments.[20] The econometric details in this literature are beyond the scope of this book, but this appendix material should help you understand the interpretative framework that now dominates research on data from such experiments.

Until recent decades, social scientists used instrumental variable (IV) methods to isolate common causal effects. To illustrate this use of IV, consider a training experiment where researchers conduct a lottery to randomly assign subsidies among a sample of applicants for a training program. Assume that these subsidies allow applicants to receive training at a deep discount. Next, assume that random assignment to these subsidies is a valid instrument for participation in the training program; that is, those who receive the subsidy are more likely to participate, and winning the subsidy is a random event that is independent of both observed and unobserved applicant characteristics. Finally, make one of two possible additional assumptions. Assume either that all applicants would receive the exact same increase in earnings from training, or at least that all applicants would receive the same expected earnings gains from training. Given these assumptions, IV applied to the data from such an experiment produces a consistent estimate of the gain in earnings that a randomly selected applicant should expect to receive, if she participates in the program.

However, beginning with the work of Angrist and Imbens (1994), economists began to devote more attention to the possibility that, in experiments like ours, the mean gains from training among those who receive training is not equal to the mean gains from training among all applicants. Even when subsidies for training are assigned randomly, an IV estimator that employs these random assignments as instruments is not necessarily a consistent estimator of the average effect of training on earnings for the entire population of applicants. Rather, IV produces an estimate of the average effect of training on earnings among a group of applicants known as compliers. These are the applicants who would attend training if and only if they won a subsidy.

To be more concrete, let $i = 1, 2, \ldots, N$ index a group of N individuals who have applied for a job training program. Assume that the program can only offer training to $K < N$ applicants. Further, assume that the training program assigns random numbers to applicants and then offers training subsidies to the applicants with the K highest random numbers.

Given this setting, we adopt the following notation:

- Y_i^0 is the earnings that i receives without training.
- Y_i^1 is the earnings that i receives with training.
- Z_i is a dummy variable that equals one if i receives an offer of a training subsidy and zero else.
- D_i is a dummy variable that equals one if i receives actual training and zero else.
- $Y_i = (1 - D_i)Y_i^0 + D_i Y_i^1$ is the actual earnings observed for i.

Now, you should remember from your econometrics class that the instrumental variables estimator of the effect of training on earnings is

$$\hat{\beta}_{IV} = \frac{\sum_{i=1}^{N} Y_i^* Z_i^*}{\sum_{i=1}^{N} D_i^* Z_i^*} \quad \text{and} \quad \text{plim } \hat{\beta}_{IV} = \frac{\text{COV}(Y, Z)}{\text{COV}(D, Z)}$$

where * indicates that a variable is measured in deviations from its sample mean. You should also remember that Z_i is a valid instrument for D_i if the receipt of the subsidy offer influences actual participation in training, which it should, and if Z_i is independent of any unobserved random factors that influence Y_i, which should also hold given that offers are random.

If the subsidy offer impacts participation, we can write $D_i = D_i^0(1 - Z_i) + D_i^1 Z_i$ where

- D_i^0 is an indicator for the training choice, D_i, that individual i would make if she were to lose the lottery, i.e., $Z_i = 0$.
- D_i^1 is an indicator for the training choice, D_i, that individual i would make if she were to win the lottery, i.e., $Z_i = 1$.

If for a given i, $D_i^0 = 1$ and $D_i^1 = 1$, we say that i is an *always taker*, meaning he always participates in the training program whether or not he receives the subsidy. If for a given i, $D_i^0 = 0$ and $D_i^1 = 0$, we say that i is a *never taker*, since he never participates in the training program even if he receives the subsidy.[21] Finally, if for a given i, $D_i^0 = 0$ and $D_i^1 = 1$, we say that i is a *complier*. Compliers only participate if they draw a favorable realization of the instrument, Z_i.

We assume that, for all i, the combination $D_i^0 = 1$ and $D_i^1 = 0$ is not possible. We assume that no one turns down training *because* he or she received the subsidy. Angrist and Imbens (1994) refer to this condition as a monotonicity assumption, and in the vast majority of IV applications that involve experimental data, this assumption is quite plausible.[22]

Given this setup and a few more assumptions that are rather innocuous in the context of the lottery studies of charter school effectiveness reviewed in this chapter, Angrist and Imbens (1994) demonstrate that

$$\text{plim } \hat{\beta}_{IV} = E[Y_i^1 - Y_i^0 | D_i^0 = 0, D_i^1 = 1] \qquad (4.1)$$

which means that IV produces a consistent estimate of the expected return from training among the compliers. Thus, Angrist and Imbens (1994) assert that IV produces a local average treatment effect (LATE). The term "Local" captures the fact that IV produces a consistent estimate of the average gain from treatment among the sample of compliers and not the entire applicant pool.[23]

This should seem strange to you if you have not encountered it before. Suppose that the same researchers conducted a second experiment on another sample of applicants for the same training program, but this time the researchers randomly offered some applicants free transportation to training sessions. Now, consider an IV estimator for the expected effects of the training program on earnings that uses the offer of transportation as an instrument for participation in training. Since applicants who face severe cash constraints may differ from applicants who have difficulty arranging transportation, the set of compliers in this second experiment, i.e., those who satisfy $D_i^0 = 0$ and $D_i^1 = 1$, may well differ from the set of compliers in the first experiment.

Further, since the limit defined in equation (4.1) depends on the distribution of both D_i^0 and D_i^1 (i.e., it depends on the nature of the experimental treatment and on how the treatment affects program participation in the population of applicants), there is no reason that the probability limit of the IV estimator associated with the free transportation experiment should be the same as the one associated with the subsidy experiment. The expected value in equation (4.1) may differ greatly over various sets of compliers defined by different experimental treatments, and this is true even if we are considering a set of potential experiments on persons drawn from the same applicant pool.

Finally, assume that a group of researchers has the power both to force lottery winners to complete the program and to prevent lottery losers from ever entering the program. In this setting, the whole applicant pool becomes the set of compliers, but IV still does not produce a consistent estimate of the expected effect of training on earnings for a randomly selected person in the population at large because the complier set only includes persons who applied for the training program. Thus, IV results derived from such experimental data do not tell us anything directly about the potential effects of the training program in the population of persons who did not apply for it.

This qualification is noteworthy. The literature on lottery studies of charter school performance is important because random assignment to offers of admission creates variation in charter school attendance but this variation is, by design, orthogonal to unobserved determinants of student outcomes. Nonetheless, we cannot assume that the estimated effects from these studies apply to populations outside the relevant applicant pools.

We saw in this chapter, and we will see again in Chapter 5, that there is no such thing as "an effect" of attending a particular type of magnet, charter, or voucher school. The value of gaining access to any given school depends, in part, on the student's fallback option. The literature on urban charters that adopt the No Excuses model does not demonstrate that these schools are the best schools in the country. Rather, it demonstrates that these schools are much better than the next best options that many of the applicants to these schools enjoy.

FIVE

Vouchers

Voucher systems embrace the idea that parents should hold educators accountable in the same way consumers hold any market producer accountable. If voucher parents are not pleased with the education their child receives in her current school, they are free to choose a different school for their child and reallocate the funds associated with their voucher to this new school.[1] The most ardent proponents of this approach argue that parents should not only be allowed to use vouchers to purchase education at any school they choose but should also be allowed to pay additional fees out of their own resources if the school they deem best for their children charges tuition greater than the face value of their voucher.

Hayek (1945) famously noted that quantities and prices change in market economies because individuals take self-interested actions based on information that they possess about their particular circumstances. Thus, markets not only create useful incentives for agents to act on the information they possess but also aggregate information in socially productive ways. These observations should apply not only to markets for agricultural products, manufactured goods, or professional services but also to markets for education. Attentive parents observe a great deal about the schools their children attend. They know whether or not their child is eager to learn and engaged in her school work. They also know whether or not their child feels safe at school, and they have opportunities to gauge the professionalism of teachers during parent-teacher conferences and other interactions. Further, caring parents who possess vouchers have both opportunity and incentive to act on the information they possess.

As voucher parents seek access to the highest-performing schools, these schools should be able to both raise tuition and expand enrollment. The resulting variation in tuition rates and enrollments created by a market for education should not only convey important information about differences in quality among schools but also creates clear financial incentives for educators to adopt the organizational and educational practices that serve children well and therefore please parents.

We begin this chapter by sketching out a simple model of the market for public and private schools that illustrates the logic behind the claims of voucher advocates. This simple model makes several predictions that existing data support. However, the model also makes predictions that are likely wrong. Education policy makers who advocate vouchers as a means of improving the quality of publicly funded education need to know why these predictions are wrong in order to design optimal voucher systems. One possibility is that some parents make poorly informed school choice decisions that do not serve the long-term interests of their children. We discuss evidence along these lines and how this possibility should affect the design of education policies.

We also discuss political barriers that may hinder efforts to implement voucher systems that improve student welfare. The social benefits of competition among publicly funded schools hinge, in part, on the rules that govern competition. Some regulations may prove beneficial for students, but others may limit competition in ways that protect incumbents in education markets. Further, some families may oppose vouchers because they realize that they may suffer losses if their local governments replace traditional public school systems with voucher plans. For example, individuals who own homes within the attendance zone of an excellent public school may oppose any reforms that increase the supply of excellent schools in surrounding neighborhoods or towns. Such individuals may fear that, if many other areas also contain excellent schools, the market value of their homes will fall.

Finally, voucher systems may not only impact the productive efficiency of schools but also the inequality of educational outcomes. So we close the chapter by discussing sorting and social stratification. Here, we comment briefly on the peer effects literature.

5.1 Baseline Model

Advocacy for voucher systems rests on the premise that competition among providers of goods and services is socially beneficial. Public school systems in many areas enjoy a legal monopoly on the provision of publicly funded education. Although public school systems do not get to choose prices or decide how many students they will serve, public educators do make numerous decisions that influence the quality of the education they provide, and at the margin, public educators find that their interests conflict with the interests of their students.

To see this conflict of interests, consider Dr. Pangloss Elementary School, which employs personnel policies and organizational practices that are efficient; that is, the school operates in a manner that, given its budget, maximizes the value of skills that children acquire. Given this starting point, imagine that the local school board offers the teachers and support staff who operate Dr. Pangloss the chance to vote on a policy change that would keep all employee salaries the same but would also shorten the school year by two weeks and give each employee five extra personal days off during the school year. How would the staff at Dr. Pangloss vote?

I conjecture they would vote yes. Further, I contend that, if public educators are politically organized and enjoy monopoly power as the sole providers of publicly funded education, we should not expect them to endorse policies that require public schools to minimize the cost of producing student skills. Decades of economics research documents that providers of all kinds of goods and services exercise monopoly power when they enjoy it, and there is no reason to believe that educators should be an exception to this rule.

Voucher advocates argue that parents are more reliable performance monitors than politicians or their appointed representatives because they have strong incentives to seek quality education for their own children. Schools in voucher systems must compete to please parents, and if they fail, they risk losing income or even their jobs.

The details of existing voucher systems differ considerably. Here, we analyze one specific type of voucher system. Our purpose is twofold. First, we seek to highlight the logic behind the claims of voucher proponents. Second, we want to understand the empirical predictions one can derive from this logic and evaluate these predictions relative to existing empirical work on vouchers.

5.1.1 Model Setup

We assume that each family has one child and that parents perfectly observe the quality of their child's school. We first describe a traditional public school equilibrium. Here, public schools receive z dollars for every student they enroll, but the government provides no support for education that takes place in private schools. Public schools are free, but parents who send their children to private schools must pay tuition.

Next, we consider a voucher system that endows each family with a voucher that is redeemable for z dollars. In this system, families choose the school, public or private, that they deem best for their children and transfer their vouchers to the schools they choose. Therefore, the budget for any particular public school equals z dollars times the number of students who enroll in the school. The budget for any particular private school equals z dollars times the number of students the school enrolls plus any additional tuition or fees that the school is able to collect from its students.

5.1.2 Families

Consider a community with a large number of families, N, and assume that each family has one school-age child. Further, assume that all families share a common utility function, $u(c, q)$. Here, c represents a composite commodity, and we normalize the price of this composite commodity to one. The second argument, q, is an index of school quality. We normalize this index so that, among schools that operate efficiently, the cost per student of providing school quality q equals q for all $q \geq 0$.

Although families have common preferences, their incomes differ. Let $n = 1, 2, \ldots, N$ index families. Each family has an income m_n that is an i.i.d. draw from $F(m)$. Parents must decide whether to send their child to public school or private school, and if the parents in family n decide to send their child to private school, they must decide what quality of private schooling, q, they desire for their child. If they send their child to public school, they pay no tuition, and their child receives school quality q_{pub}.

Given standard assumptions about preferences,[2] it is straightforward to show that, holding any level of public school quality, q_{pub}, constant, there exists a critical family income level, $\tilde{m}(q_{pub})$, such that, if $m_n = \tilde{m}(q_{pub})$, family n is indifferent between sending their child to public school or their favorite private school. Here, we adopt the convention that such families choose private school, which implies that family n chooses public school if $m_n < \tilde{m}$ and private school if $m_n \geq \tilde{m}$.

5.1.3 Private Schools

We assume that all parents observe the quality of their child's school, and we also assume that private schools exist in a competitive market with free entry. Thus, if an existing private school provides school quality q for each student, the school charges tuition equal to q, the cost of providing this level of school quality. To keep things simple, we assume that school size does not affect the cost of providing quality. Schools that choose to provide quality q for their students face the same costs per student whether they educate one student, one thousand students, or ten thousand students.

5.1.4 Public School Quality

We assume that there is one public school. Our model describes an environment where all families face only two choices: attend the local public school at no direct cost or pay tuition for private school. We assume that parents cannot move elsewhere and choose a different public school system. This public school represents a large public school district, and within this district, public educators act collectively. Further, these educators enjoy monopoly power because they are the only educators who may receive the public funds that allow parents to send their children to school without paying tuition.

Our public school receives z dollars for each student it enrolls. The educators in the public school collectively choose the quality of education in their school, $q_{pub} = \theta z$, by choosing $\theta \in [0, 1]$. This choice determines how many resources per student, $(1 - \theta)z$, educators divert away from the efficient provision of school quality and toward their own interests.

Public educators thus face the following problem:[3]

$$\max_{\theta}(1 - \theta)z F(\tilde{m})N$$

$$\text{s.t.} \quad u(\tilde{m}, \theta z) = \max_{q} u(\tilde{m} - q, q)$$

It is easy to show that $\tilde{m}$ is an increasing function of θ, and given this result, public educators face a clear trade-off. Higher values of θ reduce the rent that educators extract per student, $(1 - \theta)z$, but also increase the mass of students in public school, $F(\tilde{m})$.

The exercises at the end of the chapter allow you to work with this model and understand it better. You should be able to derive the following results.

1. The child with the lowest family income in the private school sector, $\tilde{m}$, enjoys more family income than the child from the highest-income family in the public school.

2. The lowest-quality private school is still better than the public school. Because school quality is a normal good, families with $m_n = \tilde{m}$ attend the lowest-quality private schools. However, since these families are indifferent between attending public school for free and paying tuition to attend their private school, even the quality of their private school must still be strictly greater than q_{pub}.

3. Public educators use their monopoly position to extract rents; that is, they choose $\theta < 1$.

4. If the government were to adopt a voucher system that allowed families to present a voucher worth z dollars as partial or full payment for private school tuition, public educators would no longer be able to earn rents. Because the private school sector is efficient, any family who possessed a voucher redeemable for z dollars would be able to acquire $q = z$ in the private sector without sacrificing any consumption. Thus, if public educators were to respond by choosing any $\theta < 1$, they would have no students.

5. The introduction of vouchers worth z dollars would improve the quality of education that every child receives. Public school students who choose to remain in public school would enjoy improved school quality. Those who use the voucher to switch from a public school to a private school would enjoy an increase in school quality, and those who were already in the private school sector would use the voucher to attend an even better private school.

6. Introducing vouchers worth z dollars would raise total government expenditure on education because those children who would have attended private schools in the absence of vouchers now receive public funding for their education.

Note that the first three items on this list are predictions about the characteristics of public and private schools in the absence of voucher systems. In the next section, we review the empirical literature on the performance of both public and private schools in settings without large-scale voucher systems. Existing empirical work provides clear support for prediction three but not for predictions one and two.

The fact that result one fails to hold exactly in the data should not concern us greatly. It is not a robust prediction. In our simple model, all families have the same preferences. If we allow preferences over consumption and school quality to differ among families, the income distribution for public school families may well overlap with the corresponding distribution for private school families.

However, the failure of prediction two is important. Whenever parents refuse to use free public schools and pay their own money to choose private schools, they are revealing that they find their local public schools lacking. Yet the existing literature demonstrates that a nontrivial number of private schools may be no better academically and possibly worse than nearby public schools. This raises an important question for researchers and policy makers. Why do some parents pay extra to send their children to schools that appear to be no better academically and possibly worse than their local public schools? Are these parents making decisions that serve their children well, based on information about schools that researchers do not measure? Or are these parents making choices that harm their children because they do not have the capacity and commitment required to accurately evaluate the academic performance of their children's schools?

The role of government is to fund education for children. Voucher systems allow parents to direct these funds. The social performance of voucher systems may well hinge on design elements that shape the sets of potential schools that parents consider and how they choose from these sets.

5.2 Public vs. Private School Comparisons

In recent decades, both private and public organizations in several cities and US states have introduced small-scale voucher programs and then evaluated how giving students access to private schooling changed various student outcomes. Because these small-scale programs did not represent serious competitive threats to local public schools, it seems reasonable to assert that their introduction did not affect public school quality in important ways.

5.2.1 Relative Performance

Given this assertion, we can use the results from these small-scale programs to evaluate prediction two and part of prediction five. Prediction two states that, in the absence of vouchers, existing private schools should be academically superior to public schools. Prediction five further asserts that students who use vouchers to transfer from public to private schools are moving to better schools.

The studies described in Table 5.1 speak directly to these predictions. All of the studies in Table 5.1 are lottery studies. Each program faced excess demand for vouchers, and each program used lotteries to ration the vouchers.[4] Thus, the control families in these studies took the same steps to apply for vouchers that treatment families took.

The results cast serious doubt on predictions two and five. The reported effects on math and reading achievement in Table 5.1 suggest that, often, the private schools in these voucher experiments did not actually provide superior educational services, and in some cases, these schools may have provided inferior schooling. If we assume that not only the voucher students but the incumbent students in these private schools have access to the public schools in the control groups, it seems fair to conclude that the students in these schools are likely not learning a great deal more than they could learn in their local public schools.

Nonetheless, each study that examined family satisfaction found that families who won and used vouchers were much happier with their schools than families who lost the lottery. Further, Howell and Peterson (2002) find that voucher families report higher satisfaction than public school families who never applied for vouchers.

As we note in Chapter 4, satisfaction results are not easy to interpret. Parents and students could express greater satisfaction for many reasons. Some parents and many students would be happier if their current schools shortened the school day or assigned less homework, but these changes would not necessarily serve the long-term interests of students.

Yet patterns in these results suggest that voucher parents may report higher levels of satisfaction for sound reasons. Dynarski et al. (2017) report that lottery winners in a recent voucher experiment in the District of Columbia experienced lower rates of achievement growth and no improvements in overall satisfaction. Nonetheless, parents of voucher winners did report much higher satisfaction with the safety of their children's schools.

The response rates in this DC experiment were relatively low and there may be many reasons that the program did not foster achievement growth or overall improvements in parental satisfaction. However, if the program did make children safer, we should be hesitant to label it a failure.

Other patterns in Table 5.1 also suggest that parents may observe important aspects of school performance that achievement tests do not capture. Both Chingos and Peterson (2012) and Wolf et al. (2013) report that voucher receipt improves educational attainment. Voucher students appear more likely to complete high school and to attend college.

Some may wonder how voucher schools promote attainment without generating significant improvements in achievement growth. Voucher schools may lower the nonpecuniary costs of attending school. Students who feel safe, welcome, included, and encouraged may find school less burdensome or even find school enjoyable.

In ethnographic work on Catholic schools, Bryk et al. (1993) argue that these schools achieve success in communities where public schools fail because they create a sense of community. Thus, it is noteworthy that the patterns in Table 5.1 echo results from earlier literature on Catholic schools. Neal (1997) notes that, among urban minorities who attended high school in the late 1970s and early 1980s, Catholic high schools appeared to have large positive impacts on both high school and college graduation rates.[5] In follow-up work, Grogger and Neal (2000) find similar results for later cohorts of urban minorities even though they report that urban Catholic schools have modest impacts, at best, on minority achievement.

Both the voucher literature, which has exploited experimental variation, and the early Catholic school literature, which sought to address the effects of selection with econometric models of the demand for Catholic schooling, have reached similar conclusions. Urban private schools that serve minority communities produce, at best, modest gains in achievement for their students, but often produce noteworthy attainment gains.

The earlier literature on Catholic schooling found that urban whites enjoy more modest benefits from Catholic schooling and that all forms of private schooling have little impact on the achievement or attainment of suburban students. Further, Grogger and Neal (2000) report that even among suburban students who attend nationally accredited private schools, there is no evidence that these private school students enjoy gains in achievement or attainment.

In our simple model above, there is one public school district and one public school quality. However, differences in public school quality both within and between districts are likely the keys to understanding the patterns in this earlier literature on private schooling. Parents who are not satisfied with the quality of their child's public school have two options. They can pay for private schooling, or they can find a way to get their child into a better public school.

Table 5.1 Voucher Experiments in the US

Program	Description	Maximum Voucher Value[a]	Private/Public Spending per Pupil[b]	Studies	Results
Milwaukee Parental Choice Program (I) Milwaukee, WI 1990–1994	The Program provided vouchers by lottery to eligible, low-income families, capped at 1% of Milwaukee public school students.	$2,729 in 1991–1992 (41%)	48%	Rouse (1998); Greene et al. (1999)	Modest math gains. No reading gains.
Milwaukee Parental Choice Program (II) Milwaukee, WI 2006–2011	The Program expanded to provide vouchers to a maximum of 22,500 students starting in 2005. It introduced a new accountability standard in 2010.	$6,607 in 2009–2010 (44%)[c]	—	Witte et al. (2012); Cowen et al. (2013)	Small gains in math and reading. Math gains are not statistically significant given a full set of controls. Improvements in four-year college attendance.
School Choice Scholarships Foundation New York, NY 1997–2000	The Foundation assigned vouchers by lottery to eligible, low-income families with children entering grades 1–5.	$1,400 in 1997–1998 (less than 28%)	Less than 48%	Howell and Peterson (2002); Mayer et al. (2002); Krueger and Zhu (2004); Barnard et al. (2003); Chingos and Peterson (2012)	Some evidence of noteworthy achievement gains for African American students. No noteworthy achievement impacts for other groups. Large significant positive effect on the college enrollment of African American students. Voucher families reported large increases in school satisfaction.

a. All monetary figures are presented in nominal US dollars, and represent the maximum voucher values. Entries in parentheses are expressed as fractions of per-pupil spending in local public schools. Unless otherwise noted, the data used come from the cited studies.

b. This column is calculated as the estimated per-pupil spending in schools receiving vouchers divided by estimated per-pupil spending in local public schools.

c. Source of voucher value and per-pupil spending in local public schools: see Wolf (2012).

Table 5.1 (*continued*)

Program	Description	Maximum Voucher Value	Private/Public Spending per Pupil	Studies	Results
Washington Scholarship Fund Washington, DC 1998–2001	The Fund provided vouchers by lottery to eligible families with children entering grades K-8. Voucher amounts were based on family income.	$1,700 in 1998–1999 or 60% of tuition (21%)	49%	Howell and Peterson (2002)	Achievement gains for African American students. Voucher families reported large increase in school satisfaction.
Parents Advancing Choice in Education Dayton, OH 1998–2000	The program provided vouchers by lottery to eligible families with children in grades K-12. Voucher amounts were based on family income.	$1,200 in 1998–1999 or 60% of tuition (22%)	—	Howell and Peterson (2002)	Achievement gains for African American students. Voucher families reported large increase in school satisfaction.
Cleveland Scholarship and Tutoring Program Cleveland, OH 1998–2004	The Program assigned vouchers by lottery within groups defined by family income.	$3,000 in 2003–2004 (—)	—	Plucker et al. (2006); Belfield (2006)	No significant evidence of educational gains.
Children's Scholarship Fund Charlotte, NC 1999–2000	Charlotte awarded vouchers by lottery to eligible, low-income families with children in elementary or secondary school.	$1,700 in 1999–2000 (—)	Less than 50%	Greene (2001); Cowen (2008)	Some evidence of noteworthy gains in math and reading achievement.

Table 5.1 (continued)

Program	Description	Maximum Voucher Value	Private/Public Spending per Pupil	Studies	Results
DC Opportunity Scholarship Program (I) Washington, DC 2004–2009	First federally funded school voucher program; assigned vouchers by lottery to eligible, low-income families with children in grades K-12.	$7,500 in 2004–2005 (56%) [d]	—	Wolf et al. (2013)	No robust evidence of achievement gains. Improvement in high school graduation rates.
DC Opportunity Scholarship Program (II) Washington, DC 2012–2015	(same as above)	$12,000 in 2012–2013 (58%) [e]	—	Dynarski et al. (2017)	Negative effects on math and reading achievements after one year. No effects on total parental satisfaction. Significant improvement in parental assessment of school safety.

d. Source of per-pupil spending in local public schools: see National Center for Education Statistics (2007a).
e. Source of per-pupil spending in local public schools: see National Center for Education Statistics (2007b).

Historically, finding a better public school has almost always involved moving to a place where housing costs more or helping one's child gain access to exam schools by scoring well on entrance exams. Wealthy parents possess resources that allow them to pursue these strategies. So it is not surprising to find that academic outcomes for students from wealthy families do not vary greatly as a function of whether or not they attend private schools. If privileged families send their children to public schools, they are typically not sending them to average public schools.

This same logic may shed light on patterns in the literature on No Excuses charter schools that we discussed in Chapter 4. In parallel with the older literature on Catholic schools, urban minorities appear to enjoy the greatest gains from access to these schools, although the results differ quantitatively because the gains in achievement associated with attending No Excuses charter schools are more striking than the corresponding gains in attainment. However, the importance of student background and location remains. No Excuses charters produce the most impressive results in the charter sector, and like many of the voucher experiments discussed in Table 5.1, No Excuses charters target urban students who are primarily black and Hispanic and often economically disadvantaged.

This pattern of results suggests that traditional public schools often perform poorly in urban communities that contain large populations of economically disadvantaged, minority students. These families may lack the political voice required to hold large public school systems accountable. Further, in some regions, the best public schools are in predominately white areas, and minority families may feel they are not welcome in these communities.[6]

5.2.2 Inefficiency

Prediction three above states that public educators who enjoy monopoly power use it. Therefore, it is important to consider the cost data in Table 5.1. For each program, the third and fourth columns present the maximum voucher amount and the average per-pupil spending in voucher schools. When possible, the table reports these spending levels as fractions of per-pupil spending levels in local public schools. The ratios of spending in voucher schools versus public schools are often around 50 percent.[7]

Further, the face values of the vouchers that parents receive are often only a portion of total private school spending.

Many voucher schools have produced about the same learning outcomes, better family satisfaction, and the same or better attainment outcomes while spending much less money per student than local public schools. So, it is tempting to interpret Table 5.1 as direct evidence that many of the public schools that serve students who lost these voucher lotteries are inefficient. Nonetheless, we cannot draw definitive conclusions about public versus private school efficiency based on these results.

These lottery studies examine select samples of students. Each student in these studies lives with parents or caregivers who took the initiative to apply for a voucher program. Further, they used vouchers to attend schools where other families were already paying tuition. Both of these facts raise important concerns about sample selection.

It is clear that these experiments tell us nothing about potential gains from private schooling among those who did not apply for vouchers. It is possible that students from public school families that did not apply for a voucher would have experienced much worse outcomes in the private schools that participated in these voucher programs. Further, the gains in satisfaction and attainment that voucher families enjoy may not reflect the performance of their new schools but simply the fact that these families were able to use their vouchers to place their children in a different group of peers.

It is possible that voucher schools appear to be more efficient, but in reality, are simply vehicles for providing disadvantaged students access to better peers. Students from families who make financial sacrifices to send them to private schools may be better behaved and more academically motivated. Thus, voucher systems may give recipients access to these potentially beneficial peers. However, it is obvious that policy makers cannot produce this benefit for all students by simply introducing vouchers. Someone has to go to school with the troubled kids who do not want to learn, and voucher systems cannot change this reality.

Further, even if we conclude that both urban Catholic schools and the voucher schools in the Table 5.1 experiments are much more efficient than neighboring public schools, it is not obvious that policy makers can produce these efficiency gains at scale by introducing vouchers. Many of the private schools that participate in these experiments are religious organizations or nonprofits whose missions center on helping disadvantaged children. Like the No Excuses charter schools that we examined in Chapter 4, these private schools recruit faculty who personally embrace the mission of their schools. For many of these faculty, the opportunity to effectively serve disadvantaged children is part of their compensation.

If one sought to replicate any of these schools on a large scale by introducing programs that funded universal vouchers, it is not obvious that these mission-minded schools could replicate themselves without increasing per-pupil spending. The supply curve of educators who are willing to work harder for less money may be quite inelastic.

5.3 Public School Responses

Predictions four and five from our baseline model suggest that public school students who remain in public schools following the introduction of vouchers should benefit. In our model, competition from voucher schools forces public schools to improve or lose their students.

Both Epple et al. (2015) and Rouse and Barrow (2009) survey the literature on public school performance changes in response to pressure from voucher systems. We discuss a few of these studies here.

The most noteworthy studies examine responses to voucher programs in Florida and Milwaukee. The second phase of the Milwaukee program, which began in 1998, involved more vouchers, higher voucher levels, and greater financial penalties for public schools that lost students to voucher schools.[8]

The Milwaukee program targeted families in Milwaukee who were eligible for free or reduced-price lunches at school, and since each public school in Milwaukee contains some eligible families, the program affected all Milwaukee public schools. Both Hoxby (2003) and Chakrabarti (2008) construct a sample of control schools using other public school districts in Wisconsin, and they also use data on subsidized lunch receipt in Milwaukee to create measures of treatment intensity for various public schools. Chakrabarti (2008) employs additional control-group strategies, but the overall results from both studies suggest that pressure from the voucher system did improve school-level test scores in Milwaukee public schools, at least in some subjects.

Figlio and Hart (2014) examine a means-tested voucher program introduced in Florida in 2011. The Florida Tuition Tax Credit provided relatively modest vouchers, initially 3,500 per year, that low-income students could use to attend private schools, if they were not beyond first grade and already enrolled in a private school.[9] The state announced the program one year before it issued any vouchers, so the authors have been able to examine the effect of the program on the achievement of low-income students in public schools from its announcement through many years of program growth. Figlio and Hart (2014) use five different measures of competition directly from local private schools or from funding sources for local private schools to gauge how competition for students influences public school performance. They find positive effects of competition on individual test scores of low-income students in Florida public schools, even in the announcement year, and these effects tend to grow over time.

Epple et al. (2015) concludes based on these studies and others that "competition induced by vouchers leads public schools to improve." Yet no existing voucher programs in the US provide real competitive threats to traditional public school systems.

5.4 Too Focused on Saving Money

Prediction six from our baseline model above states that universal vouchers would increase spending on public education if governments chose voucher spending levels that hold current per-pupil spending constant. This result is rather obvious. In such a scenario, spending on students who were enrolled ex ante in public schools would remain constant, and students who were enrolled ex ante in private schools would receive vouchers that they would use to offset some or all of their tuition costs. Public officials understand this reality, and therefore, many voucher proposals involve voucher funding levels that are below existing spending levels in public schools or contain targeting provisions that limit voucher offers to disadvantaged populations with low ex ante rates of private school attendance.

Policy makers defend this approach by noting the results in Table 5.1. Voucher experiments have often found that private schools produce the same learning outcomes at lower cost than local public schools, and many of the most successful No Excuses charter schools in our cities spend less per student than neighboring public schools.[10]

However, when policy makers become too focused on saving money, they may develop voucher systems that attract the least effective private providers of education. If some parents are not both willing and able to accurately evaluate the academic quality of their child's school, such voucher systems can become vehicles for allocating public funds to private schools that perform quite poorly.

Abdulkadiroğlu et al. (2015) study the Louisiana Scholarship Program (LSP), a state-wide voucher program. The program began in 2008 but became a state-wide program in 2012. Abdulkadiroğlu et al. examine the first year of data under the state-wide implementation. LSP allows students who have low incomes and who attend poorly performing public schools to apply for vouchers that they can use to attend private schools. Voucher amounts equal the minimum of either a school's tuition before it entered the program or per-pupil spending in public schools. Further, private schools that enter the program face significant application costs and must meet ongoing accountability requirements. Given these rules, the select group of private schools that chose to participate in the program contained a number of schools that charged tuition rates well below per-pupil spending in local public schools. Among private schools that participated in the LSP program during the 2012–2013 school year, the average tuition level was $4,989, or less than 60 percent of the average per-pupil spending level in the public school districts where LSP participants reside.[11]

Abdulkadiroğlu et al. (2015) find that the program did save the state money, but the program also harmed student achievement. Among students who applied for vouchers, attending a voucher school for one year lowered scores, on average, by .26, .33, and .41 standard deviations in science, social studies, and math respectively. Abdulkadiroğlu et al. also report a negative impact of voucher use on language arts achievement, but this effect is much smaller in absolute value and not statistically significant.

The LSP results are important. Any voucher program may attract some weak schools. However, this outcome is more likely when voucher programs target private schools that charge low tuition levels. Abdulkadiroğlu et al. also estimate a model that includes an interaction term between voucher use and the tuition level in LSP schools, and the results imply that, on average, the LSP schools that charge higher tuition rates produce better achievement results. In fact, at tuition levels greater than 75% of per-pupil spending in public schools, the Abdulkadiroğlu et al. (2015) results imply that LSP schools produce overall achievement gains for voucher students that are slightly better than the gains they would have expected in public schools.[12]

5.5 Voucher Systems Need Accountability Systems

Parents possess important information about how their children are doing in school, and it seems reasonable to assume that most of the parents who participated in LSP were well-intentioned. Further, press reports suggest that LSP students did feel welcome and safe in their new schools. Nonetheless, many LSP families may have lacked the information they needed to evaluate the quality of education provided in LSP schools.[13]

The Louisiana Scholarship Program did involve an accountability system, and the state sanctioned twenty-three voucher schools in the fall of 2013 based on their past performance. However, learning outcomes in sanctioned voucher schools were quite similar to those in voucher schools that did not receive sanctions. The accountability system focused primarily on score levels, and as a result, produced school ratings that provided little information about rates of achievement growth in different schools.

Although most policy discussions treat vouchers and ABI systems as policy alternatives, the results from LSP suggest that voucher systems may not be effective without strong assessment-based accountability systems. Remember where we started. In the Introduction we noted that public funding of schools is justified because some children have parents who are not both willing and able to purchase efficient levels of education for them. It seems reasonable to conjecture that some parents who do not possess the economic resources required to fund their children's schooling also lack the educational resources required to effectively evaluate the academic quality of their children's school. Concerned parents of all backgrounds know whether or not their children enjoy school and are progressing socially and emotionally. However, parents with little education may find it difficult to evaluate the academic progress that their children are making.

Thus, it seems prudent to provide voucher parents with reliable information about the relative performance of different schools in their area, and it may also be necessary to rule that certain schools are no longer eligible to receive public funds because their performance record is not acceptable. We return to this topic in the next chapter.

5.6 International Evidence

The existing literature contains results from two well-known voucher experiments in the developing world, one in India and one in Columbia. Both studies provide evidence that voucher systems may improve efficiency in these countries.

Muralidharan and Sundararaman (2015) present results from an interesting experiment in the province of Andhra Pradesh in India. This experiment involved several stages. First, the authors performed baseline testing and collected applications for a voucher program from residents of 180 villages. Then they randomly selected 90 villages as treatment villages, and in these villages they randomly assigned vouchers to a portion of the applicants. This design allows Muralidharan and Sundararaman to estimate the effect of treatment within villages and how the existence of the program in a given village affects nontreated individuals relative to their counterparts in control villages.

Muralidharan and Sundararaman report that overall rates of achievement growth for voucher winners are comparable to rates of achievement growth for applicants who do not win vouchers. However, private schools teach Hindi in addition to the standard subjects taught in public schools, so Hindi achievement growth is much greater among voucher winners. In addition, the authors find no evidence that private schools are able to educate children at lower cost simply because they are attracting the children who are easiest to teach.

Muralidharan and Sundararaman report that the private schools in their experiment spend less than one-third as much as their public school counterparts. Taken together, the achievement outcomes for voucher recipients and the spending levels in voucher schools constitute compelling evidence that public schools in these villages are inefficient. According to Muralidharan and Sundararaman (2015), the high salaries and robust employment protections that civil service teachers enjoy are key forces driving the inefficiency of public schools in rural India.

In the 1990s, Columbia ran an experimental voucher program named Programa de Amplicación de Cobertura de al Educación Secundaria (PACES). This program provided vouchers to roughly 125,000 students, and these vouchers typically covered just over half the cost of tuition in participating private secondary schools. The government assigned vouchers by lottery among applicants, who had to be in the sixth grade or higher and less than sixteen years old. Applicants who won vouchers had to earn promotions at the end of each grade in order to renew their vouchers.

Two evaluations of PACES, Angrist et al. (2002) and Angrist et al. (2006), demonstrate that lottery winners enjoyed significantly higher rates of achievement growth, repeated fewer grades, and were more likely to finish high school. The results imply that participating voucher schools produced significantly better academic outcomes than neighboring public schools.

Two features of the PACES program stand out relative to the US experiments described above and the Indian experiment in Andhra Pradesh. First, the voucher schools in the PACES program spent about as much or slightly more per student than local public schools. Second, voucher students faced a financial incentive to work hard in school since they could not renew their vouchers unless they were promoted each year. Both of these program features may have contributed to the success of PACES, but it is not possible to determine the magnitude of these potential effects.

5.6.1 Nonexperimental Evidence

Denmark, the Netherlands, Sweden, and Chile are the only countries in the world that fund public education through systems that function as national voucher systems. The systems have been present in Denmark and the Netherlands for decades. So it is really not possible to learn anything about what educational outcomes would be in these countries without vouchers.

Chile adopted its voucher system in 1981, and Sweden began using vouchers in 1993. So some modern data on outcomes exist in these countries both before and after their voucher reforms. However, both countries introduced their systems nationwide in one year. Thus, there are no control groups in either country that directly provide information about how student outcomes would have evolved in the absence of vouchers. Further, Gallego (2013) reports that Chile's voucher system has not always been a true voucher system. He claims that throughout that 1980s and 1990s, many municipalities subsidized failing local public schools, and he argues that in 2002, 30 percent of funds for public schools in Chile came from sources other than voucher revenue.

This feature of the Chilean system is not widely appreciated but is quite important. Vouchers seek to improve performance by introducing competition. The hope is that low-performing schools will be forced to improve or close because parents have the option to leave. However, if weak schools know that local governments will bail them out when parents depart, these schools face weaker incentives to improve and are able to remain open without improving.

Epple et al. (2015) provide a detailed survey of the literature that seeks to evaluate the introduction of vouchers in both Chile and Sweden. In both countries, researchers get different answers given different identifying assumptions, and we will not review these papers here. Yet two results are particularly noteworthy.

The Swedish system does not allow selective admission procedures, and it does not allow schools to charge more than the face amount of vouchers as tuition. Chile allows both practices, and the introduction of vouchers in Chile appears to have created more academic and social stratification among schools.

Aggregate test score results in Chile were not impressive during the first twenty years under vouchers, but from 2003 to 2011 Chile saw striking improvement in its performance on international tests. The timing may only be coincidental, but 2003 is the year that Chile began giving larger vouchers to low-income families. It is possible that vouchers have always improved productive efficiency in Chile, but during the first two decades, the schools that served disadvantaged students may have been funded below efficient levels.

5.7 Political Barriers

Even if we assume that vouchers can produce efficiency gains by introducing new competitors that put performance pressures on public educators, an important political obstacle should make us worry that, in many countries, policy makers cannot easily fashion large-scale voucher systems that would fully capture these gains. Denmark, the Netherlands, and Sweden already operate well-funded choice systems that are functionally equivalent to universal voucher systems, but in these countries, teachers' unions engage in collective action that constrains the capacity of schools to set pay and working conditions. The extent of these constraints varies by country and varies within countries for different types of teachers, but in some instances, union bargaining clearly limits the ability of schools to remove weak teachers and to compete for excellent ones.[14]

In many developed countries, teacher pay and pensions account for roughly half of all spending on K–12 education, and it is quite difficult for education authorities to substitute technology for classroom teachers, especially in elementary grades. Young children are not going to learn much from computer-based lessons without the supervision of adults, and for such lessons to be effective, the adults that monitor behavior and time-on-task would likely also need to provide educational assistance; in other words, these adults would need to teach.

If a national union controls the supply of teachers, it has the power to dictate much about how schools operate. Further, we expect such a union to use its monopoly power to adopt salary schedules and work rules that benefit educators and raise the cost of education services.

In most product markets, firms compete with each other, in part, by trying to find ways to organize production that improve efficiency, and a key dimension of this competition involves finding best personnel practices. In education markets, this aspect of competition is particularly salient. School leaders can significantly improve the performance of their schools by finding better ways to screen potential teachers, better ways to mentor young teachers, better ways to provide incentives for teachers, better ways to make retention and promotion decisions, and better ways to coordinate effort and share information among staff. However, if school leaders cannot compete on these dimensions, their options for innovation are limited, and their ability to develop new organizational practices that would better serve students is greatly constrained.

On the other hand, if schools are allowed to compete on these dimensions, the result should be more intense competition and increased rewards for the most skilled teachers. This competition should improve education quality by improving pedagogy, keeping more excellent teachers in their profession, and encouraging more talented persons to enter teaching.[15]

5.7.1 Housing Markets and Political Opposition to Choice

To date, large-scale voucher systems have not received strong political support in the US. Nechyba (2000) notes that political opposition to vouchers may, in part, reflect a link between housing markets and the quality of local public schools. Nechyba's model is quite complicated and beyond the scope of our text. However, one key insight is easy to grasp.

Consider a family who owns a home in a wealthy suburb of Chicago. Assume that because the families in this suburb are wealthy and well educated, parents are quite involved in the local public schools, and organized parent groups not only support public educators but also hold them accountable for many aspects of school performance. Thus, the quality of the schools in this suburb is quite high relative to the quality of schools in other towns or cities, even when one accounts for the fact that the families in this suburb pay relatively high taxes to support their schools.[16]

In the absence of vouchers, we expect home prices in this suburb to reflect the fact that residents of this suburb enjoy the right to send their children to high-quality public schools that are nearby. From this starting point, consider the introduction of universal vouchers financed through a state-wide income tax. Given the existence of a successful universal voucher system, persons who could afford to live in this wealthy suburb could also choose to live anywhere in the Chicago area and send their children to a local voucher school that provides excellent education. Given this reality, the introduction of universal vouchers would likely reduce home prices in this suburb.

In many metropolitan areas, parents bid for spaces in the best schools by buying homes in the best school districts or attendance zones. Given a successful voucher system, parents would live in the location that is optimal for their family given their work locations, hobbies, and other interests, knowing that the supply of voucher schools would respond to demand in these locations. So a successful universal voucher system would necessarily lower the prices of homes owned by families who now have access to many of the best public schools.[17]

Many residents in the best public school districts may oppose vouchers because they realize that a successful voucher system would reduce their housing wealth. Brunner and Sonstelie (2003) survey California residents concerning how they voted in a 2000 referendum on state-funded vouchers. Consistent with the insights of Nechyba (2000), Brunner and Sonstelie report that homeowners voted to protect their property values. Homeowners without children were much more likely to oppose the measure if their local public schools were excellent.[18]

5.8 Design Details, Segregation, and Inequality

We began the chapter with a simple model of the market for schooling. In this model, students from families with more than a critical level of income attend private school, and less advantaged students attend public school. Further, this form of income stratification among the private and public school sectors continues to hold if governments introduce universal vouchers and allow private schools to charge tuition rates above the common voucher amount.

Yet, in our model, the introduction of universal vouchers has many effects on the observed relationship between a family's income and the quality of the education their child receives. Children who attend public schools in the absence of vouchers enjoy higher school quality after the introduction of vouchers because competition forces public schools to raise quality, and if their families choose to combine vouchers and their own financial contributions, they will attend private schools that are even better. However, children from wealthy families who choose private schools in the absence of vouchers also attend better schools following the introduction of vouchers, since vouchers subsidize their families' spending on education. Whether or not the introduction of vouchers increases or decreases differences in school quality among children who come from different parts of the family income distribution depends on many factors. One key factor is the efficiency of public schools prior to the introduction of vouchers. When public schools are grossly inefficient, competition offers greater promise for children from low-income families who do not have access to private schools without vouchers.

In Epple and Romano's 1998 and 2008 articles, the authors consider an environment where students differ with respect to both family income and ability. By assumption, students value able peers, and this gives rise to two-dimensional sorting among private schools. The best private schools enroll the richest and most able students. They give merit scholarships to students who are brilliant but not that wealthy and charge higher tuition to students who are truly wealthy but not exceptionally gifted. Weaker private schools enroll kids who tend to be less wealthy and less gifted.

Epple and Romano (2008) show that the introduction of universal voucher systems that place no constraints on the tuition or admission policies of voucher schools generates even greater income and ability stratification among schools. On the other hand, voucher systems that do not allow private schools to charge more than a common voucher level as tuition allow governments to induce competition among schools without increasing the stratification created by the cream-skimming behavior of private schools.[19]

5.9 Peer Effects and Complications

A growing literature suggests that peer effects may be important determinants of academic achievement (see Epple and Romano (2011) and Sacerdote (2011)). Yet to this point, we have devoted little attention to peer effects. Two practical considerations motivate our decision to ignore peer effects in most of our analyses.

First, many of our analyses become much more complicated in the presence of peer effects. For example, in Chapter 3 we noted that school assignment systems that employ the deferred acceptance (DA) algorithm are strategy-proof and produce assignments that avoid justifiable envy. However, we derived these properties in a setting where students only care about the qualities of the educational programs at different schools. They do not care who their classmates happen to be. If students do care directly about the identity of their classmates, truth telling may no longer be a dominant strategy, and if students do not submit their actual preference rankings, there is no guarantee that DA will produce assignments that avoid justifiable envy.[20]

Second, the large literature on peer effects in education has not produced definitive results concerning exactly how they work in different settings. Researchers usually need some type of experimental or quasi-experimental variation to identify peer effects, and even when they have access to experimental data that contain clear evidence that peer effects exist, researchers may find it difficult to pin down mechanisms. Carrell et al. (2013) exploit random variation in the assignment of students to classes in order to estimate the magnitude of peer effects among cadets at the Air Force Academy. Although they found clear evidence of peer effects, a subsequent effort to assign students to classes in ways that exploit the observed pattern of peer effects failed to improve student learning.

EXERCISES

▶ Let i index families. Each family i with income m_i cares about both consumption and the quality of the education received by their only child. The parents must choose whether to send their child to public school or private school. If they choose public school, they do not have to pay anything and their child receives an education of quality q_{pub}, which the family takes as given. If the parents choose private school, they may pick any quality of education q, but they must also give up consumption worth q. Each family i has the same utility function over a composite good c_i and the quality of their child's education q_i.

$$u\left(c_i, q_i\right) = \alpha \log\left(c_i\right) + (1 - \alpha) \log\left(q_i\right)$$

If family i sends their child to private school, $c_i = m_i - q_i$, else $c_i = m_i$.

- Assume that public school is not an option, and derive family i's demand for school quality, $q_i = q\left(m_i\right)$.
- Assume that family i is indifferent between sending their child to private versus public school. Derive an expression for m_i in terms of q_{pub} and α.

Public School's Problem. The public school receives a fixed amount z per child enrolled. Taxpayers find it difficult to monitor the actions of public educators. So we assume that public educators divert a fraction θ of z to their own consumption. Educators cannot capture all of z because all families would choose private schooling if $\theta = 1$ and $q_{pub} = (1 - \theta) z = 0$. Educators face a trade-off. As they decrease θ, they attract more students and therefore more total funding, but they keep less revenue per student.

Normalize the number of families where the public school operates to 1 and assume their incomes are distributed uniformly from \$50,000 to \$200,000.

- Assume that public educators collectively choose θ to maximize the total revenue they capture for their own consumption. Formulate and solve the maximization problem that these educators solve.
- Let $\alpha = 0.8$ and $z = \$25,000$. How much of the instructional funds does the school keep for itself? At what level of income are families indifferent between public and private school?
- What is the difference in mean incomes between public and private school families?

SIX

Putting the Pieces Together

In the Introduction, we discussed the most common justification for public funding of K–12 education. Many children have parents who are not both able and willing to invest efficiently in their education. Governments can improve welfare by investing in these children and later taxing their enhanced future earnings to pay for these investments. In sum, government funding of education helps complete the market for investments in human capital.

Most modern countries spend more than 5 percent of national income on publicly funded education for children. So the systems that governments employ to procure education services for children may have important welfare consequences. In Chapter 1, we saw considerable evidence that traditional public schools often waste resources. Personnel policies in traditional public schools appear to be a key source of waste. Teachers' unions and other professional organizations demand work rules, employment protections, and salary schedules that shield public educators from capricious decisions by public administrators. Educators in public school systems are justifiably wary of policies that would give principals or other supervisors the type of discretion over pay, retention, and promotion decisions that many owners or managers enjoy in the private sector. Administrators in public school systems are also civil servants who may benefit from making personnel decisions based on nepotism or other personal considerations rather than merit.

Yet policies that protect public educators from capricious sanctions may also make them less accountable for their performance. Existing research suggests that many weak teachers receive tenure quite early in their careers. Further, among tenured teachers, pay is not related to available measures of teacher performance. Finally, advocates of various reform agendas often contend that public school systems are overly reluctant to close or reorganize failing schools.

Decades of reform efforts have sought to improve the quality of education by making publicly funded educators more accountable for their performance. We treat these initiatives as efforts to change the way governments procure education services. Taxpayers cannot directly observe whether the portion of their taxes allocated to education is being employed efficiently or whether, given the same spending levels, it is possible to purchase better education services for children. Thus, reform proposals typically create mechanisms that produce new information about educator performance, and in most cases, reformers also demand that education authorities use this new information to guide the reallocation of resources from less efficient to more efficient education providers.

For example, NCLB spelled out mechanisms for collecting assessment-based measures of educator performance and promised to close schools that failed to meet certain performance targets. Centralized school assignment mechanisms collect information from parents about their preferences over different schools. Even though most districts do not use this information to guide resource allocation among schools or educators, these systems may produce better matches between students and schools. Charter systems gather information from parents by giving them an opportunity to apply for seats in schools that they deem better than existing local public schools, and in many cases, school systems reallocate funds from traditional schools to charter schools in response to the expressed demands of parents. Voucher systems operate on the same principles, but these systems often make the link between parental decisions and resource allocations even more explicit.

6.1 Work to Be Done

In practice, none of these reform strategies have worked perfectly. Existing assessment-based accountability systems induce numerous hidden actions that not only contaminate information about educator performance but also harm students. Some centralized assignment systems provide incentives for parents to engage in socially wasteful gaming behaviors that may enhance inequality, and even the best assignment mechanisms do not directly impact the productivity of schools. Finally, several empirical results presented in Chapters 4 and 5 suggest that, while many parents use charter or voucher programs to choose better schools for their children, some parents choose charter or voucher schools that may not serve the long-term interests of their children.

Much work remains, but one thing is clear. Policy makers should not treat programs that expand parental choice as substitutes for accountability systems. Policy makers must combine efforts to promote competition among schools with well-designed accountability systems. Optimal education policy should employ parents as performance monitors because many parents possess important information about the performance of schools that achievement tests do not capture. Yet parents are likely to make better choices if robust accountability systems both produce public information about the relative performance of different schools and require that public education authorities withdraw funding from the weakest schools.

In sum, optimal education policies likely define a system of regulated competition among sets of education providers that education authorities deem eligible to receive public funds. A similar approach already exists in health care. Medicare allows beneficiaries to receive care at public or private hospitals, but the program does not pay for every type of care or treatment that patients may demand. Health care providers must be licensed, and Medicare will not pay for treatments that regulators deem wasteful.

Existing research tells us little about the optimal ways to blend parental choice and accountability. Barlevy and Neal (2012) propose Pay for Percentile (PFP) as the optimal assessment-based incentive scheme. However, PFP does not gather information from parents, and it does not induce educators to foster any student skills that achievement tests do not measure. Further, PFP elicits effort from a fixed set of teachers. The existing literature on assessment-based incentives has nothing to say about the design of mechanisms that both elicit optimal teacher effort and spell out optimal retention and promotion decisions, and economists have not characterized optimal mechanisms for granting and renewing school charters or determining the eligibility of schools to receive public funding. I hope that economists will soon tackle these design questions, but in the interim, let me offer a few conjectures about likely properties of the optimal regulated choice system.

6.1.1 Measure All Aspects of Performance

You may be familiar with the old adage, "you get what pay for." This saying serves as an important warning for education policy makers. If policy makers choose not to reward particular dimensions of school performance, educators may divert effort away from valuable activities. If policy makers base educator pay and job security solely on assessment-based performance metrics, they should not be surprised if schools neglect important aspects of social and emotional development. If policy makers adopt voucher programs that contain no performance-based regulations concerning the eligibility of organizations to receive public funds, such programs will produce whatever schools parents demand, and ex post, voucher schools will exist that fail to educate children well. Further, as I noted in Neal (2002), in the absence of any regulatory constraints on parental choice, large-scale voucher systems would surely produce some socially harmful schools operated by organizations like the Ku Klux Klan. Finally, policy makers should adopt policies that promote regular health and safety inspections in schools. Even the most vigilant parents are not able to monitor all conditions in their child's school.[1]

6.1.2 Invest in Better Measurement Technologies

Some form of assessment-based accountability is likely necessary to ensure that parents select from a menu of schools that actually promote learning. However, no large-scale assessment systems exist that are designed for the purpose of gathering consequential information about educator performance. The goal of ABI systems is to provide incentives for educators to teach well, which means high-stakes assessments should be designed so that educators find that it is in their best interests to promote subject mastery rather than run test-prep sessions.[2] Researchers and policy makers should spend more time and resources on the development of assessments that cover a well-defined curriculum but are less predictable and therefore less coachable than most modern assessments. Such assessments will likely vary enough in form and content each year that the results will provide little information about secular trends in achievement, but this is a good thing.[3] When high-stakes assessment systems do not produce scaled achievement scores but only percentile scores that describe where students rank in the achievement distribution, accountability policies must be built around relative comparisons among educators, and this commitment to relative performance metrics is quite valuable.

6.1.3 Relative Performance

In Chapter 2, we noted that consequential public reports about the performance of publicly funded educators must not contain judgments concerning whether or not the performance of specific students, teachers, principals, or schools meet or fail to meet certain standards. Such reports are difficult to verify and therefore easy to corrupt. Thus, it is not surprising that the literature contains evidence that rating systems built around such reports often produce inflated ratings.[4]

Policy makers can avoid these problems by building accountability systems around relative performance metrics. Imagine the set of all teachers who teach algebra to ninth-grade students in a particular district or state. If the district reports all measures of performance for these teachers in terms of percentile ranks, political pressures cannot induce evaluators to inflate teacher ratings across the board. Evaluators can only rank one teacher first, and they can only rank 10 percent of teachers in the top decile of the performance distribution. Likewise, they must assign 10 percent of teachers to the bottom decile and must designate some teacher as the worst performer. Systems that require evaluators to report only percentile ranks should reduce false reports about educator performance.[5]

6.1.4 Testing under No Stakes

Having said this, we also noted in Chapter 2 that educational standards are a necessary tool for education policy makers. Standards define objectives for educators. Further, policy makers need to assess student achievement relative to fixed standards in order to gauge what distributions of skills students possess and how achievement levels today compare to levels among previous cohorts.

This observation implies that education authorities must operate two assessment systems: one that creates consequential relative performance metrics for educators, and a second that produces scaled measures of student achievement relative to known standards. In addition, the latter must be a no-stakes system; that is, the results should create no consequences for individual students or educators. This approach removes incentives for educators to engage in coaching and other gaming behaviors that have often inflated and distorted the measures of student achievement produced by high-stakes accountability systems like NCLB.[6]

6.1.5 Collect True Parental Preferences

Pathak (2016) argues that centralized school assignment mechanisms should employ some form of the deferred acceptance algorithm in order to create an environment where families have common knowledge that truth telling is in everyone's best interest and where the final assignment of students to public schools respects the broad criteria that govern student priorities in different schools. I would go a step further and argue that it would likely be useful to force all schools that receive any public funding to participate in a common DA mechanism.

Imagine the following process. Each spring, let all schools that are eligible to receive funding from a given district (e.g., traditional public, charter, and voucher) post information about their schools online in a portal maintained by the district. Assume that the portal includes information about each school's location, teachers, past record of student achievement, safety records, measures of parental satisfaction with the school, etc. In some districts, the portal might also contain information about fee schedules in voucher or charter schools. Let schools that plan to open for the first time in the fall post a prospectus that describes the organizational and educational practices that the school will follow.

During the month of May, allow parents to visit open houses at various schools in order to gain more information about schools they deem interesting. Also, allow schools to interview families and collect information about potential students. Then, in July, require schools to submit a seating capacity for each grade and a formula that produces priority rankings over all students in each grade. Each district must determine whether and how to restrict the types of formulas that schools may submit.[7] After each school has submitted its priority formula, require all students who do not have a school assignment for the fall or who desire to change schools to submit a rank-ordered list of N schools. N should vary with the size of the district, but N should always be large enough to eliminate concerns about strategic behavior. Finally, run student-proposing DA and assign students to schools.

I have left out many design details, but regardless of how policy makers implement such a system, ex post they will possess detailed information from parents concerning their actual preferences over schools. This information should help education authorities improve resource allocation.

Consider the following scenario. Let school A be a hypothetical K–5 elementary school in such a system. Suppose that each year for the past five years, a higher fraction of the current students assigned to school A enter the DA mechanism and seek a transfer than from any other school in the district. Further, suppose no families of entering kindergarten students list A as their first choice, even though hundreds of kindergarten families live within walking distance of school A. Given many different models of how parents form preferences over schools, this information would justify enhanced scrutiny of school A, and this scrutiny could produce grounds for removing school A from the set of schools eligible to receive district funds.

Existing research does not tell us a great deal about how policy makers should use all of the information that such a mechanism would produce. We know little about how parents gather the information they use to rank schools. Further, we saw in the previous chapter that if parents rank schools based on their preferences for the peers that they expect their children to have in different schools, truth telling may no longer be an optimal strategy for parents, and it is not clear how policy makers should use the information contained in the preference orderings that parents report.

Nonetheless, the mechanism I describe here requires all schools that receive public funds to provide certain types of information for prospective students and also requires parents to submit rankings. These features may enable and motivate parents to make more informed decisions about their children's schooling. Economists must continue to explore how policy makers can best use the information that parents acquire.

6.1.6 Compete for Students by Competing for Educators

The quality of education hinges on the performance of teachers in classrooms. The best curriculum decisions, the best instructional technologies, and the best school facilities are not worth much if teachers do not teach well. So beneficial regulated competition among schools should induce innovation among schools in practices that govern the recruiting, hiring, training, compensation, retention, and promotion of educators.

It is logically possible that competition could produce labor markets for teachers that still exhibit many of the features that characterize employment relationships between teachers and public school districts now, such as pay compression, short tenure clocks, and robust employment protections. However, existing personnel practices in many successful charter schools are quite different.

Policies that govern regulated competition among schools should not require teachers in publicly funded schools to join unions or work under district-wide civil service contracts. Any organization that obtains the right to negotiate terms of employment for all teachers in publicly funded schools enjoys something close to a de facto monopoly on the supply of publicly funded education services, and we should expect such an organization to exploit its monopoly position.

If a single manufacturer enjoyed the right to act as the monopoly producer of all engines used in lawnmowers, the existence of many different lawnmower manufacturers would not imply efficient outcomes in the market for lawnmowers. The prices of various lawnmowers would likely exceed socially efficient levels because the engine manufacturer would use its monopoly position in the engine market to extract surplus from the lawnmower market.

Teachers are the educational engines of schools. If schools are not allowed to actively compete for educators by exploring ways to improve personnel and organizational practices that determine training, incentives, and job assignments for educators, the value of forcing schools to compete for students is greatly diminished.

6.2 Moving Forward

Large literatures in economics consider how governments can maximize the social surplus created from selling assets, or how governments can minimize the costs of procuring particular goods or services. Researchers who study these questions pay particular attention to information constraints, and their conclusions about the optimal design of various mechanisms hinge on assumptions concerning who gets to observe different types of actions, who has access to different types of performance information, and what types of information courts can verify.

In this book, we have examined various education reform proposals and the empirical results derived from evaluations of these reforms while trying to highlight the importance of hidden actions, hidden information, and verifiability. We have repeatedly explored problems that arise because the work of educators is difficult to monitor and the output that educators produce is difficult to measure and value. We have also seen that granting parents control over the public funds allocated for the education of their children does not solve all of these information problems.

Yet economists have only begun to explore how information problems complicate the design of education policies. Neal (2011) reviews the limited literature on the optimal design of assessment-based incentive systems, but economists who work on charter schools and voucher systems have not carefully explored the optimal strategies for constraining the school choice set available to different parents. This is a thorny problem because some parents are both well-informed and well-intentioned but others are not, and education authorities cannot directly observe the type of any particular set of parents. Finally, economists should be studying the costs and benefits of different ways to incorporate charter and voucher schools into centralized school assignment mechanisms.

Progress on these questions may yield important welfare gains. In the developed world alone, governments spend trillions of dollars on education services for children. Economists need to devote more energy to characterizing the optimal mechanisms for spending so much public money.

Notes

Introduction

1. See Table B-28 in Obama (2011).
2. See Becker (1993), Mincer (1958), Mincer (1974), and Schultz (1960).
3. See OECD (2012) for 2012 spending data from OECD countries.
4. Ben-Porath (1967) and Mincer (1974) are two canonical examples.
5. See Cunha and Heckman (2007) and Heckman et al. (2013). Deming (2009), Belfield et al. (2006), and Anderson (2008) provide empirical results that are consistent with these models.
6. To keep things tractable, we not only divide life spans into just three periods but also assume that the skills an individual acquires in one period cannot be used until the next period. This approach may seem strange, but our three-period framework illustrates key insights concerning the optimal sequencing of different types of learning. Further, these qualitative insights remain if we numerically analyze a much more cumbersome model that divides life spans into a large number of shorter periods.
7. See Sektnan et al. (2010).
8. It may have been useful to measure earnings from age 18, since most states do not mandate school attendance after age 17. However, a significant fraction of the NLSY79 respondents were older than 18 at the date of their first interview. By starting at age 20, we get many more observations per cell.
9. See Bertrand et al. (2010), Gicheva (2013), and Altonji et al. (2012).
10. For example, Figures I.1 and I.2 show that the variance of earnings among education groups from a given cohort first declines and then increases as the cohort ages. This pattern is expected within the human capital framework and has been documented in many data sets. Also, the fact that the profiles for the most educated workers peak at later ages is also expected since those with greater learning capacities invest more in productive skills.

11. See Willis and Rosen (1979), Card (1999), and Bhuller et al. (2017) for more on this topic.
12. See Becker and Tomes (1986) and Mulligan (1997).
13. See Becker and Tomes (1986). Wealthy parents should equate the marginal returns of different forms of giving to their children, which implies that they should invest efficiently in their child's education.
14. See De Nardi et al. (2015).
15. For idiosyncratic reasons, Joe or any other person may earn more or less than the expected return on their schooling, but these deviations average out if the government is financing the schooling of millions of children.
16. We could tell a similar story about Joe's education even if Joe came from a wealthy family. The only difference is that the government would be financing investments that Joe's family may have made on their own.
17. See Grossman (2006).
18. Friedman and Friedman (2002) argue that governments should fund public education so that citizens gain the skills and common values necessary for a stable democratic society. Lucas (1988) suggests that skilled workers may generate productivity spillovers that are not fully reflected in individuals' wages. Such spillovers provide another potential rationale for governments to subsidize education.
19. See Bils and Klenow (2000), Lange and Topel (2006), and Manuelli and Seshadri (2014).
20. There is nearly universal agreement among scholars and policy makers that governments should fund mandatory schooling for children. Even in less developed countries, policy makers now tout universal primary education as an important policy goal. See Bruns et al. (2011).
21. Here, we assume that all agents enjoy full information about the consequences of their actions. They know with perfect certainty how changes in skill investments will change their future earnings. This assumption simplifies the math, but the key lessons we derive from this model remain in versions that incorporate uncertainty. We also ignore the effort costs associated with learning and working. This allows us to focus on income maximization and greatly simplifies our analysis.
22. See Ben-Porath (1967).
23. See Cunha and Heckman (2007) for more on technologies that describe the production of multiple skills.
24. I thank Jorge Luis Garcia for excellent work on the numerical simulations.

Chapter 1: Resources and Outcomes

1. See https://www.bls.gov/cps/cpsaat39.htm.

2. See Dunn (2012).

3. In 1995, the Supreme Court ruled that Judge Clark should begin the process of restoring local control of the schools. See *Missouri v. Jenks*, 515 U.S. 70 (1995).

4. According to Dunn (2012), some scores for students in grades K–4 did improve, but these gains evaporated as students progressed into middle school.

5. See Ciotti (1998) and Dunn (2012).

6. The case *Abbott v. Burke* generated a series of New Jersey Supreme Court decisions that mandated increases in funding for most districts and particularly large increases for the Abbott districts, a collection of low-income districts that have large populations of minority students. Evidence on changes in student achievement among the Abbott districts has been mixed. See Coate and Vander-Hoff (1999) and Goertz and Weiss (2009). See Hanushek and Lindseth (2009) for an account of a similar episode in Wyoming. Trends in student achievement, relative to nearby states or the nation as a whole, do not provide any evidence that the large court-mandated increases in spending raised student achievement. Here, the schools involved were not urban or predominately minority.

7. See Hanushek (1986), Hanushek (2003), and Hanushek and Rivkin (2006).

8. See Flyer and Rosen (1997) and Eide et al. (2004).

9. Card and Krueger (1992) attempt to measure the relationship between school resources and the slopes of log earning profiles with respect to education among individuals who were born in different states but moved to the same state as adults. They conclude that additional school resources raise realized returns to education. However, results in Speakman and Welch (2006) suggest that, among migrants, relationships between birth states, destination states, and wage rates do not satisfy restrictions implied by the identifying assumptions that Card and Krueger (1992) employ. Further, Heckman et al. (1996) highlight reasons that differences in these state-specific slopes may not be good proxies for differences in effective school quality.

10. Yinger (2004a) provides an overview of court-ordered school finance reforms beginning with the 1971 *Serrano v. Priest* decision by the California Supreme Court.

11. See Hoxby (2001).

12. See Yinger (2004b).

13. See Downes (1992), Downes et al. (1998), and Hoxby (2001).

14. See Lafortune et al. (2016), Jackson et al. (2016), and Papke (2005).

15. Some researchers introduce peer effects in equation (1.1). In these models, the rate at which students learn is also influenced by the characteristics of their classmates. Here, we ignore peer effects. This approach simplifies the presentation of empirical models of education production.

16. Our discussion draws heavily on the material in Todd and Wolpin (2003). See Krueger (1998) and Hanushek (1997) for different perspectives on the literature.

17. However, the points we discuss also apply in some form to our simple cross-section model in equation (1.2) as well.

18. The vector, $\hat{a}_{ijt}$, is as close as possible to the vector of achievement levels, a_{ijt}, given that these fitted values must be linear combinations of the regressors. Further, $\hat{\alpha}$, $\hat{\gamma}$ and $\hat{\beta}$ are consistent estimators of the parameters in the best linear approximation of $E(a_{ijt}|a_{ijt-1}, \bar{z}_{jt}, \bar{x}_{it})$.

19. Measurement error in lagged achievement measures would not bias our estimate of the effect of class size on expected achievement if true past achievement were orthogonal to class size.

20. See Ballou and Podgursky (1997).

21. It seems reasonable to assume that most parents do not know when specific teachers in their local school acquire master's degrees. Therefore, we do not expect parents to change their behavior when their child's teacher finishes a master's program.

22. These classes could be during the regular school term. However, if policy makers worried that heavier teaching loads would diminish overall performance, teachers could teach these additional classes during summer school.

23. We are ruling out the possibility that more practice teaching could make teachers worse.

24. Some charter school organizations advocate post-graduate teacher training models that incorporate a learning-by-doing approach. These models rely heavily on supervised student teaching followed by structured feedback. For example, see http://www.sposatogse.org/ and http://noblenetwork.org/NobleRelay.

25. See Ballou and Podgursky (1997).

26. See Ballou and Podgursky (1997) and Hanushek and Rivkin (2006). Wiswall (2013) provides one set of results that stand in contrast to the rest of the literature. He finds, using data from North Carolina, that the performance of fifth-grade math teachers improves steadily, throughout their careers, as they gain more experience. He finds results for reading teachers that parallel those in the existing literature.

27. See Becker and Stigler (1974) and Lazear (1979).

28. Since many union victories in representation elections do not produce contracts, there is no reason to expect these studies to produce the same results.

29. Because current teachers would likely demand even higher salaries if public schools chose to return to 1960 class sizes, it is not possible to know exactly how much the shift to smaller classes contributes to current expenditure levels.

30. Class size is an important driver of school expenditures, but some changes in instructional staff per student are not driven by changes in class size. Teaching loads and the use of teachers for jobs outside the classroom, such as curriculum oversight or other administrative functions, also impact these ratios.

31. There is also evidence that smaller classes create achievement gains in grades 1–3, but these gains appear to be much smaller.

32. See Evans and Popova (2016), Ganimian and Murnane (2016), and Glewwe and Muralidharan (2016).

33. See Duflo et al. (2012) results from an incentive program designed to address this problem.

34. Private schools also hire more teachers per student enrolled.

35. Muralidharan and Sundararaman (2013) also report efficiency gains from staffing public schools with lower-quality but lower-cost contract teachers as opposed to civil service teachers.

36. See Gibbons and Roberts (2013) and Syverson (2011).

37. See Gibbons and Henderson (2012) and Syverson (2011).

38. See Bloom et al. (2017). Private sector firms that employ poor human resource management practices exit at much higher rates than firms that link pay and performance in systematic ways.

Chapter 2: Assessment-Based Incentives

1. See Ballou and Podgursky (1997).

2. See Mosher (1968), Meyer and Brown (1977), and Balfour (1997) for more on the history of civil service reforms in the US.

3. To this point, we have ignored curriculum design issues, and we will continue to do so. Schmidt et al. (1997) report that researchers and policy makers have not established consensus concerning optimal curriculum design, and relative to other scholars, economists have no skills that grant us a comparative or absolute advantage in solving this problem. So, for this book, we take the curriculum that an education authority selects as given, and we ask what education policies induce publicly funded educators to teach children in ways that efficiently build the skills described in this curriculum.

4. In Neal (2011), I draw distinctions between performance-pay systems that map student achievement into explicit bonuses or fines for teachers and assessment-based accountability systems that map student achievement into a variety of sanctions or rewards for educators, such as enhanced oversight, threats of school closure, reductions in funding, etc. Our ABI definition encompasses both approaches.

5. See Gordon et al. (2008), Staiger and Rockoff (2010), and Neal (2011).

6. See Kerr (1975), Campbell (1979), and Holmstrom and Milgrom (1991).

7. See Skolnick (1966), Chapter 8, pp. 167–168.

8. In some cases, these confessions may have been false.

9. See Campbell (1979), page 85.

10. This approach is standard because competition among employers for workers should pressure employers who hire many workers to choose contracts that maximize the surplus available in employer-employee relationships. Thus, the results derived from this framework should also apply to settings where many principals each employ many agents to produce the same output.

11. Impossible to verify at a cost such that production remains profitable.

12. See Besley and Ghatak (2005) for more on personnel practices in mission organizations.

13. To the extent school systems compete with other sectors for educated workers, they must raise base salaries to compensate educators for any change in compensation policies that creates more salary risk.

14. See Appendix 2.13 for the formal derivations.

15. See Georgia Public Policy Foundation (2015), Office of the Governor Special Investigators (2011), and WXIA-TV (2015).

16. See Kingdon (2007), page 181.

17. This feature of NCLB is paradoxical. The rationale for NCLB involved the claim that state education departments and the school districts under their supervision were not making efficient use of federal education funding. Yet NCLB called for the same state education departments to design the measurement systems used to hold them accountable.

18. It is logically possible that the Cronin et al. (2007) results, in part, reflect the effects of educators coaching students on the types of items that were common on their state's NCLB assessments. Nonetheless, the relationship between a student's true subject mastery and the likelihood that his state deemed him proficient changed substantially between 2003 and 2006 in many states. See Koretz and Hamilton (2006) for more on score inflation due to coaching.

19. The eighth-grade results stand out, but the math proficiency rates increases for third and fifth grade were also larger than average. The third-grade rate rose more between 2005 and 2006 than between 2002 and 2005.

20. See Stecher (2002) and Holcombe et al. (2013) for other examples.

21. See Neal (2011) and Koretz and Hamilton (2006).

22. Race to the Top also sought to constrain the capacity of states to inflate their reported proficiency levels by making their own assessments less demanding over time.

23. See http://www2.ed.gov/programs/racetothetop-assessment/index.html.

24. We may never know. In 2013, the Every Student Succeeds Act replaced No Child Left Behind. This new law gives states greater flexibility to determine

the sanctions that schools may face when their students perform poorly on assessments, and many states are moving away from high-stakes accountability systems. This trend may reduce incentives for educators to coach.

25. See Neal (2013) for more details.

26. The first was a district-level system that the city put in place in 1996. The second is the 2002 implementation of NCLB in Illinois.

27. In addition, these ABI systems did not generate clear gains for students whose baseline achievement levels placed them well beyond proficiency.

28. See footnote 44 in Neal and Schanzenbach (2010).

29. See Cronin et al. (2007) and Neal (2011). Koretz and Hamilton (2006) stress that high-stakes testing programs built around standards generate standards-driven instruction that contains many elements that are functionally test-preparation drills and therefore inflate student test scores relative to available low-stakes measures of student achievement. In a sense, Koretz and Hamilton (2006) are describing coaching behaviors that may not fit the technical definition of corruption. However, these coaching behaviors do inflate scores and compromise the meaning of proficiency reports. Further, in some cases, assessment items are so closely tied to the wording of specific learning standards that the line between coaching and cheating becomes blurred.

30. See Koretz and Hamilton (2006), Holcombe et al. (2013), and Neal (2013) for more details.

31. See Koretz (2015) for a more detailed discussion of related issues.

32. It is easy to create examples where teacher A earns a higher PPI score than teacher B, but teacher B produced more valuable learning gains in her classroom.

33. Recall that PFP requires testing agencies to only report assessments results in terms of ranks, that is, within-year percentile scores. Thus, Barlevy and Neal (2012) impose the same information restrictions present in Lazear and Rosen (1981).

34. Barlevy and Neal (2012) point out that policy makers may find it difficult to directly measure P^*. Policy makers who implement PFP may have to experiment with different prize structures in order to learn more about the optimal prize rate.

35. Gains were slightly larger in the treatment arm with higher bonus rates.

36. This gain is an average gain over two different PFP implementations. PFP treatment based on team performance produced a gain of .196 sd, while PFP based on individual performance produced a gain of .178.

37. See Neal (2013) for more.

38. I refuse to participate in any debates concerning whether or not the Common Core standards are the correct standards from society's perspective since I am not qualified to offer an informed opinion.

39. See Neal (2011) for a detailed treatment of this topic.

40. Yet even Chetty et al. (2014b) do not evaluate potential firing rules that are based on absolute performance standards. Rather, they consider replacing different fractions of the left tail of the teacher performance distribution.

41. The exact result would depend on the correlation between effort norms and the marginal cost of exceeding these norms. If those with strong norms face marginal higher costs of exceeding their own personal standards, we expect compression. Since optimal firing rules depend crucially on the variance of potential teacher performance, such compression would invalidate the existing firing and tenure rule calculations in the literature.

42. See Koretz and Hamilton (2006) and Neal (2011) for surveys of this literature. See Taylor and Tyler (2012) for evidence that evaluation and training can improve teacher performance in a setting where teachers face severe consequences if they fail to improve.

43. The performance-pay scheme in Springer et al. (2011) involved performance targets that many educators had little or no chance of meeting. The targets in the New York City experiment described by Goodman and Turner (2013) and Fryer Jr. (2013) were so low that 90% of the control group earned a bonus. In Neal (2011), I point out that incentive systems built around targets and bonuses may elicit no response from workers when targets are so high that workers see them as not attainable or so low that workers believe they can meet them without supplying extra effort.

44. In the United Kingdom, the Office for Standards in Education, Children's Services and Skills (Ofsted) runs a rigorous and consequential school inspection system. These inspections are not announced. They address both academic performance and issues of safety and wellness for the students.

45. See Rothstein (2010), Chetty et al. (2014a), and Jackson et al. (2014).

46. See http://web.mit.edu/rgibbons/www/903%20LN%201%20S10.pdf.

47. HINT: Look up the moment-generating function for a normal random variable.

48. Note that in this example, the base salary would likely be negative. Given this contract, the farmer transfers all the revenue from his farm stand to the picker. In order to cover the costs of growing the tomatoes, the farmer would need to charge the picker a fixed fee for the opportunity to pick and sell. If the picker were risk averse, we would expect a lower bonus rate and a lower fixed fee. In this case, it would be optimal for the farmer to provide partial insurance for the picker.

49. Here, we have assumed $\sigma^2 = 0$, so there are no shocks to the signal. However, if $f \cdot p = 0$, the optimal contract still involves a fixed salary for cases where $\sigma^2 > 0$. Given a fixed salary, the agent bears no effort costs and no salary risk.

Chapter 3: Letting Parents Choose

1. In the balance of this chapter, I draw heavily on material by Pathak (2011 and 2016). I thank Parag Pathak for many helpful discussions of the literature on school assignment mechanisms.
2. See Neal (2009).
3. See http://iipsc.org/projects/ for a list of some US cities that have adopted or are considering such systems.
4. See Roth and Sotomayor (1990) for a detailed treatment of this problem.
5. We require students to submit complete rankings because schooling is mandatory in modern countries. One implication of mandatory schooling is that each student must prefer his least favorite school to not attending school at all.
6. In our example, the total number of lockers in the district is greater than the total number of students, and each student must submit a complete preference ranking over all schools. In practice, some school systems run DA based on preference orderings from students that contain roughly their top five to ten choices. Thus, in practice, the algorithm treats all schools that a student did not rank as schools that she is not willing to attend, which implies that, as in the marriage application, some students may remain unmatched when the algorithm stops.
7. The established convention of endowing students or families with preferences and endowing schools with priorities highlights the idea that schools are objects and not persons.
8. In most instances, we care about the case where $N \geq M$. If this condition fails, some students never get initial room assignments. These students remain without rooms because they have no assignment to claim as their own and therefore no assignment to trade with other students.
9. Recall that no room can belong to two cycles in the same round.
10. The result in Abdulkadiroğlu et al. (2009) is even stronger. Fix the priorities of schools, and consider two mechanisms A and B. Now, imagine comparing the matchings produced by these two mechanisms for each possible set of student preferences. If for all possible preferences, the matching produced by mechanism A weakly Pareto dominates the matching produced by mechanism B, and if there is at least one set of preferences such that the matching produced by A strictly Pareto dominates the matching produced by B, we say that mechanism A dominates mechanism B. Abdulkadiroğlu et al. show that, in settings with coarse priorities and random tiebreaking, no strategy-proof mechanism

dominates DA. Thus, it is immediate that no variation on the two-step procedure proposed by Erdil and Ergin (2008) can be strategy-proof, if the procedure
actually facilitates Pareto improvements in the second step.

11. See Pathak and Sönmez (2008) and Kapor et al. (2017).

12. This priority ranking may rely on random numbers as tiebreakers.

13. See Chen and Sönmez (2006) for experimental results that support the hypothesis that DA is more transparent than TTC.

14. Both now employ DA mechanisms.

15. See iipsc.org.

16. See Abdulkadiroğlu et al. (2011a).

17. Given the limited prerequisites for this book, we cannot explore the details
of the econometric models employed in these papers. Yet you should recognize that researchers must make strong assumptions in order to build empirical
models that take the ordinal preference rankings that families submit to school
assignment mechanisms as inputs and then produce cardinal estimates of the
relative willingness of families to pay for different school assignments as outputs. Return to our story about Jack and Jill, but instead of assuming that Jack
has a much stronger preference for school A than Jill, assume that Jack is risk
loving, and Jill is risk averse. In this alternative scenario, we would again expect
that Jack is more likely to list school A as his first choice, but in this scenario,
Jack is signaling something about his attitudes toward risk and not the strength
of his desire to attend school A.

Chapter 4: Charter Schools

1. Charter authorizers may be agencies within state governments or private, nonprofit organizations that state governments allow to make decisions about charter applications and renewals.

2. See   http://www.chicagotribune.com/news/opinion/commentary/ct-charter-
schools-cap-teachers-union-perspec-20161014-story.html.

3. It is worth nothing that ABI systems may provide metrics that authorizers
consider when making renewal decisions.

4. We return to this topic below when we discuss the dramatic recent expansion
of charter schools in New Orleans. See Abdulkadiroğlu et al. (2016).

5. In our setting, TOT also equals the average treatment effect (ATE) among the
population of lottery applicants. We use TOT terminology to make clear that
these lottery studies only provide information about the population of lottery
applicants. These lottery samples do not allow researchers to estimate the ATE
of lottery schools among the entire population of students.

6. There is also no a priori reason to claim that a given LATE effect should be bigger or smaller than the corresponding TOT average for the entire applicant pool.

7. Black-white test score gaps in math and reading among high school students typically range from about .7 standard deviations to .9 standard deviations. Most of the University of Chicago Charter Schools (UCCS) students in the Hassrick et al. (2017) study began their formal schooling in a UCCS school and never left. Thus, the 6–8 results imply that the cumulative gains for middle school students exceed many measures of the overall black-white test score gap.

8. See Abdulkadiroğlu et al. (2011b) and Hassrick et al. (2017).

9. This is a key potential benefit of both charter and voucher competition. If the leaders of a given school know that they are going to lose their jobs if their school performs poorly, they have strong incentives to search for ways to recruit, train, motivate, and retain excellent teachers. They also face strong incentives to dismiss teachers who cannot or will not teach well. Thus, properly regulated competition among schools for students may provide incentives for schools to compete in the market for teachers in ways that generate rewards for excellence and penalties for poor performance. See Hoxby (2002). In the balance of the book, we will have more to say about the details of proper regulation. This will not involve simply letting all parents choose whatever school they desire.

10. The authors restricted the Pilot sample to students who listed a Pilot school as their first choice. Given that random numbers create strict priorities in the school assignment system, those who gain entrance to Pilot schools are also lottery winners.

11. These conversions are known as takeovers. The authors also present evidence that similar takeovers in Boston have also been successful, but the scale of charter expansion in Boston is much smaller.

12. In private correspondence with the authors, I learned that the point estimate for the total cumulative reading impact is actually larger than the corresponding estimate for the math impact, but this difference is not statistically significant.

13. The increase in four-year college attendance rate is 8.9 percentage points, a 35 percent increase.

14. See Booker et al. (2007), Imberman (2011b), Zimmer et al. (2012), and Cremata et al. (2013).

15. Imberman (2011b) provides evidence that charter schools may improve student attendance and reduce the frequency of conduct infractions that require disciplinary action.

16. The details of the empirical methods in Walters (2014) are beyond the scope of our text, but the key step in his estimation procedure is the estimation of a selection model that allows him to predict expected achievement outcomes

in both charter and public schools for all students. Given this information, he poses a model of school choice where families trade off expected achievement gains against the commuting costs required to attend different schools, holding their current places of residence constant.

17. Location matters because different districts have different rules concerning the transfer of funds from public schools to charter schools based on enrollment flows.

18. See Hoxby (2003), Bettinger (2005), Imberman (2011a), and Winters (2012).

19. Further, the program could verify how funds are used by requiring students to return their laptops to the program after four years. The program could then verify that program members used their computers for school work and did not simply buy laptops and sell them.

20. See Angrist and Imbens (1994), Vytlacil (2002), and Heckman and Vytlacil (2005).

21. You may be asking why anyone would bother applying if he is a never taker. The idea is that new information may arrive between application and the assignment of subsidies by lottery. The same holds in the charter school lottery studies described in this chapter. After families apply for admission to charter schools but before they learn whether or not they win a slot in the admission lottery, they may receive new opportunities (e.g., scholarship to private schools, admission to magnet programs, etc.).

22. See Vytlacil (2002) for a formal treatment of the equivalence between the LATE assumptions and the assumptions that are implicit in most economic models of selection into education, training programs, or other investment activities.

23. Note that, if we assume that all applicants expect the same return from training, this common return must equal our LATE.

Chapter 5: Vouchers

1. Given the presence of fixed operating costs, voucher schools that suffer revenue losses should usually suffer net income losses.

2. For example, assume that preferences are monotonic and that both c and q are normal goods.

3. Here, N is so large that we let $F(\cdot)$ serve as a proxy for the empirical distribution of income in the community.

4. Rouse and Barrow (2009) provide additional details concerning the execution of many of these studies.

5. Evans and Schwab (1995) also report significant attainment gains for minority students and urban students in Catholic schools, but they do not estimate separate effects for urban minorities.

6. See http://www.newsweek.com/race-schools-592637.

7. Some may argue that this cost differential simply reflects the fact that voucher schools often do not enroll students with disabilities. However, the Digest of Educational Statistics reported in 2013 to 2014 that less than 13 percent of students receive services under the Individuals with Disabilities Act. Even if per-pupil spending on these students is double the spending required for other students, the underrepresentation of these students in voucher schools cannot explain the cost savings that voucher schools generate.

8. The second phase also allowed students to use vouchers in religious schools.

9. In 2010–2011, public schools in Florida spent roughly $6,900 per student. See http://www.famisonline.org/wp-content/uploads/2016/06/16-17-FAMIS-FEFP-PPT.pdf.

10. In addition, the literature on public housing demonstrates that it is much more cost effective for governments to give disadvantaged families housing vouchers than to operate public housing projects, and recent research suggests that cities realize large savings when they privatize bus services. See Olsen (2008) and Jerch et al. (2016).

11. Abdulkadiroğlu et al. (2015) report $8,605 as the average per-pupil spending in public schools. This average is an LSP enrollment-weighted average of district spending levels. The LSP enrollment-weighted average tuition in private schools that receive LSP vouchers is $5,311, which is slightly higher than the unweighted average of $4,989.

12. The 75% spending level corresponds to $6,454 per student, which is roughly $1,465 more than the average tuition in LSP schools. Given the results in Abdulkadiroğlu et al. (2015), table 11, predicted achievement changes for LSP students, at this tuition level, are positive in all subjects except science, and the predicted loss in science is quite small.

13. Abdulkadiroğlu et al. (2015) cite an April 22, 2014 *Times-Picayune* article by James Varney that presented results from a survey of over 1,500 LSP parents. Almost all LSP parents felt that their children were both welcome and safe in their new schools. LSP parents were less satisfied with the academic quality of their schools, but roughly 92% still reported that they were satisfied with their child's academic performance.

14. We noted above that Gallego (2013) claims that municipal governments in Chile have often subsidized failing public schools. He also contends that employment protections in the unionized public sector made it difficult for municipal schools to respond to competitive pressure from private schools.

15. For more on this theme, see Hoxby (2003).

16. Nechyba (2000) does not take a stand on how families with high income and high ability create positive externalities, but it is reasonable to conjecture that

such families create positive spillovers, at least in part, through being involved in the monitoring and operation of public schools.

17. Some of the simulation results in Nechyba (2000) imply that these families could lose close to 20 percent of their housing wealth. The model in Nechyba (2000) is quite stylized. There are only three possible districts, and income segregation between districts is limited. It would be easy to construct scenarios that would imply even larger losses for homeowners in small, exclusive suburbs.

18. See Brunner et al. (2001) for related results from an earlier 1993 voucher initiative in California.

19. See Ferreyra (2007) for work on how making religious schools eligible to receive vouchers changes levels of voucher use and patterns of sorting among schools.

20. Interested students may consult Echenique and Yenmez (2007) and Pycia (2012) to begin exploring this literature.

Chapter 6: Putting the Pieces Together

1. It is possible that, given a fully developed voucher system, private accreditation services would emerge to provide these inspections, and government inspections would not be necessary.

2. Hanushek (2009), Koretz and Béguin (2010), and Koretz et al. (2016) propose systems that may deter coaching, but none of these proposals have been implemented on a large scale.

3. See Neal (2013).

4. Neal (2011) describes case studies from England and Portugal, and the literature on dilution of proficiency standards under NCLB.

5. Percentiles are most useful when they describe relative performance within proper comparison sets. For example, teachers should be compared with other teachers who teach the same subject to students from similar backgrounds.

6. See Neal (2011) for a detailed treatment of this topic.

7. All of the policy decisions that shape sorting in choice systems can be conveyed in the set of restrictions that determine how schools may express capacity and priorities. For example, regulators could allow a school to divide its capacity into a number of different mini-schools that each charged different fees and used different rules for prioritizing students. On the other side, families would list their preferences over these mini-schools.

Bibliography

A. Abdulkadiroğlu and T. Sönmez. 2003. School choice. *American Economic Review*, (3): 729–747.

A. Abdulkadiroğlu, P. A. Pathak, A. E. Roth, and T. Sönmez. 2006. Changing the Boston school assignment mechanism. Technical report, National Bureau of Economic Research.

A. Abdulkadiroğlu, P. A. Pathak, and A. E. Roth. 2009. Strategy-proofness versus efficiency in matching with indifferences: Redesigning the NYC high school match. *American Economic Review*, 99(5): 1954–1978.

A. Abdulkadiroğlu, Y.-K. Che, and Y. Yasuda. 2011a. Resolving conflicting preferences in school choice: The "Boston mechanism" reconsidered. *American Economic Review*, 101(1): 399–410.

A. Abdulkadiroğlu, J. D. Angrist, S. M. Dynarski, T. J. Kane, and P. A. Pathak. 2011b. Accountability and flexibility in public schools: Evidence from Boston's charters and pilots. *The Quarterly Journal of Economics*, 126(2): 699–748.

A. Abdulkadiroğlu, P. A. Pathak, and C. R. Walters. 2015. Free to choose: Can school choice reduce school achievement? Technical report, National Bureau of Economic Research.

A. Abdulkadiroğlu, J. D. Angrist, P. D. Hull, and P. A. Pathak. 2016. Charters without lotteries: Testing takeovers in New Orleans and Boston. *American Economic Review*, 106(7): 1878–1920.

A. Abdulkadiroğlu, Yeon-Koo Che, P. A. Pathak, A. E. Roth, and O. Tercieux. 2017. Minimizing justified envy in school choice: The Design of New Orleans' OneApp. *National Bureau of Economic Research*. Working paper.

N. Agarwal and P. Somaini. 2014. Demand analysis using strategic reports: An application to a school choice mechanism. Technical report, National Bureau of Economic Research.

J. G. Altonji, E. Blom, and C. Meghir. 2012. Heterogeneity in human capital investments: High school curriculum, college major, and careers. *Annual Review of Economics*, 4: 185–223.

M. L. Anderson. 2008. Multiple inference and gender differences in the effects of early intervention: A reevaluation of the Abecedarian, Perry Preschool, and Early Training Projects. *Journal of the American Statistical Association*, 103(484): 1481–1495.

J. D. Angrist and G. W. Imbens. 1994. Identification and estimation of local average treatment effects. *Econometrica*, 62(2): 467–475.

J. D. Angrist and V. Lavy. 1999. Using Maimonides' rule to estimate the effect of class size on scholastic achievement. *The Quarterly Journal of Economics*, 114(2): 533–575.

J. D. Angrist, E. Bettinger, E. Bloom, E. King, and M. Kremer. 2002. Vouchers for private schooling in Colombia: Evidence from a randomized natural experiment. *American Economic Review*, 92(5): 1535–1558.

J. D. Angrist, E. Bettinger, and M. Kremer. 2006. Long-term educational consequences of secondary school vouchers: Evidence from administrative records in Colombia. *American Economic Review*, 96(3): 847–862.

J. D. Angrist, S. M. Dynarski, T. J. Kane, P. A. Pathak, and C. R. Walters. 2012. Who benefits from KIPP? *Journal of Policy Analysis and Management*, 31(4): 837–860.

J. D. Angrist, P. A. Pathak, and C. R. Walters. 2013. Explaining charter school effectiveness. *American Economic Journal: Applied Economics*, 5(4): 1–27.

J. D. Angrist, S. R. Cohodes, S. M. Dynarski, P. A. Pathak, and C. R. Walters. 2016. Stand and deliver: Effects of Boston's charter high schools on college preparation, entry, and choice. *Journal of Labor Economics*, 34(2): 275–318.

S. Aud, et al. 2013. The condition of education 2013. NCES 2013–037. *National Center for Education Statistics*.

D. L. Balfour. 1997. Review: Reforming the public service: The search for a new tradition. *Public Administration Review*, 57(5): 459–462.

D. Ballou and M. Podgursky. 1997. *Teacher Pay and Teacher Quality*. W.E. Upjohn Institute.

G. Barlevy and D. Neal. 2012. Pay for percentile. *American Economic Review*, 102(5): 1805–1831.

G. S. Becker. 1993. *Human Capital: A Theoretical and Empirical Analysis, with Special Reference to Education*, 3. University of Chicago Press.

G. S. Becker and G. J. Stigler. 1974. Law enforcement, malfeasance, and compensation of enforcers. *Journal of Legal Studies*, 3(1): 1–18.

G. S. Becker and N. Tomes. 1986. Human capital and the rise and fall of families. *Journal of Labor Economics*, 4(3, Part 2): S1–S39.

C. R. Belfield, M. Nores, S. Barnett, and L. Schweinhart. 2006. The High/Scope Perry Preschool Program: Cost-benefit analysis using data from the age-40 followup. *Journal of Human Resources*, 41(1): 162–190.

Y. Ben-Porath. 1967. The production of human capital and the life cycle of earnings. *Journal of Political Economy*, 75(4, Part 1): 352–365.

M. Bertrand, C. Goldin, and L. F. Katz. 2010. Dynamics of the gender gap for young professionals in the financial and corporate sectors. *American Economic Journal: Applied Economics*, 2(3): 228–255.

T. Besley and M. Ghatak. 2005. Competition and incentives with motivated agents. *American Economic Review*, 95(3): 616–636.

E. Bettinger. 2005. The effect of charter schools on charter students and public schools. *Economics of Education Review*, 24(2): 133–147.

M. Bhuller, M. Mogstad, and K. G. Salvanes. 2017. Life-cycle earnings, education premiums, and internal rates of return. Forthcoming in *Journal of Labor Economics*.

M. Bils and P. J. Klenow. 2000. Does schooling cause growth? *American Economic Review*, 90(5): 1160–1183.

N. Bloom, E. Brynjolfsson, L. Foster, R. S. Jarmin, M. Patnaik, I. Saporta-Eksten, and J. Van Reenen. 2017. What drives differences in management? Technical report, National Bureau of Economic Research.

K. Booker, S. M. Gilpatric, T. Gronberg, and D. Jansen. 2007. The impact of charter school attendance on student performance. *Journal of Public Economics*, 91(5): 849–876.

K. Bradsher. 1999. Detroit mayor is step closer to control of schools. *New York Times*, Mar. 5.

E. Brunner and J. Sonstelie. 2003. Homeowners, property values, and the political economy of the school voucher. *Journal of Urban Economics*, 54(2): 239–257.

E. Brunner, J. Sonstelie, and M. Thayer. 2001. Capitalization and the voucher: An analysis of precinct returns from California's Proposition 174. *Journal of Urban Economics*, 50(3): 517–536.

B. Bruns, D. Filmer, and H. A. Patrinos. 2011. *Making Schools Work through Accountability Reforms*, chapter 5, pp. 211–251. The World Bank.

A. S. Bryk, V. E. Lee, and P. B. Holland. 1993. *Catholic Schools and the Common Good*. Harvard University Press.

C. Calsamiglia, C. Fu, and M. Güell. 2017. Structural estimation of a model of school choices: The Boston mechanism vs. its alternatives, mimeo.

D. T. Campbell. 1979. Assessing the impact of planned social change. *Evaluation and Program Planning*, 2(1): 67–90.

D. Card. 1999. The causal effect of education on earnings. In O. C. Ashenfelter and D. Card, eds., *Handbook of Labor Economics*, volume 3, chapter 30, pp. 1801–1863. Elsevier.

D. Card and A. B. Krueger. 1992. Does school quality matter? Returns to education and the characteristics of public schools in the United States. *Journal of Political Economy*, 100(1): 1–40.

S. Carrell, B. Sacerdote, and J. West. 2013. From natural variation to optimal policy? The importance of endogenous peer group formation. *Econometrica*, 81(3): 855–882.

R. Chakrabarti. 2008. Can increasing private school participation and monetary loss in a voucher program affect public school performance? Evidence from Milwaukee. *Journal of Public Economics*, 92(5-6): 1371–1393.

Y. Chen and T. Sönmez. 2006. School choice: An experimental study. *Journal of Economic Theory*, 127(1): 202–231.

R. Chetty, J. N. Friedman, N. Hilger, E. Saez, D. W. Schanzenbach, and D. Yagan. 2011. How does your kindergarten classroom affect your earnings? Evidence from Project STAR. *The Quarterly Journal of Economics*, 126(4): 1593–1660.

R. Chetty, J. N. Friedman, and J. E. Rockoff. 2014a. Measuring the impacts of teachers I: Evaluating bias in teacher value-added estimates. *American Economic Review*, 104(9): 2593–2632.

R. Chetty, J. N. Friedman, and J. E. Rockoff. 2014b. Measuring the impacts of teachers II: Teacher value-added and student outcomes in adulthood. *American Economic Review*, 104(9): 2633–2679.

M. M. Chingos. 2012. The impact of a universal class-size reduction policy: Evidence from Florida's statewide mandate. *Economics of Education Review* 31.5: 543–562.

M. M. Chingos and P. E. Peterson. 2011. It's easier to pick a good teacher than to train one: Familiar and new results on the correlates of teacher effectiveness. *Economics of Education Review*, 30(3): 449–465.

M. M. Chingos and P. E. Peterson. 2012. The effects of school vouchers on college enrollment: Experimental evidence from New York City. Technical report, Brown Center on Education Policy at Brookings.

P. Ciotti. 1998. *Money and School Performance: Lessons from the Kansas City Desegregation Experiment*. Number 298. Cato Institute.

D. Clark and P. Martorell. 2014. The signaling value of a high school diploma. *Journal of Political Economy*, 122(2): 282–318.

C. T. Clotfelter, H. F. Ladd, J. L. Vigdor, and R. A. Diaz. 2004. Do school accountability systems make it more difficult for low-performing schools to attract and retain high-quality teachers? *Journal of Policy Analysis and Management*, 23(2): 251–271.

D. Coate and J. VanderHoff. 1999. Public school spending and student achievement: The case of New Jersey. *Cato Journal*, 19(1): 85–99.

County of Los Angeles District Attorney, news release, May 9, 2014. Two charged With stealing $5.4 million from LAUSD through false invoices.

E. Cremata, E. Cremata, D. Davis, K. Dickey, K. Lawyer, Y. Negassi, M. E. Raymond, and J. L. Woodworth. 2013. National charter school study. Technical report, Center for Research on Education Outcomes, Stanford University.

J. Cronin, M. Dahlin, D. Adkins, and G. G. Kingsbury. 2007. The proficiency illusion. Technical report, Thomas B. Fordham Institute.

F. Cunha and J. J. Heckman. 2007. The technology of skill formation. *American Economic Review*, 97(2): 31–47.

F. Cunha, J. Heckman, and S. Schennach. 2010. Estimating the technology of cognitive and noncognitive skill formation. *Econometrica*, 78(3): 883–931.

V. E. Curto and R. G. Fryer Jr. 2014. The potential of urban boarding schools for the poor: Evidence from SEED. *Journal of Labor Economics*, 32(1): 65–93.

D Magazine, April 1998. White collar robbery?

M. De Nardi, E. French, and J. B. Jones, 2015. Couples' and singles' savings after retirement. Working paper.

D. Deming. 2009. Early childhood intervention and life-cycle skill development: Evidence from Head Start. *American Economic Journal: Applied Economics*, 1(3): 111–134.

J. Dixon. 2013. Ex-accountant gets 70 months in prison for stealing from Detroit Public Schools. *Detroit Free Press*, Dec. 18.

W. Dobbie and R. G. Fryer Jr. 2011. Are high-quality schools enough to increase achievement among the poor? Evidence from the Harlem Children's Zone. *American Economic Journal: Applied Economics*, 3(3): 158–187.

W. Dobbie and R. G. Fryer Jr. 2013. Getting beneath the veil of effective schools: Evidence from New York City. *American Economic Journal: Applied Economics*, 5(4): 28–60.

W. Dobbie and R. G. Fryer Jr. 2015. The medium-term impacts of high-achieving charter schools. *Journal of Political Economy*, 123(5): 985–1037.

T. A. Downes. 1992. Evaluating the impact of school finance reform on the provision of public education: The California case. *National Tax Journal*, 45(4): 405–419.

T. A. Downes, R. F. Dye, and T. J. McGuire. 1998. Do limits matter? Evidence on the effects of tax limitations on student performance. *Journal of Urban Economics*, 43(3): 401–417.

E. Duflo, R. Hanna, and S. P. Ryan. 2012. Incentives work: Getting teachers to come to school. *American Economic Review*, 102(4): 1241–1278.

J. M. Dunn. 2012. *Complex Justice: The Case of Missouri v. Jenkins*. UNC Press Books.

M. Dynarski, N. Rui, A. Webber, and B. Gutmann. 2017. *Evaluation of the DC Opportunity Scholarship Program: Impacts after One Year (NCEE 2017-4022)*. National Center for Education Evaluation and Regional Assistance, Institute of Education Sciences, US Department of Education.

S. Dynarski, J. Hyman, and D. W. Schanzenbach. 2013. Experimental evidence on the effect of childhood investments on postsecondary attainment and degree completion. *Journal of Policy Analysis and Management*, 32(4): 692–717.

F. Echenique and M. B. Yenmez. 2007. A solution to matching with preferences over colleagues. *Games and Economic Behavior*, 59(1): 46–71.

E. Eide, D. Goldhaber, and D. Brewer. 2004. The teacher labour market and teacher quality. *Oxford Review of Economic Policy*, 20(2): 230–244.

M. Eng. 2014. Still more questions in case of deceased CPS worker who stole school funds. WBEZ, Jan. 14.

D. Epple and R. E. Romano. 1998. Competition between private and public schools, vouchers, and peer-group effects. *American Economic Review*, 88(1): 33–62.

D. Epple and R. E. Romano. 2008. Educational vouchers and cream skimming. *International Economic Review*, 49(4): 1395–1435.

D. Epple and R. E. Romano. 2011. Peer effects in education: A survey of the theory and evidence. In J. Benhabib, A. Bisin, and M. O. Jackson, eds., *Handbook of Social Economics*, volume 1B, chapter 20, pp. 1053–1163. Elsevier.

D. Epple, R. E. Romano, and M. Urquiola. 2015. School vouchers: A survey of the economics literature. *Journal of Economic Literature*, 55(2): 441–492.

D. Epple, R. E. Romano, and R. Zimmer. 2016. Charter schools: A survey of research on their characteristics and effectiveness. In E. A. Hanushek, S. J. Machin, and L. Woessmann, eds., *Handbook of the Economics of Education*, chapter 3, pp. 139–208. Elsevier.

A. Erdil and H. Ergin. 2008. What's the matter with tie-breaking? Improving efficiency in school choice. *American Economic Review*, 98(3): 669–689.

D. K. Evans and A. Popova. 2016. What really works to improve learning in developing countries? An analysis of divergent findings in systematic reviews. *The World Bank Research Observer*, 31(2): 242–270.

W. Evans and R. Schwab. 1995. Finishing high school and starting college: Do Catholic schools make a difference? *The Quarterly Journal of Economics*, 110(4): 941–974.

M. M. Ferreyra. 2007. Estimating the effects of private school vouchers in multidistrict economies. *American Economic Review*, 97(3): 789–817.

D. Figlio and C. M. D. Hart. 2014. Competitive effects of means-tested school vouchers. *American Economic Journal: Applied Economics*, 6(1): 133–156.

F. Flyer and S. Rosen. 1997. The new economics of teachers and education. *Journal of Labor Economics*, 15(1, Part 2): S104–S139.

P. Fredriksson, B. Öckert, and H. Oosterbeek. 2012. Long-term effects of class size. *The Quarterly Journal of Economics*, 128(1): 249–285.

M. Friedman and R. D. Friedman. 2002. *Capitalism and Freedom*, fortieth anniversary. University of Chicago Press.

R. Fryer, S. Levitt, J. List, and S. Sadoff. 2013. Enhancing the efficacy of teacher incentives through loss aversion: A field experiment. Working paper.

R. G. Fryer Jr. 2013. Teacher incentives and student achievement: Evidence from New York City public schools. *Journal of Labor Economics*, 31(2): 373–407.

R. G. Fryer Jr. 2014. Injecting charter school best practices into traditional public schools: Evidence from field experiments. *The Quarterly Journal of Economics*, 129(3): 1355–1407.

D. Gale and L. S. Shapley. 1962. College admissions and the stability of marriage. *The American Mathematical Monthly*, 69(1): 9–15.

F. Gallego. 2013. When does inter-school competition matter? Evidence from the Chilean "voucher" system. *The B.E. Journal of Economic Analysis & Policy*, 13(2): 525–562.

A. J. Ganimian and R. J. Murnane. 2016. Improving education in developing countries: Lessons from rigorous impact evaluations. *Review of Educational Research*, 86(3): 719–755.

Georgia Public Policy Foundation. 2015. The Atlanta Public Schools cheating scandal. Technical report, Georgia Public Policy Foundation.

R. Gibbons and R. Henderson. 2012. What do managers do? Exploring persistent performance differences among seemingly similar enterprises. In R. Gibbons and J. Roberts, eds., *The Handbook of Organizational Economics*, chapter 17, pp. 680–731. Princeton University Press.

R. Gibbons and J. Roberts. 2013. Introduction. In R. Gibbons and J. Roberts, eds., *The Handbook of Organizational Economics*, pp. 1–8. Princeton University Press.

D. Gicheva. 2013. Working long hours and early career outcomes in the high-end labor market. *Journal of Labor Economics*, 31(4): 785–824.

D. Gilligan, N. Karachiwalla, I. Kasiyre, A. Lucas, and D. Neal. 2017. Educator incentives and educational triage in rural primary schools. Technical report, mimeo.

P. Gleason, M. Clark, C. C. Tuttle, and E. Dwoyer. 2010. The evaluation of charter school impacts: Final report. Technical report, National Center for Education Evaluation and Regional Assistance, Institute of Education Sciences, US Department of Education.

P. Glewwe and K. Muralidharan. 2016. Improving education outcomes in developing countries: Evidence, knowledge gaps, and policy implications. In E. A. Hanushek, S. Machin, and L. Woessmann, eds., *Handbook of the Economics of Education*, chapter 10, pp. 653–744. Elsevier.

M. E. Goertz and M. Weiss. 2009. Assessing success in school finance litigation: The case of New Jersey. Education, equity, and the law, no. 1. Technical report, Campaign for Educational Equity, Teachers College, Columbia University.

D. Gollin. 2002. Getting income shares right. *Journal of Political Economy*, 110(2): 458–474.

S. F. Goodman and L. J. Turner. 2013. The design of teacher incentive pay and educational outcomes: Evidence from the New York City bonus program. *Journal of Labor Economics*, 31(2): 409–420.

R. Gordon, T. J. Kane, and D. O. Staiger. 2008. Identifying effective teachers using performance on the job. In J. E. B. Jason Furman, ed., *Path to Prosperity: Hamilton Project Ideas on Income Security, Education, and Taxes*, pp. 189–226. Brookings Institution Press.

J. Grogger and D. Neal. 2000. Further evidence on the effects of Catholic secondary schooling. *Brookings-Wharton Papers on Urban Affairs*, pp. 151–201.

M. Grossman. 2006. Education and nonmarket outcomes. In E. A. Hanushek and F. Welch, eds., *Handbook of the Economics of Education*, chapter 10, pp. 577–633. Elsevier.

E. A. Hanushek. 1986. The economics of schooling: Production and efficiency in public schools. *Journal of Economic Literature*, 24(3): 1141–1177.

E. A. Hanushek. 1997. Assessing the effects of school resources on student performance: An update. *Educational Evaluation and Policy Analysis*, 19(2): 141–164.

E. A. Hanushek. 2003. The failure of input-based schooling policies. *The Economic Journal*, 113(485): F64–F98.

E. A. Hanushek. 2009. Building on No Child Left Behind. *Science*, 326(5954): 802–803.

E. A. Hanushek and A. A. Lindseth. 2009. *Schoolhouses, Courthouses, and Statehouses: Solving the Funding-Achievement Puzzle in America's Public Schools*. Princeton University Press.

E. A. Hanushek and S. G. Rivkin. 2006. Teacher quality. In E. A. Hanushek and F. Welch, eds., *Handbook of the Economics of Education*, volume 2, chapter 18, pp. 1051–1078. Elsevier.

E. M. Hassrick, S. W. Raudenbush, and L. Rosen. 2017. *The Ambitious Elementary School: Its Conception, Design and Implications for Educational Equality*. University of Chicago Press.

F. Hayek. 1945. The use of knowledge in society. *American Economic Review*, 35(4): 519–530.

Y. He. 2016. Gaming the Boston School Choice Mechanism in Beijing. Working paper.

J. Heard and M. O'Connor. 1995. Ex-city school official indicted. Bribery, price-fixing schemes are alleged. *Chicago Tribune*, Dec. 1.

J. J. Heckman and E. Vytlacil. 2005. Structural equations, treatment effects, and econometric policy evaluation. *Econometrica*, 73(3): 669–738.

J. J. Heckman, A. Layne-Farrar, and P. E. Todd. 1996. Human capital pricing equations with an application to estimating the effect of schooling quality on earnings. *The Review of Economics and Statistics*, 78(4): 562.

J. J. Heckman, R. Pinto, and P. Savelyev. 2013. Understanding the mechanisms through which an influential early childhood program boosted adult outcomes. *American Economic Review*, 103(6): 2052–2086.

R. Holcombe, J. L. Jennings, and D. M. Koretz. 2013. The roots of score inflation: An examination of opportunities in two states' tests. In G. L. Sunderman, ed., *Charting Reform, Achieving Equity in a Diverse Nation*, chapter 7, pp. 163–190. Information Age Publishing.

B. Holmstrom and P. Milgrom. 1991. Multitask principal-agent analyses: Incentive contracts, asset ownership, and job design. *Journal of Law, Economics, and Organization*, 7(Special Issue): 24–52.

W. G. Howell and P. E. Peterson. 2002. *The Education Gap: Vouchers and Urban Schools*. Brookings Institution Press.

C. M. Hoxby. 1996. How teachers' unions affect education production. *Quarterly Journal of Economics*, 111(3): 671–718.

C. M. Hoxby. 2000. The effects of class size on student achievement: New evidence from population variation. *The Quarterly Journal of Economics*, 115(4): 1239–1285.

C. M. Hoxby. 2001. All school finance equalizations are not created equal. *The Quarterly Journal of Economics*, 116(4): 1189–1231.

C. M. Hoxby. 2002. Would school choice change the teaching profession? *The Journal of Human Resources*, 37(4): 846–891.

C. M. Hoxby. 2003. School choice and school productivity: Could school choice be a tide that lifts all boats? In C. M. Hoxby, ed., *The Economics of School Choice*, chapter 8, pp. 287–341. University of Chicago Press.

C. M. Hoxby, J. L. Kang, and S. Murarka. 2009. How New York City's charter schools affect achievement. Technical report, The New York City Charter Schools Evaluation Project.

S. Hwang. 2016. A robust redesign of high school match. *EAI Endorsed Transactions on Serious Games*, 3(11).

S. A. Imberman. 2011a. The effect of charter schools on achievement and behavior of public school students. *Journal of Public Economics*, 95(7–8): 850–863.

S. A. Imberman. 2011b. Achievement and behavior in charter schools: Drawing a more complete picture. *Review of Economics and Statistics*, 93(2): 416–435.

C. K. Jackson, J. E. Rockoff, and D. O. Staiger. 2014. Teacher effects and teacher-related policies. *Annual Review of Economics*, 6: 801–825.

C. K. Jackson, R. C. Johnson, and C. Persico. 2016. The effects of school spending on educational and economic outcomes: Evidence from school finance reforms. *The Quarterly Journal of Economics*, 131(1): 157–218.

B. A. Jacob and S. D. Levitt. 2003. Rotten apples: An investigation of the prevalence and predictors of teacher cheating. *The Quarterly Journal of Economics*, 118(3): 843–877.

B. A. Jacob and J. Rothstein. 2016. The measurement of student ability in modern assessment systems. *Journal of Economic Perspectives*, 30(3): 85–108.

R. Jerch, M. E. Kahn, and S. Li. 2016. Efficient local government service provision: The role of privatization and public sector unions. Technical report, National Bureau of Economic Research.

T. J. Kane, D. F. McCaffrey, T. Miller, and D. O. Staiger. 2013. Have we identified effective teachers? Validating measures of effective teaching using random assignment. Technical report, Bill & Melinda Gates Foundation.

A. Kapor, C. A. Neilson, and S. D. Zimmerman. 2017. Heterogeneous beliefs and school choice mechanisms. Working paper.

B. Keller. 1997. 7 Dallas employees suspended in suspected fraud. *Education Week*, Jun. 5.

S. Kerr. 1975. On the folly of rewarding A, while hoping for B. *Academy of Management Journal*, 18(4): 769–783.

T. Kim. 2001. FBI ends corruption probe that plagued Dallas District. *Education Week*, Dec. 12.

G. G. Kingdon. 2007. The progress of school education in India. *Oxford Review of Economic Policy*, 23(2): 168–195.

D. M. Koretz. 2015. Adapting educational measurement to the demands of test-based accountability. *Measurement: Interdisciplinary Research and Perspectives*, 13(1): 1–25.

D. M. Koretz and A. Béguin. 2010. Self-monitoring assessments for educational accountability systems. *Measurement: Interdisciplinary Research & Perspective*, 8(2–3): 92–109.

D. M. Koretz and L. S. Hamilton. 2006. Testing for accountability in K-12. In R. L. Brennan, ed., *Educational Measurement*, chapter 15, pp. 531–578. Praeger, 4.

D. M. Koretz, J. L. Jennings, H. L. Ng, C. Yu, D. Braslow, and M. Langi. 2016. Auditing for score inflation using self-monitoring assessments: Findings from three pilot studies. *Educational Assessment*, 21(4): 231–247.

A. B. Krueger. 1998. Reassessing the view that American schools are broken. *Federal Reserve Bank of New York Economic Policy Review*, 4(1): 29–43.

A. B. Krueger. 1999. Experimental estimates of education production functions. *The Quarterly Journal of Economics*, 114(2): 497–532.

A. B. Krueger and D. M. Whitmore. 2001. The effect of attending a small class in the early grades on college-test taking and middle school test results: Evidence from Project STAR. *The Economic Journal*, 111(468): 1–28.

J. Lafortune, J. Rothstein, and D. W. Schanzenbach. School finance reform and the distribution of student achievement. Forthcoming in *American Economic Journal: Applied Economics*.

F. Lange and R. Topel. 2006. The social value of education and human capital. In E. A. Hanushek and F. Welch, eds., *Handbook of the Economics of Education*, chapter 8, pp. 460–509. Elsevier.

E. P. Lazear. 1979. Why is there mandatory retirement? *Journal of Political Economy*, 87(6): 1261–1284.

E. P. Lazear and S. Rosen. 1981. Rank-order tournaments as optimum labor contracts. *Journal of Political Economy*, 89(5): 841–864.

M. F. Lovenheim. 2009. The effect of teachers' unions on education production: Evidence from union election certifications in three midwestern states. *Journal of Labor Economics*, 27(4): 525–587.

P. Loyalka, S. Sylvia, C. Liu, J. Chu, and Y. Shi, 2016. Pay by design: Teacher performance pay design and the distribution of student achievement. Working paper.

R. E. Lucas. 1988. On the mechanics of economic development. *Journal of Monetary Economics*, 22(1): 3–42.

Mackinac Center for Public Policy, Nov. 17, 2002. Financial scandals exposed in Michigan school districts.

R. E. Manuelli and A. Seshadri. 2014. Human capital and the wealth of nations. *American Economic Review*, 104(9): 2736–2762.

M. W. Meyer and M. C. Brown. 1977. The process of bureaucratization. *American Journal of Sociology*, 83(2): 364–385.

B. Miller. 1998. Founder of Kedar School convicted of wire fraud. *Washington Post*, Mar. 12.

J. Mincer. 1958. Investment in human capital and personal income distribution. *Journal of Political Economy*, 66(4): 281–302.

J. Mincer. 1974. *Schooling, Experience, and Earnings: Human Behavior & Social Institutions No. 2*. National Bureau of Economic Research.

F. C. Mosher. 1968. *Democracy and the Public Service*. Oxford University Press.

C. B. Mulligan. 1997. *Parental Priorities and Economic Inequality*. University of Chicago Press.

K. Muralidharan and V. Sundararaman. 2013. Contract teachers: Experimental evidence from India. Technical report, National Bureau of Economic Research.

K. Muralidharan and V. Sundararaman. 2015. The aggregate effect of school choice: Evidence from a two-stage experiment in India. *The Quarterly Journal of Economics*, 130(3): 1011–1066.

R. Nardoza. 2005. Sixteen New York City Public School custodian engineers and one vendor charged with theft and misapplication of Department of Education funds. More than one-half million dollars misapplied, embezzled or stolen, and more than $329,000 received in kickbacks. United States Attorney's Office, May 5.

National Center for Education Statistics. *Digest of Education Statistics*, 2007a: Table 172, Total and current expenditures per pupil in fall enrollment in public elementary and secondary education, by function and state or jurisdiction: 2004–05, total current expenditure.

National Center for Education Statistics. *Digest of Education Statistics*, 2007b: Table 236.75, Total and current expenditures per pupil in fall enrollment in public elementary and secondary education, by function and state or jurisdiction: 2012–13, total current expenditure.

D. Neal. 1997. The effect of Catholic secondary schooling on educational attainment. *Journal of Labor Economics*, 15(1, Part 1): 98–123.

D. Neal. 2002. How vouchers could change the market for education. *Journal of Economic Perspectives*, 16(4): 25–44.

D. Neal. 2009. Private schools in education markets. In M. Berends, M. G. Springer, D. Ballou, and H. J. Walberg, eds., *Handbook of Research on School Choice*, chapter 26, pp. 447–460. Routledge.

D. Neal. 2010. Aiming for efficiency rather than proficiency. *Journal of Economic Perspectives*, 24(3): 119–132.

D. Neal. 2011. The design of performance pay in education. In E. A. Hanushek, S. J. Machin, and L. Woessmann, eds., *Handbook of the Economics of Education*, volume 4, chapter 6, pp. 495–550. Elsevier.

D. Neal. 2013. The consequences of using one assessment system to pursue two objectives. *The Journal of Economic Education*, 44(4): 339–352.

D. Neal and D. W. Schanzenbach. 2010. Left behind by design: Proficiency counts and test-based accountability. *Review of Economics and Statistics*, 92(2): 263–283.

T. J. Nechyba. 2000. Mobility, targeting, and private-school vouchers. *American Economic Review*, 90(1): 130–146.

OECD. 2012. *Education at a Glance 2012: OECD Indicators.* OECD Publishing.

Office of the Governor Special Investigators. 2011. Special investigation into test tampering in Atlanta's school system. Technical report, Office of the Governor, Georgia.

B. Obama. 2011. Economic Report of the President, February 2011. Washington: Government Printing Office.

B. Obama. 2015. Economic report of the President, February 2015. Washington: Government Publishing Office.

E. O. Olsen. 2008. Getting more from low-income housing assistance. Technical report, The Hamilton Project: Brookings Institution.

L. E. Papke. 2005. The effects of spending on test pass rates: Evidence from Michigan. *Journal of Public Economics*, 89(5–6): 821–839.

P. A. Pathak. 2011. The mechanism design approach to student assignment. *Annual Review of Economics*, 3: 513–536.

P. A. Pathak. 2016. What really matters in designing school choice mechanisms. In L. Samuelson, ed., *11th World Congress of the Econometric Society*. Cambridge University Press.

P. A. Pathak and T. Sönmez. 2008. Leveling the playing field: Sincere and sophisticated players in the Boston mechanism. *American Economic Review*, 98(4): 1636–1652.

P. A. Pathak and T. Sönmez. 2013. School admissions reform in Chicago and England: Comparing mechanisms by their vulnerability to manipulation. *American Economic Review*, 103(1): 80–106.

J. Perez and J. Gormer. 2015. 5 charged in theft of more than $870,000 from Chicago Public Schools. *Chicago Tribune*, May 13.

M. Peters. 2015. Former Chicago schools chief to plead guilty in kickback scheme. *Wall Street Journal*, Oct. 8.

M. Pycia. 2012. Stability and preference alignment in matching and coalition formation. *Econometrica*, 80(1): 323–362.

A. E. Roth. 1982. The economics of matching: Stability and incentives. *Mathematics of Operations Research*, 7(4): 617–628.

A. E. Roth and M. A. O. Sotomayor. 1990. *Two-Sided Matching: A Study in Game-Theoretic Modeling and Analysis.* Cambridge University Press.

J. Rothstein. 2010. Teacher quality in educational production: Tracking, decay, and student achievement. *The Quarterly Journal of Economics*, 125(1): 175–214.

J. Rothstein. 2015. Teacher quality policy when supply matters. *American Economic Review*, 105(1): 100–130.

C. E. Rouse and L. Barrow. 2009. School vouchers and student achievement: Recent evidence and remaining questions. *Annual Review of Economics*, 1: 17–42.

B. Sacerdote. 2011. Peer effects in education: How might they work, how big are they and how much do we know thus far? In E. A. Hanushek, S. Machin, and L. Woessmann, eds., *Handbook of the Economics of Education*, volume 3, chapter 4, pp. 249–277. Elsevier.

W. H. Schmidt, C. C. McKnight, and S. Raizen. 1997. *A Splintered Vision: An Investigation of U.S. Science and Mathematics Education*. Springer.

T. W. Schultz. 1960. Capital formation by education. *Journal of Political Economy*, 68(6): 571–583.

M. Sektnan, M. M. McClelland, A. Acock, and F. J. Morrison. 2010. Relations between early family risk, children's behavioral regulation, and academic achievement. *Early Childhood Research Quarterly*, 25(4): 464–479.

L. S. Shapley and H. Scarf. 1974. On cores and indivisibility. *Journal of Mathematical Economics*, 1(1): 23–37.

L. A. Shepard and K. C. Dougherty. 1991. Effects of high stakes testing on instruction. In *Annual Meetings of the American Educational Research Association and the National Council on Measurement in Education*. Working paper.

J. Siedel, D. Mihalopoulos, and L. Fitzpatrick. 2015. Feds: Ex-CPS CEO "fraudulently" steered $40M contract in Detroit. *Chicago Sun Times*, Nov. 2.

J. Skolnick. 1966. *Justice Without Trial: Law Enforcement in Democratic Society*. Wiley.

Smith, Adam. 1827. *An Inquiry into the Nature and Causes of the Wealth of Nations*. No. 25202. Printed at the University Press for T. Nelson and P. Brown.

D. Smith. 2000. School district sues developers over Belmont. *Los Angeles Times*, Jun. 28.

T. D. Snyder and S. A. Dillow. 2015. Digest of education statistics 2013. National Center for Education Statistics.

R. Speakman and F. Welch. 2006. Using wages to infer school quality. In E. A. Hanushek and F. Welch, eds., *Handbook of the Economics of Education*, volume 2, chapter 13, pp. 813–864. Elsevier.

M. Spence. 1973. Job market signaling. *The Quarterly Journal of Economics*, 87(3): 355–374.

M. G. Springer, D. Ballou, L. S. Hamilton, V.-N. Le, J. R. Lockwood, D. F. McCaffrey, M. Pepper, and B. M. Stecher. 2011. Teacher pay for performance: Experimental evidence from the project on incentives in teaching (POINT). Technical report, Society for Research on Educational Effectiveness.

D. O. Staiger and J. E. Rockoff. 2010. Searching for effective teachers with imperfect information. *Journal of Economic Perspectives*, 24(3): 97–117.

B. M. Stecher. 2002. Consequences of large-scale, high-stakes testing on school and classroom practice. In L. S. Hamilton, B. M. Stecher, and S. P. Klein, eds., *Making Sense of Test-Based Accountability in Education*, chapter 4, pp. 79–100. RAND.

C. Syverson. 2011. What determines productivity? *Journal of Economic Literature*, 49(2): 326–365.

J. A. Taylor. 2007. Former top District charter schools official sentenced to prison for embezzlement, kickbacks, and tax evasion. United States Attorney's Office, District of Columbia, Nov. 29.

J. A. Taylor. 2008. United States reaches $1,750,000 settlement with the District of Columbia to resolve allegations regarding fraudulent misuse of federal grant funds by the District of Columbia Public Schools. United States Attorney's Office, District of Columbia, Sep. 12.

E. S. Taylor and J. H. Tyler. 2012. The effect of evaluation on teacher performance. *American Economic Review*, 102(7): 3628–3651.

P. E. Todd and K. I. Wolpin. 2003. On the specification and estimation of the production function for cognitive achievement. *The Economic Journal*, 113(485): F3–F33.

United Press International, Mar. 17. 1998. More charges in school fraud probe.

United States Attorney's Office, Central District of California, Sep. 2, 2015. Eight indicted in fraud case that alleges $50 million in bogus claims for student substance abuse counseling.

Eastern District of Michigan, Sep. 19, 2011. Former Detroit Public Schools official sentenced.

United States Attorney's Office, Northern District of Texas, Nov. 12, 2008. Former Dallas Independent School District executive sentenced to 11 years in federal prison.

United States Attorney's Office, Office of the Inspector General, Jan. 23, 2014. Former District of Columbia Schools Compliance Officer pleads guilty to wire fraud and conflict of interest charges, defendant's private transportation company collected more than $460,000 in fraudulent payments.

M. Urquiola. 2006. Identifying class size effects in developing countries: Evidence from rural Bolivia. *Review of Economics and Statistics*, 88(1): 171–177.

M. Urquiola and E. Verhoogen. 2009. Class-size caps, sorting, and the regression-discontinuity design. *American Economic Review*, 99(1): 179–215.

E. Vytlacil. 2002. Independence, monotonicity, and latent index models: An equivalence result. *Econometrica*, 70(1): 331–341.

C. Walters. 2014. The demand for effective charter schools. Technical report, National Bureau of Economic Research.

R. J. Willis and S. Rosen. 1979. Education and self-selection. *The Journal of Political Economy*, 87(5, Part 2): S7–S36.

B. Winegarner. 2013. 6 surrender in $15M San Fran school embezzlement case. *Law360*, May 15.

M. A. Winters. 2012. Measuring the effect of charter schools on public school student achievement in an urban environment: Evidence from New York City. *Economics of Education Review*, 31(2): 293–301.

M. Wiswall. 2013. The dynamics of teacher quality. *Journal of Public Economics*, 100: 61–78.

P. J. Wolf. 2012. The comprehensive longitudinal evaluation of the Milwaukee Parental Choice Program: Summary of final reports (SCDP Milwaukee Evaluation Report, no. 36). *School Choice Demonstration Project*, Figure 7: Maximum voucher amount compared to MPS average per-pupil expenditures.

P. J. Wolf, B. Kisida, B. Gutmann, M. Puma, N. Eissa, and L. Rizzo. 2013. School vouchers and student outcomes: Experimental evidence from Washington, DC. *Journal of Policy Analysis and Management*, 32(2): 246–270.

WXIA-TV. Apr. 1, 2015. 11 Atlanta educators convicted in cheating scandal. *USA Today*.

E. Wyatt. 2000. Ex-Queens school chief charged in $6 million bid-rigging scheme. *New York Times*, Nov. 2.

J. Yinger, ed. 2004a. *Helping Children Left Behind: State Aid and the Pursuit of Educational Equity*. MIT Press.

J. Yinger. 2004b. Introduction. In J. Yinger, ed., *Helping Children Left Behind: State Aid and the Pursuit of Educational Equity*. MIT Press.

R. Zimmer, B. Gill, K. Booker, S. Lavertu, and J. Witte. 2012. Examining charter student achievement effects across seven states. *Economics of Education Review*, 31(2): 213–224.

Index

Pages followed by an 'n' indicate endnotes.

Skolnick, J., 65
Smarter Balanced Assessment Consortium
(SBAC), 73–74
Smith, Adam, 2–3
Social gains and retention policies, 88–90
Socially harmful schools as voucher program
risk, 178
Somaini, P., 123
Sönmez, T.: deferred acceptance and Top
Trading Cycles, 115–118, 120; empirical
work on school assignments, 122
Sonstelie, J., 171
South America, resources and outcomes in,
50
Speakman, R., 187n
Spence, M., 10
Spending. See Resources and outcomes
Springer, M. G.: performance-pay scheme
targets, 191n; social gains and retention
policies, 90
Staiger, D. O., 88–90
Standards in assessment-based incentive
systems, 77–78
STAR (Student/Teacher Achievement Ratio)
experiment, 47
Strategy-proof mechanisms: deferred
acceptance, 110, 120; parent choice,
118–122; Top Trading Cycles, 114
Student/Teacher Achievement Ratio (STAR)
experiment, 47
Studies without lotteries for charter schools,
140–142
Study effort in education production
function, 35
Sundararaman, V.: developing countries,
50–51; voucher program achievement
results, 167–168
Supreme Court rulings on local control of
the schools, 187n
Sweden: class size, 48, 57; voucher programs,
168–169

Takeovers, 195n
Teacher effects literature, 62–63
Teachers. See Educators
Tenure and teacher performance, 63, 175–
176

Texas, charter schools in, 128
Three-period model for investments, 4–7,
185
Time investment in skills development, 5
Time series evidence for resources and
outcomes, 30–31
Tomes, N., 41
Top Trading Cycles (TTC): vs. deferred
acceptance, 115–118; in deferred
acceptance, 111–112; locker example,
114–115; process, 112–114
Trades in Top Trading Cycles, 112–113
Treatment on the treated (TOT), 132–133
Triage in assessment-based incentive
systems, 75–76
Tuition charges for charter schools, 128
Turner, L. J.: performance-pay scheme
targets, 191n; social gains and retention
policies, 90
Tutoring in No Excuses model, 135

Uganda: education reform, 52; Pay for
Percentile system in, 84
Uniform CPA Examination, 74, 80, 86
Unions: charter schools, 128; No Excuses
model, 136; pilot schools, 137; salary
schedules, 42–46; voucher programs, 170
United Kingdom, school inspection system
in, 192n
United States: class size experiments, 56–
57; education spending and pupil-teacher
ratio, 25; voucher program support,
170–171
University of Chicago Charter Schools
(UCCS) achievement results, 134–135,
139
Urban charter schools, achievement results
in, 134
Urquiola, M., 48–49
Uttar Pradesh, assessment-based incentive
system corruption in, 71

Value-added model (VAM): in education
production function, 36–39; experimental data, 40–42; limitations, 38–39;
teacher quality, 92–96
Varney, James, 197n